COLONIAL WRITING
AND THE NEW WORLD
1583–1671

Until recently most scholars of Anglo-American colonial history have treated colonialism either as an exclusively American phenomenon or, conversely, as a European one. *Colonial Writing and the New World 1583–1671* argues for a reading of the colonial period that attempts to render an account of both the European origins of colonial expansion and its specifically American consequences. The author offers an account of the simultaneous emergence of colonialism and nationalism during the early modern period, and of the role that English interactions with native populations played in attempts to articulate a coherent English identity. He draws on a wide variety of texts ranging from travel narratives and accounts of the colony in Virginia to sermons, conversion tracts and writings about the Algonquin language.

THOMAS SCANLAN has taught at the University of Virginia and Ohio University where he is now Assistant Professor of English. He has published articles and reviews in *American Literature* and *Spenser Studies*.

COLONIAL WRITING
AND THE NEW WORLD
1583–1671
Allegories of Desire

THOMAS SCANLAN

CAMBRIDGE
UNIVERSITY PRESS

PUBLISHED BY THE PRESS SYNDICATE OF THE UNIVERSITY OF CAMBRIDGE
The Pitt Building, Trumpington Street, Cambridge, United Kingdom

CAMBRIDGE UNIVERSITY PRESS
The Edinburgh Building, Cambridge CB2 2RU. UK http://www.cup.cam.ac.uk
40 West 20th Street, New York, NY 10011-4211, USA http://www.cup.org
10 Stamford Road, Oakleigh, Melbourne 3166, Australia

First published 1999

Printed in the United Kingdom at the University Press, Cambridge

Typeset in Baskerville 11/12.5 [wv]

A catalogue record for this book is available from the British Library

Library of Congress cataloguing in publication data

Scanlan, Thomas.
Colonial writing and the New World. 1583–1671: allegories of desire/Thomas Scanlan.
    p.   cm.
Includes index.
ISBN 0 521 64305-8 (hardback)
1. American prose literature – Colonial period. ca. 1600–1775 – History and criticism. 2.
English prose literature – Early modern, 1500–1700 – History and criticism. 3. United
States – History – Colonial period, ca. 1600–1775 – Historiography. 4. Indians of North
America – First contact with Europeans. 5. Great Britain – Colonies – America – Histori-
ography. 6. Colonies in literature. 7. America – In literature. 8. Desire in literature. 9.
Allegory. I. Title.
PS367.S33 1999
818'.10809–dc21   98-30999   CIP

ISBN 0 521 64305 8 hardback

For Laurie with love

Contents

Illustrations

All illustrations are reproduced by permission of the Tracy W. McGregor Library, Special Collections Department, University of Virginia.

Acknowledgments

I would like to acknowledge here the tremendous debt I owe to my family, friends, students, and colleagues. I cannot possibly mention by name all of the people who have helped me to see this project through from its earliest stages to its current incarnation, but suffice it to say that this book would never have been written without the support of the various communities to which I have been fortunate enough to belong. I would therefore like to thank the faculty and students of the Graduate Program in Literature at Duke University, colleagues at the University of Virginia, and the staffs of the John Carter Brown Library and the University of Virginia Library's department of Special Collections.

I owe my next largest debt to the various friends and colleagues who have offered criticism and support during the past several years. Tan Lin was one of the first people to figure out what this book was really about, and I am grateful that he was kind enough to share that with me. Jonathan Flatley is the kind of friend and colleague without whom books could not be written: he read large chunks of unwieldy prose on short notice and always managed to make the ideas clearer and the argument stronger. Steve Arata read the whole book and offered invaluable suggestions and comments. Steve Cushman read the whole book twice and offered the kind of criticism and support that helped me to keep believing in the project. Peter and Kris Onuf have taught me many things by example: how to write, how to make beautiful things, how to enjoy life. Many other people helped to make this book better, and I would like to thank them for everything they added: Uschi Appelt, Larry Buell, Michelle Burnham, Eric Lott, V. Y. Mudimbe, Dana Nelson, Teju Olaniyan, Sally Poor, Yael Schlick, Terry Toulouse, Cindy Wall, Mary Catherine Wimer, and Peter Wood.

As a graduate student I benefited immeasurably from the criticism and support of my mentors. Cathy Davidson possesses the rare gift of being able to deliver criticism with just the right amount of enthusiasm. Stanley Fish has been unwavering in his support of the project and unsparing with his time. Annabel Patterson, in some very real sense, taught me how to do scholarly work, as well as how to love it.

I owe a great debt to all of the people associated with Cambridge University Press, who helped to bring this book into print. I cannot imagine a better editor than Josie Dixon, who supported the project from the outset and provided much needed guidance as I prepared the manuscript for publication. Mary Fuller and Peter Hulme, who read the manuscript for the press, functioned as ideal readers, offering the kinds of critical comments and helpful suggestions that a writer might hope for but never expect. And Rachel Coldicutt was as cheerful as she was efficient in copy-editing a less than perfect typescript.

Only my parents, Joe and Robin Scanlan, know how much I owe them, and so I will not try to thank them for everything here. My brothers and sisters – Margaret, Vincent, Michael, Brian, Kate, and Daniel – have contributed more to this book than they know. And finally, from my son Quinn who was born during the writing of this book, I have learned more (about living and writing) than I can possibly say in a sentence or two. He has my undying gratitude and admiration.

I have saved the greatest debt for last. I owe so much more to Laurie Fox than these few words. Not only have her critical rigor and flawless sense of style made each sentence better, but more importantly her love and friendship have made the most trying moments of the writing of this book infinitely more bearable. Without her good humor and endless patience I could never have finished the book. It is dedicated to her with love.

Introduction

Fifteen-hundred-and-eighty-three might strike some readers as an odd date to use as the starting-point for a study of English colonial writing. Its significance lies not in its marking a decisive act, such as the embarkation of a voyage, the founding of a colony, a hard-fought battle with intransigent natives. Rather, 1583 marks the date of publication of an extremely influential and significant colonial text. I am referring to the translation into English and the publication in London of Bartolomé de Las Casas's *Brevíssima relación de la destrucción de las Indias*. That text, which Tom Conley and others have suggested marks the genesis of the so called "Black Legend," could also be said to mark the beginnings of the English attempts to fashion a national identity through colonial endeavor.[1]

If nothing else, the first English translation of *Brevíssima relación* demonstrates the extent to which England's colonial project was born, at least in part, out of a conscious desire to compete with its Catholic rivals (especially Spain) for power and prestige on the world stage. In spite of the complex European geopolitical context in which English colonialism was conceived, however, most scholars of Anglo-American colonial history have, until recently, treated the colonial phenomenon either as an exclusively American phenomenon or, conversely, as a European one. Accordingly, the study of the colonial period has remained surprisingly insular, as scholars from two distinct fields have consistently failed to engage in a dialogue. Scholars working in the field of American Studies have attempted to account for the origins of what has come to be known as the American self. It is my contention that these conventional – American exceptionalist – accounts are fundamentally anachronistic, insofar as they read back the later construction of an American national identity to its putative colonial "beginnings." Just as problematic, however, are some attempts

1

by scholars of the English renaissance that construct the colonial phenomenon as something that was exported intact from Europe. Rather than regarding colonialism as a complicated set of negotiations between the imperial nation and its colonies, these scholars have asserted that renaissance beliefs and perceptions were determinant in the construction of Europe's colonial empires.[2] To offer these critiques is not to suggest that the colonial period should be regarded as somehow detached from the subsequent emergence of an American nation. Nor is it to suggest that the study of renaissance themes cannot offer insight into Europe's colonial expansion. But it is to say that the study of the colonial period could benefit from a dialogue between these two approaches. In a sense, I intend this study as an attempt to inaugurate precisely such a dialogue.

In the pages ahead, I attempt to continue the recent work of American Studies scholars, who have painstakingly argued that the encounter between the European settlers and the indigenous populations should be placed at the center of our study of colonialism. But I also suggest that, by returning to the questions asked by an earlier generation of American Studies scholars, we can understand more fully the complicated role that the native populations played in England's attempts to articulate both a national identity and a colonial one. In so doing, I am pushing the the study of the colonial period in two new directions. First, I argue for a reading of the colonial period that attempts to render an account of both the European origins of colonial expansion and its specifically American consequences. Secondly, I argue for a broadening of the earlier interpretive framework, which focused almost exclusively on soteriological questions, to include a discussion of the colonial phenomenon in a multitude of contexts. More specifically, I suggest that we establish as our goal the understanding of colonial desire in all of its religious, political, psychological, cultural, social, and economic complexity. Although readers will inevitably perceive this study to have fallen short of this ambitious goal, I would ask them to treat it as a modest first step toward that ultimate goal.

As a means of achieving this synthesis of approaches to the colonial period, I have focused on what we might call the interpretive status of the native people. Rather than assuming that the exploitation and destruction of native populations and their cultures could only signify something to a subsequent, more enlightened, generation, I argue that the native populations figured in complicated and not necessarily predictable ways in the writings of those who were doing the colonizing. Before we can understand the role that the native populations played in the English attempts to articulate a national identity through their colonial enterprise, we must first re-examine our assumptions about English national identity. Rather than functioning as a stable concept, against which colonists could define their various projects, English national identity was very much in flux. Indeed, it is my argument that the colonial project became one of the primary ways that the English used to articulate and define their own emerging sense of nationhood. Moreover, it is my purpose here to explore the interesting and complex ways that the native populations functioned in English attempts to accomplish the task of defining themselves.

As a prerequisite to our understanding the colonial period, I suggest that we recognize the allegorical dimensions of colonial writing, particularly those writings that offer representations of native persons. If allegory involves the construction of a narrative that points toward, and yet operates at a distance from, another narrative, then almost by its very nature, colonial activity would seem to encourage allegorical writing. Colonial endeavor is never an end in itself. It is always a means to an end. As such, the narration of the events in the colonial space always must connect itself to some ultimate goal, which is inevitably removed from the colony. Colonial writing therefore tells two stories: It narrates events in the colony, while referring to the desires of the nation. In suggesting that we read colonial texts as allegories, I should say that I am merely attempting to give substance to a claim that has formed the implicit basis of much of the work known as post-colonial studies. As one scholar of post-colonial literature has put it, "If allegory identifies a process of signification in which an image in a literary text is interpreted against a pre-existing master code or typological system," then one must recognize that "a similar process of interpreting signs has been used in imperial thinking to read the world and to legitimise the power relations it established within it."[3] My concern in this study has accordingly been that of attempting to uncover the system of signification, within which colonial writing and its representations of native peoples functioned.

In the first chapter, I attempt to establish a theoretical and historical rationale for the reading of colonial texts as allegories. Rather than suggesting, however, that we can perform this task by resorting to simple "codes," I attempt to demonstrate the complex relationship among the interlocking discourses of nation and colony, Catholic and Protestant, and Self and Other. To grasp the complexity of these relationships, I suggest, is to begin to describe the notion of colonial desire. And rather than situating that desire entirely within a psychoanalytic framework, I argue for its historicization. As a means of achieving that historical understanding, I offer readings of Richard Hakluyt's *Discourse of Western Planting* and of the prefaces of two English translations of Bartolomé de Las Casas's *Brevíssima relación de la destrucción de las Indias*. Finally, I conclude the chapter with an examination of contemporary accounts of the development of national identity as a way to point us toward an understanding of the relationship between that phenomenon and colonialism.

In chapter 2, I focus on the first and third volumes of Theodor DeBry's *Great Voyages*, which are re-publications of Thomas Harriot's *Briefe and True Report* and Jean de Léry's *History of a Voyage*, respectively. It is my contention that these two texts and the accompanying engravings by Theodor DeBry can be read allegorically, and that the crucial keys to that allegory are to be found in a phrase uttered by Thomas Harriot, who argued that the goal of English colonial settlement was to get the "natives" to "fear and love" the English. DeBry, who saw in the Spanish atrocities in the New World simply another version of the persecution that he suffered as a Protestant in Europe, was determined to situate the colonial endeavors of the Protestants in the context of a narrative balanced between fear and love. In other words, the terror instilled by the Spanish would serve as the backdrop to the more moderate approach of Protestant colonizers, who recognized the value of both fear and love. To this end, DeBry subtly manipulates the ethnographic content of his images to produce a narrative that is as much about Protestant colonial ambitions as it is about ethnographic realism. DeBry's project, therefore, represents the beginnings of a Protestant ethnography – or, more precisely, the Protestant appropriation of ethnographic images – that gives readers the first visual and textual renditions of the dynamic of fear and love that will inform much of subsequent Protestant colonial writing.

If the English, as they attempted to embody the ideals of Protestant colonialism, strove to construct their relationships with native populations as guided by love, the case of Ireland would seem to offer a significant counter-example. In chapter 3, therefore, I examine Edmund Spenser's infamous *A View of the Present State of Ireland*. But rather than asserting, as other critics have, that Spenser's most extreme pronouncements are driven exclusively by a profound racism, I urge us to look at the way that Spenser constructs the identities of the colonizing English and colonized Irish. Read in this way, Spenser's text becomes a lament on the failure of English identity within the colony. Ironically, Spenser is unable to perceive that the Protestant faith of the English could be used as a tool to construct an identity that could, in turn, ensure the success of the colony. Spenser, in other words, fails to perceive that the discourses of nation, colony, and faith could be constructed in allegorical relation to one another.

The English recognition of the power of Protestantism in promoting the colonial enterprise – and, conversely, of the power of colonialism in advancing the Protestant cause – would have to wait until influential members of the English clergy embraced England's colonial ambitions as their own. In chapter 4, I examine several sermons that were written, delivered, and published during the early days of the English colony in Virginia by Robert Gray, William Symonds, William Crashaw, Alexander Whitaker, and John Donne. These sermons suggest not only that a well-disciplined colony will be the product of love and fear, but also that the colonial project itself stands in allegorical relation to a much larger and more important set of goals. What is important is not simply the way one achieves control over one's colony, but also how that colonial control will contribute to the larger narrative of England's survival and advancement. If DeBry's *Great Voyages* offers readers an idealistic portrait of Protestant colonialism, then the Virginia sermons show a willingness to wrestle with the hard facts of colonialism. No longer tied to the restrictive notion that the integrity of English colonial identity can only be ensured by a bloodless colonialism, these ministers develop a subtle and powerful rhetoric that allows them to incorporate the use of force into a colonial program, whose stated goal was the protection of the native populations.

In contrast to the Virginia divines, who provide a compelling rationale for situating England's colonial efforts within the context of the narrative of European geopolitical conflict, Roger Williams demonstrates that the colonial endeavor can offer English readers an allegory of the various internal doctrinal and political conflicts that threatened the integrity of their nation. This set of conflicts, and Williams's brilliant intervention in them in his *A Key into the Language of America*, serve as the subject of chapter 5. In his *Key*, Williams uses his representations of the native people to construct a devastating polemic against his rivals in the neighboring colony of Massachusetts Bay. The real power of Williams's text, however, lies in his ability to deploy Protestant colonial rhetoric against his fellow Protestants. By portraying himself as the lone practitioner of a colonialism committed to a loving and peaceful relationship with the native inhabitants, Williams demonstrates the enduring power of the Protestant commitment to love before fear in colonial matters. Moreover, Williams's text, and its subsequent reception, reveals England's own continuing desire to find in its colonies an idealized version of itself.

In the final chapter, we explore John Eliot's attempt to construct a Protestant colonial identity, not for readers in England, but for an explicitly colonial audience. Unlike Williams, who attempts to exploit the divisions among the colonists in order to gain support from English readers, Eliot attempts to heal those divisions by promoting his own efforts to convert the Indians. In his *Indian Dialogues*, Eliot confronts the paradoxical position that missionary work occupied in the English colonial scheme. Central to the rhetoric and yet marginal to the day-to-day operations of the colony, missionary work seemed to function as the marginal activity that ensured the stability and integrity of the core of Puritan colonial endeavor. Even in the praying towns themselves, Eliot's attempts to arrange the native populations into Christian communities, seemed indicative of this paradoxical status of missionary work. Located on the outskirts of Puritan settlements, the praying towns constituted in a literal/geographical sense the margins of Puritan culture in New England. Eliot's goal in the *Indian Dialogues*, therefore, is to move the missionary project from the margins to the center. In other words, Eliot's project is deeply allegorical. By pursuing what has hitherto functioned as a marginal goal, namely the conversion of the Indians, Eliot suggests that his fellow colonists will actually be ensuring the achievement of their primary goal, namely the survival of English Protestantism in the New World.

Before turning to the task I have just outlined, I would like to situate my work in a slightly more personal context by saying that, in some very real sense, this book began in a graduate seminar on Milton. During that seminar, I couldn't help asking questions similar to the ones that propel me in this study – questions for which the complete answers lie on both sides of the Atlantic. What struck me then, and continues to strike me now, is the artificiality of the boundaries between the two seventeenth centuries – the British one and the American one. It is not my intention to account in this book for this separation, but rather to urge us to repair it. It is my contention that historical events that profoundly shaped the course of British history – the St. Bartholomew's Day massacres, the defeat of the Spanish Armada, the Laudian purges of the English clergy, the English Civil War, the execution of Charles I, the restoration of Charles II to the throne – also exerted an influence, more or less directly, upon England's emergence as a colonial power. Although it is not my purpose here to trace all of these connections, I believe that this study will demonstrate their importance, and it is my hope that this study will function as the beginning of a conversation that has been very long in coming.

CHAPTER ONE

The allegorical structure of colonial desire

When he published his *Brevíssima relación de la destrucción de las Indias* in 1552 in Seville, Bartolomé de Las Casas almost certainly did not foresee the use to which the tract would be put over the next century-and-a-half.[1] To be sure, he intended his brutal exposé of the cruelty and inhumanity of the Spanish in the New World to bring about changes in Spanish colonial policy, but it is highly unlikely that Las Casas, a Catholic Bishop, would have anticipated, or even approved of, the Protestant appropriations of his text with which I will be concerned in this chapter. Translated into English and published in London four times between 1583 and 1699, the *Brevíssima relación* provided the English Protestants with justification for both their foreign policy toward Spain and their colonial policy in the New World. The cruelty so graphically described in the *Brevíssima relación*, which the English figured as typically Catholic and Spanish, enabled the English to see colonial endeavor as a means of defining what it meant to be English and what it meant to be Protestant. Moreover, the Protestant appropriation of this quintessentially Catholic text speaks to the methodology that I will employ in this study, for it is with the cultural work of colonial texts in the construction and maintenance of a national identity that I will be most concerned in the pages ahead.

It would be a gross oversimplification to suggest that the publication of one text set the course that English colonialism would take for the next one-hundred-and-fifty years. But it would be correct to say that one can see in the English republication of *Brevíssima relación* an attempt to fashion a coherent identity for a nation, whose commitment to colonialism and Protestantism, at least at the end of the sixteenth century, was in doubt. The two prefaces I will examine demonstrate the ease with which colonial writing can be made to do domestic work. By suggesting what might distinguish an imagined Protestant colonial undertaking, these prefaces implicitly ask what it meant to be a Protestant. By asking how the English as a nation would fashion their colonial enterprise, they were also asking what it meant to be English. And finally, in their insistent focus on the cruelty of the Spanish toward the native populations, the prefaces forge the crucial link between the behavior of colonizing nations and their identities.

That link between colonization and the construction of national and religious identities – and the role that the native populations played in rendering the connection visible – constitutes the subject of this study. It will be my argument that colonial writers frequently turned to allegory as a means of giving shape to this complicated and multivalent set of relations. Allegory, which I will suggest is the mode one turns to when the concept one is trying to articulate seems just out of reach – or, conversely, hopelessly lost to the past – gave colonial writers (and their readers) a means of imagining and expressing the tremendous religious, ideological, and economic potential implicit in the colonial undertaking itself. Before turning to Las Casas's *Brevíssima relación* and Richard Hakluyt's *Discourse of Western Planting*, as examples of the power of allegorical reading and writing, however, I will undertake to consider some of the theoretical issues implicit in my move toward allegory. I will conclude this chapter with a meditation on some of the possible connections between notions of allegory and notions of national identity.

TYPOLOGY, ALLEGORY, DESIRE

As one might expect, descriptions of encounters between Indians and English settlers abound in the narratives generated during the colonial period. But until relatively recently, scholarly accounts of the history of the colonization of North America had rendered the native populations of this continent all but invisible. For Perry Miller, whose massive three-volume study of "the New England mind" constitutes the most comprehensive and complete study of colonial Puritanism we have, the Indians figure only in the margins. Indeed, so marginal are Indians in his study that they don't even merit a heading in his index. Miller implicitly accounts for his omission when he tells his readers that he has sought to tell the story of what he calls the "the intellectual culture of New

England."[2] And the unlettered Indians figured in that story only insofar as they constituted one of "the long list of afflictions an angry God had rained on" the Puritans.[3] Rather than seeing the Puritan interactions with the Indians as signifying something fundamental about the character of their colonization, Miller instead examined the way that the Puritans chose to *interpret* their own struggles with the Indians.[4] As Roy Harvey Pearce has aptly described the Puritan interpretation of the Indian, "The Puritan writer on the Indian was therefore less interested in the Indian's culture than in the fallen spiritual condition which that culture manifested."[5] It was in these *manifestations* that Miller was able to discern the contours of that phenomenon that would occupy him for most of his career, namely "the New England mind."

In an attempt to correct for what now seems an egregious omission, scholars of the colonial period have, during the past two decades, gradually placed the encounter between Europeans and Native Americans at the center of their work.[6] As a result, our understanding of the moment of initial contact and of the subsequent relationship between Europeans and native peoples has evolved dramatically from what it was a generation ago.[7] Although Pearce's groundbreaking study dates back to 1953, it was not until the 1970s that significant numbers of scholars set out to produce sweeping accounts that would alter the very terms in which we understood the colonial period of American history.[8] The nature and scope of this revision cannot adequately be summarized in a few sentences, as it was performed by scholars from a variety of disciplines using an array of sometimes overlapping, sometimes contradictory, methodologies. But it is safe to say that the result of this work was the recognition that the English treatment of the native populations constituted a legitimate and important object of study.[9]

It would be fair to say that most, if not all, of these revisionist histories of the colonial period remain committed to the project of recovering and reconstructing what we might call, for lack of a better word, the "real" terms of the encounter between the English and the Indians. In so proceeding, the revisionists have (sometimes explicitly, sometimes implicitly) repudiated the providential framework in which Perry Miller and his followers situated their analyses of the colonial period. Such a repudiation seems only reasonable. After all, in the typological framework deployed by the Puritans, there were really only two roles available to the Indians. They either functioned as "types" of unregenerate humanity, linked with Satan and Roman Catholicism, or they represented the power of a merciful God to bring about conversion and redemption among the heathens. In either case, the Indians functioned not as independent subjects, but as manifestations of the elect status of the Puritan community in New England. In order to uncover the "real" barbarity and cruelty of the English colonizers, historians have necessarily had to dismantle the interpretive framework that enabled the Puritans to construct the Indians as signifying figures in their own soteriological narratives.

As crucial as this move away from typology has been, it seems to have had the unintended consequence of obscuring the fact that the English men and women who colonized the New World were, in the broadest possible sense, interpretive creatures. It would be a mistake, in other words, to assume that the colonizers' interpretations only followed along soterioligical lines. My goal in this study is to show the central importance of the Indian in other interpretive registers, other than a strictly soteriological one. It will be my aim in the pages ahead to show how the Indian functioned in English Protestant accounts not simply as an instance of unregenerate man – as a device in various soteriological narratives – but also as a crucial figure in the English attempt to generate and sustain a coherent national and religious identity. To put it another way, my goal here is to renew the emphasis on the questions of interpretation that were necessarily rendered so central when typology was all we talked about.

Perhaps the most important lesson to be drawn from the revisions of our accounts of the colonial period is that not all of the desires of the colonists were, strictly speaking, godly. These accounts reveal the limitations of typology – or rather the limitations of any exclusively typological reading of the colonial period. In the pages ahead, I argue for the usefulness of the notion of allegory which, while maintaining the important focus on interpretation, is also a term that is capacious and flexible enough to account for narratives and events that fall outside the narrow confines of typology. This is the case for several reasons, not least of which is the capacity of allegory to narrate desires other than strictly religious ones.

The move toward allegory might at first seem an odd one to make, given the considerable debate that has swirled around the very question of what constitutes the difference between typology and allegory. According to Sacvan Bercovitch, in what probably still stands as the most brilliant reworking of Miller's argument to date, "Typology recommended itself to the Reformers as an ideal method for regulating spiritualization, since it stressed the literal-historical (as opposed to a purely allegorical) level of exegesis, and then proceeded to impose the scriptural pattern upon the self, in accordance with the concept of *exemplum fidei*."[10] While Bercovitch does not deny the prevalence of allegorical writing during the colonial period, he does suggest that reformed Christianity privileged literal, historical typology over what he calls the more "allegorical" forms of writing.[11]

For our purposes, the most important feature of Bercovitch's argument is his recognition that figural interpretations of all sorts abounded during the colonial period. Moreover, as he so convincingly shows, there was a vigorous debate surrounding the question of which kinds of figural interpretations were to be encouraged and which were to be condemned. In any event, as Thomas H. Luxon notes in his study of English Puritan writing, any attempt to justify one method over another proved difficult. "Reformed Christianity," he argues, "for all its insistence on literalism, remains profoundly committed to an allegorical ontology. It is incessantly about the business of othering. It others the world into God's allegory of himself and his kingdom; it others the past as an allegory of the present and the present as an allegory of the future."[12] I do not mean to suggest that the differences between typology and allegory were all semantic, or that any attempt to make a distinction between the two is spurious. But I do mean to suggest that the idea of typology cannot begin to accommodate the considerable body of figurative writing that does not posit a literal connection between the past and the present or, more precisely, a connection between ancient Israel and seventeenth-century Massachusetts. My point here is that Protestants in general, and the English Puritans in specific, were constantly allegorizing everything. They lived in a world, in which every person, object, and event was filled with signifying potential. Accordingly, one of the central claims of this study is that Protestant colonial writings on Indians operated not simply within a narrow, typological framework, but also within a much more broadly allegorical one – not just within a soteriological context, but within a political one as well.

I should like to make clear at this point what I mean (and what I do not mean) by allegory. Like Angus Fletcher, I adhere to the literal definition of allegory as meaning "other speaking." I would also embrace his eloquent suggestion that "in the simplest terms, allegory says one thing and means another."[13] It is important to recognize that such a definition could encompass writings from any number of different genres, and not simply writing that proclaims itself as allegory in the way that, say, Spenser's *Faerie Queene* or Bunyan's *Pilgrim's Progress* do.[14] For my purposes, allegory does not refer to a particular *genre* of writing but rather to a *mode*, which is of course the word that Fletcher used to define and describe allegory. There is, for our purposes, an obvious reason to reject the idea of allegory as an exclusively literary genre, and that has to do with the fact that none of the texts I will concern myself with in this study are explicitly literary, and so strictly generic (or literary) definitions of allegory are of limited use. More importantly, however, it is important to recognize that to proclaim one's interest in the "modality" of allegory rather than its "genericness" is implicitly to declare one's conviction that no discussion of allegory can be complete without a consideration of reception as well as production. Following Fletcher, therefore, I shall be less interested in using the theory of allegory as means of accounting for the genesis of a particular kind of text, and more interested in using it as a way of interpreting texts.[15]

In his insistence on the modal qualities of allegory, Fletcher follows C. S. Lewis's assertion that it is neither theme nor content that defines allegory, but structure.[16] Such an assertion seems to demand the recognition on our part that many different sorts of texts posit a relationship between themselves and some other, external text – and that text could be constituted as a set of events, as a body of knowledge, or even as an entire system of beliefs. There are, in other words, texts that explicitly declare themselves as allegories and others that, by virtue of their implicitly asserted connection to a context shared by their readers, demand of their readers an act of allegorical interpretation. The object of most of the texts discussed here was to encourage readers to forge just such a connection between a distant colonial scene and their own immediate circumstances. In the case of England in particular, whose entry into the competition for colonies in the New World was much later than that of its Catholic rivals, the task of generating interest in and commitment to the colonial enterprise was an especially urgent one. The authors of these colonial texts, although they do not explicitly announce their writings as allegories, do require their readers to draw a connection between the two apparently distinct narratives of colonial adventure and national advancement. It is my contention that this interpretive requirement is fundamentally an allegorical one.[17] It will also, therefore, be my contention that the colonial texts we will examine in this study function as "implicit allegories".

Although he doesn't call them "implicit allegories," Walter Benjamin makes a similar claim for the reading of Baroque German dramas. In Baroque representations of Golgotha, for instance, Benjamin suggests that we can discern not simply the workings of allegory, but indeed its very essence. In his reflection on Golgotha, Benjamin asserts that allegory presents us with two worlds that seem hopelessly sundered from each other, and it therefore requires what he calls a faithless leap on the part of the reader. The allegorical structure of these representations merely brings the two opposites into a dialectical relation with one another, and the reader does the rest. Allegory, according to Benjamin, is a structure that embodies both a sense of loss and confusion and the possibility of hope and coherence. Or, to put it another way, the essence of allegory, as Benjamin defines it, lies in the demands it places on the reader. Unlike the simplest definintions of literary allegory that posit a one-for-one correspondence between concrete characters, settings, and actions and their "real-life" counterparts, Benjamin's notion of allegory is marked by the uncertainty of the relationship between the signifier and what it might ultimately signify.

As Fredric Jameson has eloquently suggested with respect to Benjamin, "allegory is precisely the dominant mode of expression of a world in which things have been for whatever reason utterly sundered from meanings, from spirit, from genuine human existence." Jameson goes on to point out that allegory can be useful for more things than simply the Christian project of connecting the incoherence and misery of this world with the harmony and bliss of the next. Allegory becomes "the dominant mode of expression" in any world where what is hoped for exists at a remove from what is, where the incoherent present is posited against a resolutely coherent future, or where the connection between the present and the past or the present and the future requires a leap of faith. The world from which colonial writing sprung was one marked by social and economic dislocation, religious and political controversy, periodic famine, and devastating world war. It was, in other words, a world marked more by loss than by plenitude. And as such, it was a world ideally suited to the allegorical mode.[18]

For Benjamin, allegory becomes the privileged mode in a world marked by loss, decay, and rupture precisely because of its unique power to embody temporality. Thus it is that Benjamin approves of Friedrich Creuzer's distinction between symbol and allegory: "The distinction between the two modes is therefore to be sought in the momentariness which allegory lacks. There [in the symbol] we have momentary totality; here [in allegory] we have a progression in a series of moments."[19] In an attempt to clarify precisely what allegory is and how it functions, Benjamin offers the following helpful analogy:

In the ruin history has physically merged into the setting. And in this guise history does not assume the form of the process of an eternal life so much as that of irresistible decay. Allegory thereby declares itself to be beyond beauty. Allegories are, in the realm of thoughts, what ruins are in the realm of things.[20]

Just as the ruin embodies, in a poignantly concrete way, history, so does allegory embody thought. Both thoughts and things will be subject to "irresistible decay." The by-product of one process of decay is ruin, of the other, allegory.[21] In a sense, I will be treating the texts I read in this study as ruins. The idea of the ruin is a particularly useful image for dealing with colonial texts. Ruins are objects that cry out for interpretation, but they are not objects whose proper interpretation will ever be located in some definitive notion of authorial intention. This is not to say that intention is irrecoverable, but rather that it is inevitably layered with history.

There is one thing that remains to be said about the indeterminacy of allegory before we turn to a discussion of the specific ways in which allegory lends itself to the narration of colonial desire. In Benjamin's definition, an allegorist, if such a creature even existed for him, gestures at a meaning without ever being certain of whether the meaning is even able to be articulated. In other words, both the construction and interpretation of allegory involve more than simple substitution. Since allegory proceeds dialectically, by both preserving things *and* reminding the reader of their fragility and transience, it is a phenomenon that cannot be reduced to a simple equation or translation. I would therefore urge us to resist readings of the colonial period that discover beneath the overtly religious writings of the Puritans a simple and straightforward discourse of conquest. As appealing as the notion of a "manichean allegory" might be – that is, an allegory whose code always renders what is native as inferior and/or evil – Protestant writings about native populations almost always operated according to much subtler and more complicated rules.[22]

Although it is not my intention to provide a psychoanalytic reading of colonial texts *per se*, I should say that parts of my argument strongly suggest connections between allegorical structures of desire and psychoanalytic ones. I am of course not the first scholar to observe that psychoanalytic theory can be used to explain and understand the allegorical mode. Joel Fineman, for instance, has persuasively argued that allegory not only contains an expression of desire – it is itself a structure of desire. According to Fineman, the very structure of allegory holds out the promise either of recovering something that has been lost or of attaining a deferred desire. Allegory's literal surface, therefore, points to a moment when desire merges with reality. The structure of allegory, in other words, implies a series of crucial separations: the separation of desire from its fulfillment, the separation of the literal from the figurative, the separation of the signifier from the signified. It is precisely because of these separations that allegory manages to contain and portray "continual yearning" and "insatiable desire."[23]

Fineman's analysis of allegory builds on the Lacanian notion that desire operates in much the same way as language, where plenitudinous, satisfactory meaning always falls victim to the slippage between the signifier and the signified.[24] It seems to me that this idea offers a useful point of entry into colonial discourse, which is indeed a form of writing that, by its very nature, must always promise more than it can deliver. The Lacanian vocabulary offers us two other useful insights into the workings of colonial discourse. The first of these, as Jacqueline Rose has suggested in her reading of Lacan, is the notion that desire is always constituted by loss. And the second is to be found in Lacan's profoundly suggestive assertion that "man's desire is the desire of the Other."[25] As Rose has observed, however, these two insights are not easily separable. That is to say, in her reading of Lacan, the desire for the Other is necessarily implicated in narratives of loss.[26] For the purposes of reading colonial texts – or more specifically, colonial texts about native Others – the power of these two interdependent assertions would seem to lie in their ability to offer insight into one of the most prominent features of the texts we will be examining, namely the consistent attempt by colonial writers to narrate the colonial experience as the most readily available means to overcome an almost overwhelming sense of national loss. Moreover, it is through their encounters with the native populations that the English seem to feel that they can articulate an identity that seems always on the verge of disappearing into nothingness.

In a discussion of Franz Fanon's *Black Skins, White Masks* that proceeds along the lines I have been suggesting, Homi Bhabha describes how the process of identification with the Other works to generate an identity for the colonizer. Significantly, what Bhabha calls the "ambivalent identification of the racist world," turns not on the notion of "Self and Other but [on] the otherness of the Self inscribed in the perverse palimpsest of colonial identity." Fanon's work, Bhabha suggests, rather than affirming notions of the Self and Other as static categories, "reveals the deep psychic uncertainty of the colonial relation itself." Ultimately, for Bhabha, "the question of identification is never the affirmation of a pre-given identity, a *self*-fulfilling prophecy – it is always the production of an image of identity and the transformation of the subject in assuming that image."[27] I take it that Bhabha's intention here is, in part, to foreclose any attempt to describe the colonial relation in crude or reductionist psychoanalytic terms. Rather than suggesting that psychoanalysis can offer scholars a template onto which they can map what he calls "that bizarre figure of desire," Bhabha merely asserts that psychoanalysis can give us a language and a set of tools for coming to terms with the intricate phenomenon of colonial desire – a phenomenon, he insists, whose complexity resides as much within the psyche of the colonizer himself as it is embodied within the relations between colonizer and colonized. The usefulness of Bhabha's work, for our purposes here, lies in its consistent refusal to suggest that the recovery of the unconscious desires of the colonizers can help us to produce a predictably linear narrative of total suppression and conquest.[28]

Readers will no doubt discern in the pages ahead an affinity, albeit not always explicitly articulated, between the notions of colonial desire I attempt to trace and Bhabha's own work. Just as significantly, readers will detect a reluctance on my part to cast my argument entirely in the idiom of psychoanalysis. This hesitation derives from two sources. First, I have tried at every turn to respect the historical specificity of the early colonial period, which consitutes the subject of this book. Psychoanalytic models, therefore, to the extent that they offer us a vocabulary for describing colonial desire, are useful. Insofar as they posit a transhistorical or transcendent narrative of desire, however, these models would seem to lead us astray. For similar reasons, I would urge us to recognize that the history of the early colonial period cannot be adequately narrated by rendering it in terms that make it appear to be nothing more than an earlier version of the same colonial phenomenon that appeared much later. While one can no doubt discern similarities between the colonial encounters depicted in the writings of say Kipling, Conrad, and Forster and those found in early English colonial narratives, those similarities must, it seems to me, always be narrated within an historical framework that respects the historical differences between the late nineteenth century and the early seventeenth century.

The second reason for my reluctance to embrace psychoanalysis wholeheartedly has to do with the fact that, as I hope will become obvious in a moment, not all the repression on the part of early English colonial writers was a function of unconscious drives. That is to say, the English did indeed seek to repress their desire to subjugate the native populations, or at least to narrate that subjugation as something other than the desire for domination and economic gain. But that repression was largely, if not wholly, due to their *conscious* attempt to fashion a colonial identity that would stand in stark contrast to that of the Spanish. To be sure, the effect of the English determination not to reproduce the rapacity and cruelty of the Spanish, was to generate a colonial ideology that allowed its adherents to avoid confronting their darker motives. But that is not a story that can be completely or satisfactorily narrated within the discourse of psychoanalysis. It is to that story that we will now turn, as we explore the genesis of the "black legend" and its apparent hold on the English colonial imagination.

TRANSCENDING MASSACRES

I suggested at the outset that we begin our study of English colonial writing by looking at the English translations of the work of Bartolomé de Las Casas. My interest in Las Casas stems from two features that are readily apparent in the English translations and their editorial apparatus. First, the English publication and dissemination of Las Casas's text demonstrates the fact that colonial writing could signify something to people who lived outside the immediate context of its initial production. That is, colonial practices and their subsequent narrations could be transformed into allegories. What these early translations show is that Spanish colonization – or, more precisely, the Spanish treatment of the native populations in the colonial setting – could be made to signify something about the Spanish as a nation. Implicit in the English interest in Las Casas, in other words, is the hope that English colonial endeavor could be used to construct a very different narrative of English national identity. The translations of Las Casas, however, do more than simply reveal the allegorical potential of colonial writing. They – and this will constitute my second concern here – in effect articulate a critique of Spanish colonial desire. And, as such, they seem to construct the limits of English colonial desire – or at least the limits of the articulation of that desire.

Before turning, however, to England, I need to say more about the *Brevíssima relación* and its author. Born in Seville in 1474, Las Casas was the son of Don Francisco de Las Casas who himself traveled to America with Christopher Columbus in 1493. The son made his first voyage to America in 1502 as a Dominican missionary, and his experiences there convinced him both of the humanity of the native populations and of the injustice of the Spanish treatment of them. He thus became known as a tireless advocate for Indian rights and as a proponent of a colonialism driven not by commercial interests but by the zeal for converting the native populations to Catholicism. Originally composed in 1542, the *Brevíssima relación* was intended to provide support for the so called New Laws enacted in that year to protect Indian rights. Within three years these laws were revoked by the Crown, and Las Casas felt the increasing necessity of making known to the public the atrocities which their fellow Spaniards were committing in the New World.

Although Las Casas is perhaps best known today for his *Historia de las Indias*, the only one of his works published during his lifetime was the *Brevíssima relación*. And the publication of this work, which significantly was written in Spanish and not in Latin, sparked a bitter public debate over the goals of colonialism and the status of the native peoples. In this debate, Las Casas attempted to discredit the thinking of opponents, such as Juan Ginés de Sepúlveda, who used the Aristotelian concept of natural slavery to justify what might otherwise seem unconscionable behavior. According to Aristotle, a Greek citizen was not allowed to enslave a fellow citizen, but slaves could legally and morally be drawn from other racial and ethnic groups.[29] Thus, following Aristotle's logic, the Spanish were enslaving the native populations of America. In the *Brevíssima relación*, Las Casas provides his countrymen with a gruesome, colony-by-colony description of the barbarity of the Spanish explorers. The inventory of atrocities includes, among other horrors, murdering children, impaling pregnant women, and burning people alive, all in the service of a colonial project whose primary aim was to discover gold and other hidden treasure. Whether it be in Hispaniola, Nicaragua, Guatemala, or Cuba, Las Casas relentlessly tells the same story over and over again. Indeed, part of the power of this text is its seemingly endless repetition of the same story with only the names of places changed. In contrast to the cruelty of the Spanish, Las Casas offers numerous examples of the compassion and kindness of the Indians, and thereby he attempts to refute claims that they were not fully human. Thus, in the face of the treachery of the colonizers, the Indians in *Brevíssima relación* mourn the deaths of their children and other loved ones and attempt to dissuade their attackers with generosity and kindness.

The *Brevíssima relación* was neither anti-colonial nor anti-Catholic. To the contrary, it was intended to shape further Spanish colonial efforts into an expression of Catholic missionary doctrine. In spite of its origins, however, the *Brevíssima relación* anticipated, in a sense, the tensions that underlay subsequent English colonial activity, tensions between those who saw in colonialism an opportunity for personal gain and others who hoped to transform colonial ventures into harvests of souls. And even more crucially, the *Brevíssima relación* seemed to offer the English a means of resolving those tensions by revealing the implicit potential in the colonial undertaking for articulating a Protestant identity that would in turn help to generate a coherent national identity. In any event, Las Casas would probably have found it strange that his tract was published as a piece of anti-Catholic propaganda some thirty years after it first appeared in Seville. And he would almost certainly have found it remarkable that his text continued to enjoy a readership in England in 1699, almost one-hundred-and-fifty years after its first printing in Spanish.

That a text, which was intended to be an intervention in a specific political debate, could experience such longevity in a context completely outside that of its original composition and dissemination indicates that the issues it confronts are of more than a passing interest. The enduring English distrust and dislike for the Spanish would, in part, account for the periodic rejuvenations of the *Brevíssima relación*, which certainly does not paint a very flattering picture of the Spanish. But there is more at work here than simple national or religious prejudice. The English could only safely reprint Las Casas's text if they felt certain that their own colonial project bore absolutely no resemblance to that of the Spanish. In fact, in the prefaces that accompany the various English editions of the *Brevíssima relación*, one can see the workings of an ideology that would enable the English to distinguish their brand of colonialism from that of other nations, particularly the Spanish.

In the two prefaces that I will examine here one can roughly discern the trajectory of this study, which starts in late Elizabethan England and is particularly concerned with the evolution of colonial ideology in the Civil War and Protectorate period – the mid-seventeenth century – and, passing through the Restoration of the English monarchy, ends in the late seventeenth century with the publication of John Eliot's *Indian Dialogues* in 1671. From its deployment in 1583 as an argument in favor of English intervention in the Low Countries, to its use as a Catholic foil in 1656 against which England's own Protestant colonial operations might be renovated under the auspices of Oliver Cromwell, the *Brevíssima relación* proves itself a remarkably malleable text open to strategic re-interpretation. The popularity, if we may call it that, of the *Brevíssima relación* is, I believe, only partly to be explained by the enduring English hostility toward the Catholics and the Spanish from the late sixteenth through the seventeenth centuries. Although, as I shall suggest in the pages ahead, nascent English colonialism presented itself as a practical and economical means to counter Spanish aggression both in Europe and elsewhere, it also promised to do the cultural work of constructing the Spanish as emblematic figures against whom the English could define their own colonial enterprise as uniquely Protestant.

Expressed another way, one can see in the early English printings of Las Casas the conviction that colonial endeavor could nourish an emerging sense of national and religious identity. In other words, from its earliest stages English colonialism presented itself as a means of achieving geopolitical and economic goals, and as a way of advancing certain religious and ideological causes. In both of these arenas, the Spanish had a role to play. Whether expressed as the foreboding military menace that took the very real shape of the Armada, or as the more subtle threat of a wily Catholicism that sought quietly to subvert an otherwise unsuspecting Protestant culture, the Spanish provided the English with a convenient enemy against whom to fight and against whom to define themselves. Gradually, an English Protestant colonial ideology emerged that, although it privileged religious and spiritual purity, also allowed for the pursuit of economic gain and geopolitical dominance. And a crucial component of that ideology was what the English saw as their uniquely humane and compassionate approach toward the native populations they encountered. In the service of such an ideology, Las Casas's document of the barbarism of the Spanish provided, of course, the ultimate counter-example.

The first English edition of *Brevíssima relación* was entitled *The Spanish Colonie, or briefe chronicle of the acts and gestes of the Spaniards in the West Indies, called the Newe World*, and it was published by William Brome in London in 1583.[30] Wasting no time in unfolding his agenda to the reader in his preface, the editor, who is perhaps Brome himself, hopes that this tract will "serve as a President and warning to the xii Provinces of the lowe Countries."[31] The context of this remark is the Elizabethan Dutch Wars, which were urged upon the queen by the so-called Leicester-Walsingham-Sidney faction of her court. This staunchly Protestant coterie advocated an activist and interventionist foreign policy that would keep the aggressive Spanish at bay not just in the Netherlands but elsewhere in the world. In the minds of these royal advisers, the goals of foreign and colonial policy merged in their attempts to thwart Spanish expansion around the globe. But the case of the Low Countries, which were under Spanish control in the 1580s, was a complicated one. Although Elizabeth was not pleased with such a strong Spanish (and Catholic) presence so close to England, she was reluctant to engage in the costly business of fighting a war. And her ambivalence was only heightened by the necessity of having to intervene on behalf of the Protestant faction who had rebelled with the intention of establishing a republic.

The author of the preface to *The Spanish colonie* seems less concerned with the overtly colonial context of the tract he is introducing than he is with its European implications. The prefatory remarks thus continue with an elaboration on the relationship between the Spanish involvement in the New World and their interference in the Low Countries:

> But two reasons have moved me to publishe this preface, which I do dedicate to all the provinces of the Lowe countreys: The one, to the end, awaking theselvs [sic] out of their sleep, may begin to thinke upon Gods judgements: and refraine from their wickedness and vice. The other, that they may also consider with what enemie they are to deale, and so to beholde as it were in a picture or table, what stay they are like to be at, when through their rechlessnesse [sic], quarrels, controversies, and partialities themselves have opened the way to such an enemie: and what they may looke for.[32]

The author posits the quite literal possibility that what the Spanish have done to the Indians they are able and willing to do to the Dutch. In so doing, however, he seems to imply that the Dutch, whom he begs to "refraine from their wickednes and vice," are not completely blameless. Perhaps he is referring to the attempts by the Dutch to overthrow a monarchy and set up a republic, and if so, this was a message that was necessarily to be delivered with delicacy where Elizabeth was concerned. In any case, such a depiction of the Dutch was different from the ways in which Las Casas would construct the Indian victims of the Spanish massacre as completely innocent.

In addition to encouraging the Dutch to take stock of their enemy, the above passage issues a call for unity and solidarity that would continue to inform many Protestant causes, including the colonial one, throughout the next hundred years. And although the preface uses Spanish colonial excesses to make a point that has nothing to do with colonial policy as such, it seems unwittingly to join together two issues that would become inextricably connected in the subsequent colonial adventures of the English, namely the question of the status of native victims and that of English Protestant identity. In fact, the cause of native conversions will emerge, as we shall see in the chapters ahead, as perhaps the one cause that Protestants of all persuasions could wholeheartedly support. And various English colonizers, notably Roger Williams and John Eliot, recognizing the power of the discourse on native peoples, would proceed to portray their own programs as protecting the interests of the native populations, and thereby rendering themselves unassailable.

Although he raises questions about the legitimacy of the Spanish claims to the new world, the editor of *The Spanish colonie* does not encourage the English to contest those claims, at least not militarily. His interests seem limited to the Netherlands. In 1656, however, the *Brevíssima relación* was published again in London under the title of *The Tears of the Indians*, and this time its translator, one J. Phillips, suggests that Las Casas's tract would justify English intervention in the New World.[33] More specifically, Phillips argues that the English have a moral obligation to drive the Spanish from the West Indies. Phillips's prefatory remarks are a subtle piece of work that, on the one hand, extoll the virtues of the past colonial efforts of the English and, on the other, explore the advantages of depriving the Spanish of their colonies in the New World. And if words are not enough, Phillips includes engravings that give visual renditions of the cruelties and tortures that are already graphically described within the tract.[34]

It is possible that Phillips's choice of a title for his translation, echoing as it does John Eliot's *Tears of Repentance*, was intended to call to the readers' minds what was viewed as England's most ambitious and successful attempt to convert the native populations of America. Such a gesture, by juxtaposing a humane Protestant colonial operation to a brutal Catholic one, would give added force to Phillips's argument that England make a move on the West Indies. In any event, the title seems to play on the widely held perception among the English that Indians never cry, a phenomenon that John Eliot describes.

Indians are well known not to bee much subject to teares, no not when they come to feele the sorest torture, or are solemnly brought forth to die; and if the Word workes these teares, surely there is some conquering power of Christ Jesus stirring among them, which what it will end in at last, the Lord best knows.[35]

By the time *The Tears of the Indians* was published, the connection between Las Casas and Eliot had already been established. Eliot's contemporaries, deliberately echoing the sobriquet that had been bestowed upon Las Casas, called Eliot "the Apostle to the Indians."[36] The difference, however, was that Las Casas was perceived as the lone moral voice in a colonial operation unsurpassed in its rapacity. Eliot and his supporters, on the other hand, attempted to depict their work as wholly consistent with a colonial project consumed with the task of performing God's will on earth.

By 1656, the English had been colonizing in North America for more than half a century, and so the publication of *Brevíssima relación* could speak directly to their own colonial experience. Given Cromwell's bloody campaign in Ireland to suppress the rebellious Irish and the Puritans' ruthless prosecution of the war against the Pequots in America, however, Phillips had more than a little rhetorical work to perform in his attempt to distinguish English colonial practices from those of the Spanish. He begins with Ireland in a dedicatory Epistle to Cromwell:

Pardon me, Great Sir, if next my zeal to Heaven, the loud Cry of so many bloudy Massacres, far surpassing the Popish Cruelties in *Ireland*, the Honour of my Country, of which You are as tender as of the Apple of Your own eye, hath induced me, out of a constant Affection to your Highness Service, to publish this Relation of the *Spanish Cruelties*; whereby all good men may see and applaud the Justness of your Proceedings: Being confident that God, who hath put this Great Designe into your Hands, will also be pleased to give it a signal Blessing.[37]

Phillips most likely refers in the above passage to the mistreatment of Protestants by the Catholics in Ulster during the 1640s – a situation which Cromwell's expedition to Ireland brutally remedied. The publication of *Brevíssima relación*, therefore, seems intended to do two things. First, it provides justification for

Cromwell's "proceedings" in Ireland by offering demonstrable proof of the lengths to which the Spanish are willing to go in their search for power and wealth. Secondly, and perhaps more significantly, the tract shows that Ireland was just the beginning of a much larger conflict against the forces of the anti-Christian papists.

Given the constant Spanish attempts to undermine the English control of Ireland, the Spanish and the Catholic Irish would have been associated in most English readers' minds. And this association is what enables Phillips to draw what might otherwise seem a far-fetched parallel. To suggest that the Protestant settlers in Ulster and the native Irish were the counterparts of the Indians and Spanish respectively would of course contradict geographical, historical, and political logic. And yet, because of the ties between the Spanish and the native Irish, such a parallel would probably have seemed plausible to many English readers. Moreover, as I shall suggest in the subsequent chapters, this trope of Protestant colonists portraying themselves as the righteous victims of Catholic injustice will persist as a means of justifying their own most brutal acts. Phillips himself seems aware of the need to explain away acts and events that might at first seem to incriminate the English.

When our own Case had a small Resemblance of this, how Sensible the People were, and how they mourned at the burning of a poor Village; the usual Accidents, or rather, things to be expected, in a tedious and necessitated War: but had you been Eye-witnesses of the transcending Massacres here related; had you been one of those that lately saw a pleasant Country, now swarming with multitudes of People, but immediately all depopulated, and drown'd in a Deluge of Bloud . . . your Compassion must of necessity have turned into Astonishment: the tears of Men can hardly suffice; these are Enormities to make the Angels mourn. . .[38]

Although Phillips does not specify which "case" of the English it was that resembled the Spanish depopulation of America, there were, by 1656, several examples to chose from. A likely possibility would have been the Puritans' war against the Pequot Indians in New England in 1636–7, which was first brought home to England through a series of eye-witness accounts and then later through colonial histories. In this war, English settlers, under cover of darkness, burned an entire Indian village to the ground and thereby caused the deaths of hundreds of Indians, including women and children.[39]

Phillips tellingly describes the misdeeds of the Spanish as "*transcending* massacres," a choice of words that emphasizes the power of colonial narratives to extend beyond their immediate temporal and geographical contexts. Unlike the English slaughter of the native inhabitants, Phillips seems to imply, the Spanish slaughter can signify something fundamental about their identity as a colonizing nation. Indeed, the English response to their own acts of brutality would seem to indicate their implicit deployment of this strategy. Although there was some outcry against the violence from the Puritans themselves, by and large, they regarded the episode precisely as Phillips framed it: one of "the usual Accidents... in a tedious and necessitated War." Rather than allowing his readers to draw what might seem the obvious parallel between the English and Spanish slaughters of Indians, Phillips suggests that they are in fact different: one was "transcendent" while the other was not; one was the unfortunate and inevitable result of a just war, while the other was the product of unmitigated greed and cruelty. This persistence in occupying the moral high ground served to reinforce Phillips's ultimate goal of convincing Cromwell and the English of the wisdom and efficacy of driving the Spanish from the West Indies.

Should we chase him from his Indian Treasures, he would soon retire to his Shell, like a Snail tapt upon the horns. And perhaps it would not a little avail to the General Peace of Europe, whereby we should be strengthened against the Common Enemy of Christianity. For doubtless it hath been the Satanical Scope of this Tyrant, To set all the European Princes at Variance, and to keep them busie at home, that they might not have leasure to bend their Forces against his Golden Regions.[40]

In suggesting that Spain's power and influence in Europe could be curtailed by depriving it of its colonial wealth, Phillips was merely articulating explicitly an argument that had been implicit in the writings of Elizabethan colonial theorists, namely that colonies could lend ideological and material support to English attempts to project their national identity onto a world stage.

The re-translation and publication of a tract that, by 1656, was more than one-hundred years old was not simply the gratuitous attempt to justify English colonial aggression by pointing to Spanish atrocities that were almost one-hundred-and-fifty years old.

There was also the very real matter of the expanding English colonization in the West Indies. What had hitherto constituted for the Puritans in parliament an implicit program of attempting "to enrich England at the expense of the Spanish Indies" became, under Cromwell, an explicit policy.[41] More generally, however, Phillips's translation of and preface to *Brevíssima relación* is indicative of the enduring need the English felt to define their own sense of national identity through colonial endeavor.

Between the prefaces of the 1583 and 1656 editions, we can discern a modulation from concerns that are entirely geopolitical to preoccupations with both geopolitics and ideology. It would not be an understatement to suggest that from very early on in their colonizing history, the English would have to define their intentions toward the native populations as fundamentally different from those of the Spanish. Las Casas's vivid and horrifying accounts of Spanish cruelty, which offered the English a tangible and concrete example against which to define their own colonial practices, meant that the English could never openly advocate the slaughter of the native populations. In short, the English would always be forced to represent their encounters with native populations as markedly different from the slaughters perpetrated by the Spanish.

The English response to the early translations of *Brevíssima relación*, while generally acknowledged to be widespread and far reaching, is not a subject that has received a great deal of attention from scholars. Such a gap in the scholarship is surprising since it could be argued that most of the English injunctions against cruelty to the natives can find their origins in Las Casas's revelations of the scandalous behavior of his countrymen. It lies outside the scope of this study to provide a detailed account of those reactions to Las Casas, but I would like in the next few pages to examine Richard Hakluyt's *Discourse of Western Planting*, a text that explicitly acknowledges the importance of Las Casas in the formulation of a colonial ideology. What will concern me in my reading of Hakluyt, however, is not simply the extent to which he echoes Las Casas's critique of Spanish colonial desires, but also the ways in which that critique can be used in an attempt to construct a positive colonial ideology for the English. Moreover, Hakluyt's text provides further evidence of the English conviction that narratives of colonial adventure would need to be constructed as allegories.

That is to say, writers of these narratives would need to render the colonial enterprise in terms that allowed their readers to embrace it as an essential part of their own story. Richard Hakluyt seems to have recognized this necessity, when he argued that colonialism would offer England a chance to improve its economic position within the European world, remedy internal social and economic divisions, mollify religious differences, and stabilize the English colonial rule of Ireland.[42] Indeed, Hakluyt's ambitious colonial vision, which he lays out in his *Discourse of Western Planting*, could be said to represent an invitation to the allegorical narration of colonial adventure. Implicit in this influential tract is the notion that would-be colonial adventurers could, while directly participating in the narratives of colonization, indirectly influence the story of the English nation.[43]

As any reader of Hakluyt's *Discourse* will recall, Hakluyt held out the hope that England's putative colonial involvement in the New World would bring about a peaceful solution to the seemingly intractable problems that had engulfed Ireland since the English had first colonized it.[44] England's colonial efforts in North America, Hakluyt argued, would relieve the queen of having to spend endless amounts of money to keep the Irish in check. In other words, Hakluyt asserted that Ireland would guarantee the profitability of the North American ventures and vice-versa. In his vision, the English colonial empire would be constructed of a series of interlocking enterprises, each of which would support the others: to participate in the colonization of Ireland was simultaneously to contribute to England's efforts in the New World; and to particpate in the colonization of the North America colonies was to aid in England's quest to bring Ireland under its control. This was a vision that lent itself to allegorical writing because it emphasized the interchangeability and interconnectedness of the various narratives of colonizing and nation-building.

Hakluyt's belief that Elizabeth's disastrous colonial efforts in Ireland could be salvaged, or at least helped, by engaging in an even more ambitious colonial project halfway across the world might have seemed naive to some. The successful English suppression of Desmond's 1583 rebellion gave Hakluyt the unwarranted impression that things in Ireland were under control. Of course, a seasoned Ireland-watcher at the end of Queen Elizabeth's reign would have seen the squelching of Desmond's rebellion for what it was, namely a Pyrrhic English victory. No matter what the source of his optimism was, Hakluyt's assertion that the material gains of North American colonial activity would bring Ireland firmly under English control proved wrong. And yet much of what he proposed in his *Discourse of Western Planting* indeed found a sympathetic audience among some of the queen's most favored councillors.

The notion that England's various colonial enterprises could synergistically support each other was a novel one, but Hakluyt's suggestion that the capital to fund colonial adventure could be obtained from private sources was not new. In 1568, Sir Henry Sidney, in his capacity as Lord Deputy of Ireland, proposed an ambitious scheme that utilized private sources of funding for colonizing Ulster. As Nicholas Canny notes, the so-called "Ulster Project" would serve "as a precedent not only for future plantations in Ireland but for colonization also in the new world."[45] Some four years later, Sir Thomas Smith, who served Elizabeth as Ambassador to France, Privy Councillor, and Secretary of State, took Sidney's idea one step further in his bid to colonize the Ards Peninsula in Ireland. According to Canny, not only did he seek no financial backing from the government, but he also engaged in two new practices. First, and most crucially for our purposes, he tried to generate interest and support for his project by publishing pamphlets, which described the advantages of investment and were specifically targeted at the younger sons of the gentry. Secondly, Smith's venture was the first to utilize, for the purposes of colonization, the notion of the "terminable joint-stock principle."[46] This idea, by which many investors provided the capital and shared the risk of a colonial undertaking, would prove indispensable in England's subsequent efforts of colonization.[47] Just as the early versions of the joint-stock company provided models upon which later colonial efforts were based, the joint-stock company itself was a successor of the privateers. These ships, which brought merchant seaman together with men of arms, made their money in part through trade and in part through acts of piracy directed principally at the Spanish and French.[48] These anti-Catholic impulses that justified and motivated the privateers would become a distinguishing feature of later, more sophisticated, English colonial operations. Moreover, the notion of a joint-stock company itself is one filled with allegorical implications. By investing money in a company in England that would put that money to work in the New World, these investors seem to have understood that they were participating in an enterprise whose narrative could be interpreted in a number of ways: as a declaration of national self-interest, as an expression of religious commitment, and as a manifesto of economic salvation.

There was little that was new in and of itself in Hakluyt's *Discourse*. What was new about Hakluyt's memorandum, however, was the range of national problems which he proposed to solve by means of a brand of colonial adventure that presented itself as virtually risk-free, at least to the crown. Not only would the Queen realize a financial profit on her share of the capital investment, but she would also increase her own domestic political capital both by alleviating religious tensions, and by providing relief to economic distress. In an oddly prescient passage, Hakluyt suggests that the queen might find in her colonial ventures a previously unthought of solution to internal religious division:

But also many inconveniences and strifes amongest ourselves at home in matters of Ceremonies shalbe ended; For those of the Clergye which by reason of idlenes here at home are nowe alwayes coyninge of newe opynions, havinge by this voyadge to sett themselves on worke in reducinge the Savages to the chefe principles of our faithe, will become less contentious, and be contented with the truthe in Relligion alreadie established by aucthoritie.[49]

In Hakluyt's analysis, religious division was only one of the problems caused by idleness, the other principal difficulty being economic discontent as evidenced by the "multitudes of loyterers and idle vagabondes. . . whereby all the prisons of the lande are daily pestred and stuffed full." For this social ill too, Hakluyt proposed colonization as the answer, suggesting that, as a result of the economic demand generated by colonial activity, these idlers "shalbe made profitable members by employing them in England in makinge of a thousande triflinge thinges."[50]

In addition to the financial and domestic political gains, Hakluyt argued that colonizing would represent a way for the Queen to increase her country's moral capital as well. Referring his readers to the 1583 English translation of Las Casas's *Brevíssima relación de la destrucción de las Indias,* Hakluyt suggests that it "woulde require more than one chapiter especially where there are whole bookes extant in printe not onely of straungers but also even of their own countrymen (as of Bartholmewe de las Casas a Bisshope in Nova Spania.)"[51] Hakluyt goes on to urge the Queen, through English colonial intervention, to put a stop to the Spanish cruelty, and thereby he implicitly suggests that colonial activity, in addition to easing economic pain and social unrest, could directly enhance England's geopolitical position.

Hakluyt's *Discourse* reveals him to be one of the first English colonial promoters to realize that the representations of England's colonial adventures could prove as crucial to their success as any single voyage or expedition. He seems implicitly to have grasped one of the most significant differences between the colonialism practiced by the English and that practiced by the other European powers, namely the fact that English colonial endeavor, because it was never centrally funded or directed, would literally have to be sold to the English people. Moreover, Hakluyt was the first col-onial writer to give voice to the idea that England's colonial efforts could serve its national interests, a simple notion that appeared nowhere near as obvious to his contemporaries as it does to us today. After – although almost surely not because of – Hakluyt, English colonialism would become not simply a collection of actions but also a collection of writings. These writings, some of which serve as the immediate focus of this study, are fundamen-tally allegorical in nature because they consistently, if at times only implicitly, assert that England's far-flung colonial projects could be rendered central to the construction and narration of an English national identity. More specifically, allegory is a term that allows us to account for the specifically national component in colonial writing. And it allows us to see that the writings about the native populations were inextricably intertwined with attempts to formulate and describe an English national identity. Before we turn to the writings themselves, however, we will need to say a few things about the status of England's national identity during the early colonial period.

ALLEGORY AND NATIONAL IDENTITY

In recent years, a number of scholars have argued persuasively for the emergence during the Elizabethan period of "a specifically national sense of self."[52] If, however, one believes as Claire McEa-chern has asserted, that "the nation is an ideal of community that is, by definition, either proleptic or passing, ever just beyond reach," then we should be careful not to attribute to "Englishness" during the Elizabethan period the status of a fully imagined or articulated national identity.[53] Indeed, such a caution seems warranted, given the tendency of earlier scholars of the colonial period to assume that the colonists defined their own uniquely American identity against an already established and fixed notion of English national identity.[54] As I hope will become clear in the pages ahead, such an assumption – long a staple of the American exceptionalist line of thinking – is unwarranted, as the English themselves were struggling with the vexing questions of who they were and how they might constitute themselves as a nation. The early stages of the colonial phenomenon, therefore, mark not the beginning of a separate, independent American identity, but rather an attempt to give shape to an English identity that seemed always in danger of dissolving in the ferment of social, political, religious and economic turmoil.

Although religious controversy constantly threatened to unravel the delicate fabric of English national identity, Protestantism itself was a term to which most Englishmen clung as they attempted to define themselves and their nation. To put it another way, it wasn't a question of *whether* Protestantism would or could define the nation, but rather *which version* of Protestantism would become synonomous with Englishness. Such an assertion is supported by the recent work of scholars who have studied the development of nationalism in the early modern period. Liah Greenfeld, for instance, asserts that Protestantism was "perhaps the most significant among the factors that furthered the development of English national consciousness." But, in addition to shaping the character of English national identity, Protestantism also influenced both its timing and its scope. According to Greenfeld, "it was owing to the Reformation, more than to any other factor, that nationalism spread as wide as it did in the sixteenth century."[55] Ultimately, Greenfeld claims that, "because of the association between the Reformation and English national identity, Protestantism not only provided the yet voiceless nationalism with a language, but also secured it a sanctuary and protection which it needed in order to mature."[56] Echoing Greenfeld's argument, Linda Colley eloquently and succinctly describes the relationship between Protestantism and the English nation as follows:

"Protestantism was the foundation that made the invention of Great Britain possible."[57] As I shall argue in the chapters ahead, Protestantism and the English nation are always presented as mutually dependent in the context of colonial discourse. It would be impossible, in fact, to conceive of the one without the other. Indeed, the most significant contribution of colonial writing to the development of an English identity would consist in its promise to weave Protestantism into the fabric of a national identity.

In addition to recognizing the connection between religion and the development of national identity in England, scholars have also argued for some time that Europe's period of initial colonial expansion coincided with the emergence of nationalism as a coherent ideology. Robert Berkhofer, Jr., for instance, argues that "exploration and expansion overseas resulted from and reinforced nationalism at the same time that it promoted an overall collective vision of a Europe in contradistinction to the rest of the world."[58] Arguing more narrowly than Berkhofer, Robert A. Williams astutely suggests that, in the particular case of the English, colonial discourse combined with "Protestant discourses" to function as an especially effective means of defining "a distinct national identity in the world system."[59] In other words, it was at the nexus of Protestantism and English nationalism that English colonialism was born. In the end, the colonial project became an indispensable component in the English nation's search for a coherent identity. In large part, due to the self-conscious efforts of colonial promoters, the colonies themselves were represented simultaneously as extensions of the nation and as the most effective way of articulating England's commitment to Protestantism.

In attempting to discuss the emergence of national identity, I have found it helpful to employ a term coined by Benedict Anderson, who examines the emergence of nationalism in the modern era. For Anderson, "nation-ness is the most universally legitimate value in the political life of our time." Anderson's word, "nation-ness," means the act of thinking *and feeling* in terms of nation, which he defines as "an imagined political community – and imagined as both inherently limited and sovereign." Although the idea of nation-ness involves the attempt to imagine a political community, Anderson argues that national consciousness is as much a product of culture as (if not more than) it is a product of

political ideology.[60] For Anderson, the emphasis on culture is crucial because he sees the emergence of this idea of nation-ness as
the result of the decline of the "unselfconscious coherence" of
the "great religiously imagined communities." In other words, the
emergence of nationalism is inextricably linked to the transition
from a world of communities imagined primarily in religious
terms to a world of communities imagined primarily along political lines. Therefore, to attempt to account for the transition
exclusively in terms of political ideologies is to commit an anachronism. These communities couldn't have been driven by political
ideologies at a moment when those political ideologies were at
best weak and nascent. The vocabulary that Anderson chooses to
narrate this decline is, therefore, necessarily a cultural one.[61]

Anderson traces the decline of the great religiously imagined
communities to two things: first the "exploration of the non-
European world," and second the decline of Latin as the sacred
language. For Anderson, this latter phenomenon, "exemplified a
larger process in which the sacred communities integrated by old
sacred languages were gradually fragmented, pluralized, and terri-
torialized."[62] Anderson is interested in examining a process in
which cultural identities were gradually eroded. No longer held
together by stable notions of linguistic and geographic identity,
these imagined communities began to construct themselves along
national lines. The idea of "nation-ness," therefore, becomes
necessary at precisely the moment when older notions of imagined
communities cease to function.

The importance of Anderson's formulation for our purposes lies
in its construction of nation-ness as a concept that implies a narrative of loss. Although he does not describe that sense of loss in
psychoanalytic terms, it could be said to function analogously to
the Lacanian discourse of desire we discussed earlier. In such a
reading, nation-ness could be described as that insatiable yearning
that persists in the face of the satisfaction of its most immediate
demands. In other words, it would seem that Anderson's nation-
ness is constituted as a desire which, because it is never wholly or
completely fulfilled, must exist at the level of fantasy. As a way
of getting at this feature of nation-ness Anderson, appropriating
language from Walter Benjamin, argues that each national group
inevitably comes to imagine itself as "a sociological organism
moving calendrically through homogenous, empty time."[63] At any

point in a nation's history, the people have a sense of the past as well as a hope for the future. To experience one's nation, however, is also to be conscious of a sense of eternity, a sense of the nation as a transhistorical reality. By existing in time and space, the idea of the nation lends itself to expressions of loss and desire that are experienced both vertically (in time) and horizontally (in space). Rather than conceiving of the development of the nation in exclusively positivist terms, as an inevitable sign of our progress into modernity, Anderson correctly identifies it, at least in part, as a process of loss and decay.

As I shall demonstrate in the next chapter, there emerged early on in Protestant colonial discourse the conviction that the representational potential of the native populations could be harnessed to help construct and define a Protestant identity. As a Protestant nation, England implicitly embraced the notion that its involvement with the native populations in the New World could serve as an allegory for its own ongoing struggle to define a coherent national identity. In this study, I attempt to connect the English discourses of native populations to England's emerging sense of itself as a nation. It is my argument that the discourse of the native populations was intimately connected to England's attempts to conceive of and represent itself as a Protestant nation.

As I attempt to explore the interrelationships of the discourses of nation, native, and religion, I suggest that the colonial narrative offers a unique way of weaving these three discursive strands together. It will be my argument in the chapters ahead that a secure and coherent national identity lay just outside the grasp of English colonial writers. The colonial project served the dual function, therefore, of providing a language and a set of experiences that could satisfy the English desire to represent itself as a Protestant nation. As the English sought ways to distinguish their Protestant nation from the Catholic nations of Europe, they turned increasingly to their colonial projects. And as they attempted to derive a national identity from their colonial adventures, they seized upon their treatment of the native populations as the defining feature. Very early on in England's narration of its colonial experiences the discourse of the native began to function for England as an allegory of the Protestant nation. The texts I examine in the pages that follow are a varied and diverse group, but they can all be read as allegories of that struggle to establish a distinctly English national identity. Colonial exploration, in these texts, becomes the most effective way of expressing national identity. "Nation-ness," in other words, needs "colonial-ness."

CHAPTER TWO

Fear and love:
two versions of Protestant ambivalence

One of the most dramatic realizations of the allegorical potential of colonial adventure was Theodor DeBry's *Great Voyages*. Described by one recent critic as "perhaps the most massive and magnificent illustrated travel collection of all time," DeBry's *Great Voyages* assembled a wide range of texts and images in thirteen volumes published over forty-five years.[1] This impressive undertaking, which DeBry began in 1590 by publishing Thomas Harriot's *Briefe and True Reporte* along with engravings based on the watercolors by John White, was continued by DeBry's sons Jean Théodor and Jean Israel, after the death of their father in 1598. Although the colonial enterprise operated in the margins of the known geographical world, DeBry understood that it could be rendered central to Europe's struggle between Protestants and Catholics. DeBry, I would suggest, offered Europeans the most forceful articulation of the notion that Protestant identity could achieve its fullest expression through colonialism. It will be my argument in this chapter that the texts and images that constituted the *Great Voyages* functioned as components in a compelling allegory of the ongoing Protestant struggle for survival in a predominantly (and menacingly) Catholic Europe. This assertion will in turn form part of the larger argument of this book, namely that through their colonial involvement in the New World the English discovered a means of connecting their religious identity with their emerging sense of national identity – a process that would consistently find its most succesful articulation in representations of English relations with native populations.

Born in 1527 or 1528 in Liege, DeBry was exiled from his home in 1570 after being accused by the Catholic authorities of sympathizing with the Reformation. Forced to forfeit all of his property in Liege, DeBry fled first to Strasbourg, where he worked as an engraver, and then to Frankfurt, where he worked as a publisher and bookseller until his death in 1598. DeBry's own experience at the hands of the Catholic church enabled him to perceive intuitively the connection between the Inquisition and the Spanish treatment of the native populations in the New World. This connection would, of course, eventually receive its most dramatic treatment in the seventeen engravings that accompanied DeBry's edition of Las Casas's *Brevíssima relación de la destruición de las Indias* in 1598. As Bernadette Bucher notes, those engravings, which render in unrelenting detail the atrocities described by Las Casas, undoubtedly "mirrored, for the Protestant victims of the Spanish Inquisition, their own misfortune."[2] Although he is probably best known for his portrayal of Spanish atrocities, in the first three volumes of his *Great Voyages*, DeBry concerned himself not with Catholic misdeeds but with Protestant achievements in the New World. My focus in this chapter will be volumes one and three of the *Great Voyages*, in which DeBry published Thomas Harriot's *Briefe and True Report* and Jean de Léry's *History of a Voyage to the Land of Brazil*.[3] Since the writing and first printing of Léry's work precedes that of Harriot's work, I shall be considering them in that order, and not in the order that DeBry published them. And I shall defer my treatment of DeBry's engravings until the conclusion of the chapter.

Within two years of its first printing as a quarto in 1588, Thomas Harriot's *A Briefe and True Report* was published again by Théodore DeBry with what he called "the true pictures and fashions of the people in that parte of America now called Virginia." This first volume of the *Great Voyages*, with its copperplate engravings based on the watercolor drawings by John White, the artist who had accompanied Harriot to Virginia in 1585–6, was indeed stunning. Two years later, in 1592, in the third volume of the *Great Voyages*, DeBry published Léry's *History of a Voyage* along with Hans Staden's account of his captivity among the Indians of Brazil in the decade preceding Léry's brief visit to that country. Since both Léry and Staden had produced woodcuts to accompany the earlier editions of their works, DeBry had an easy and reliable source from which he could generate the engravings that accompany the two texts in his volume.

With DeBry it is easy for readers to forget that his books are as much the product of his own genius as they are the work of the individual authors and artists he publishes.[4] On the surface, DeBry would seem merely to have produced a compilation of text and images that really belonged together in the first place. After all, John White had accompanied Thomas Harriot to Virginia and, according to Paul Hulton, had been supervised closely by Harriot in the making of his drawings.[5] DeBry's first volume, therefore, takes advantage of the technology of copperplate engraving to gather together material that, although produced at the same time and in the same place, had never before been presented as a single work.[6] In other words, so "natural" is the publication of Harriot's text with White's images that one is hardly aware at all that DeBry has played a role in the construction and manipulation of the material. Similarly, in volume 3, DeBry simply brought together the texts and images of two narratives about the same place. Again, he would appear not to have done anything very remarkable at all.

It is my belief that DeBry grasped the complexities and potential contradictions that would confront Protestants as they engaged in colonial activity. Accordingly, each of these texts offers us a glimpse of one of the fundamental components of the ambivalence that will characterize Protestant encounters with (and representations of) the native populations in the New World for the better part of a century. It is not my aim to provide an exhaustive reading of DeBry's work in this chapter, but rather to use his work as a means of perceiving and exploring what I will argue in this book are the dynamics of Protestant colonial writing. Borrowing a phrase from Thomas Harriot, I will argue that English Protestants consistently constructed their encounters with the "natives" of the New World in terms of "fear and love." Although, as I will show in a moment, Harriot specifically intended his phrase to refer to the feelings of "the natives" themselves, colonizing Protestants also confronted the native inhabitants with the same mixture of fear and love.

The visual representations of the native inhabitants contained in the first and third volumes of the *Great Voyages* reveal Harriot's binary at work. If Protestants felt compelled to represent their encounters with the natives as driven by love – or at least kindness – they also had to acknowledge the considerable fear that native customs and behavior might provoke among European settlers. In his work, DeBry accordingly gives play to both of these powerful emotions, but he does so in an almost paradoxical way. Accompanying the text of Léry, whose explicit commitment is to a Protestantism that seems to transcend national boundaries, are frightening images intended to communicate the necessity of Protestant colonial intervention. And accompanying the text of Harriot, who commits himself to an undertaking that promises to strengthen a Protestant nation, are images that reveal the potential for love in the well managed Protestant colony. Insofar as they offer DeBry two different versions of the Protestant potential of colonialism, Léry and Harriot furnish their Protestant readers with a means of resolving the tension between two different modes of perceiving the colonial encounter. And as a result, from this moment forward, fear and love will function as the poles in an antinomy that will continue to inform Protestant colonization for at least another century.

WHAT OF FRANCE?

As any reader of Jean de Léry's *History of a Voyage to the Land of Brazil* will immediately recognize, the author did not need Théodore DeBry to tell him that the recounting of his New-World adventures could serve as an allegory of the Protestant plight within Europe. What began as Léry's attempt "to escape from religious strife in France and establish a new community where Catholic and Protestant alike could live under a free and tolerant government," ended with Léry's discovery of the perfect way to comment on that religious strife.[7] Léry, in other words, went to the New World hoping to discover a *literal* space where Protestantism might flourish, but upon his return to Europe, he would realize that he had instead found a *figurative* space from which he might articulate a compelling critique of Catholic Europe and a powerful new notion of European Protestant identity.

There were probably many things that drew DeBry to publish *Histoire d'un voyage faict en la Terre du Bresil*, but one was almost certainly the biography of its author Jean de Léry. A Protestant like DeBry, Léry witnessed and survived the bloody religious conflicts that engulfed Europe during the sixteenth century. Born in 1534 in Burgundy, Léry went as a young man to Geneva to receive training for the ministry in the Church of Geneva. In September of 1556, while in Geneva, Léry interrupted his training to travel with thirteen other men to Brazil to join the first Protestant mission to the New World. They had been invited there by one Nicholas Durand de Villegagnon, who had left France the year before with the backing of the Huguenot Admiral Gaspard de Coligny and the Cardinal of Lorraine.[8] According to Léry, "Before leaving France,Villegagnon promised several honorable persons who accompanied him that he would establish the pure service of God in the place where he would reside."[9] Léry, in other words, was under the impression that Villegagnon would be committed to help establish and support the Reformed Church in his colony. But Villegagnon, whom Claude Lévi-Strauss described as "a strange character, who had tried every profession in turn," showed himself at the outset to be an unreliable friend to Reform, and in the end he proved downright treacherous to Léry and his companions.[10]

Disallusioned and embittered, Léry returned to France, arriving in January of 1558, after a harrowing voyage in which many of his ship's crew died of starvation. From France, Léry went immediately back to Geneva to continue his studies for the ministry, a career which he began in earnest in 1562. Although Léry appears to have begun writing his *History of a Voyage* in 1563 in Geneva, the manuscript, which met with enough mishaps to make any writer foreswear writing forever, would not be published until 1578.[11] In the meantime, in August, 1572, Léry would witness first-hand the St. Bartholomew's Day Massacre from his church in La Charite-sur-Loire. Escaping to Sancerre, Léry would there survive the siege of Sancerre that lasted from January until August of 1573. Almost immediately after emerging safely from the siege, Léry produced one of the best known narratives of the Protestant struggles for survival in the wake of the St. Bartholomew's Day Massacre. That narrative, the *Histoire memorable de la ville de Sancerre*, was published in 1574.

Although the Massacre occurred some sixteen years after Léry had left Brazil, and although Léry had already composed a draft of his *History of a Voyage*, the effects of that subsequent series of horrifying events would leave an unmistakable imprint on the narrative of his earlier experiences. In the words of Frank Lestringant, "The trauma of this second experience is superimposed on the first."[12] The *History of a Voyage*, therefore, repeatedly invokes the bloody events of 1572–3 as a point of reference for understanding what he saw and did in Brazil. As the following passage passionately demonstrates, Léry found it impossible not to connect the cannibalism he saw in Brazil with that he witnessed in Sancerre.

> Furthermore, if it comes to the brutal action of really (as one says) chewing and devouring human flesh, have we not found people in these regions over here, even among those who bear the name of Christian, both in Italy and elsewhere, who, not content with having cruelly put to death their enemies, have been unable to slake their bloodthirst except by eating their livers and hearts? I defer to the histories. And, without going further, what of France? (I am French, and it grieves me to say it.) During the bloody tragedy that began in Paris on the twenty-fourth of August 1572 – for which I do not accuse those who are not responsible – among other acts horrible to recount, which were perpetrated at that time throughout the kingdom, the fat of human bodies (which, in ways more barbarous than those of the savages, were butchered at Lyon after being pulled out of the Saone) – was it not publicly sold to the highest bidder? The livers, hearts, and other parts of these bodies – were they not eaten by the furious murderers, of whom Hell itself stands in horror? Likewise, after the wretched massacre of one Coeur de Roy, who professed the Reformed Faith in the city of Auxerre – did not those who committed this murder cut hiš heart to pieces, display it for sale to those who hated him, and finally, after grilling it over coals – glutting their rage like mastiffs – eat of it?[13]

The horror with which Léry recounts "the brutal action of *really* (as one says) chewing and devouring human flesh," recalls his earlier disputations with Villegagnon and his followers who insisted on the validity of the Catholic doctrine of transubstantiation: "they wanted not only to eat the flesh of Jesus Christ grossly rather than spiritually, but what was worse, like the savages named *Ouetaca*, of whom I have already spoken, they wanted to chew and swallow it raw."[14] It would seem that the horrific actions of his countrymen during the siege merely function as an extension of their belief in transubstantiation. Although there is something predictable and logical to the idea of Catholics eating *real* human flesh – not just the bread and wine of the Eucharist – there is in the end what Lestringant calls the "unassimilable horror" of cannibalism. It is this "unassimilable horror" that leads to Léry's ambivalent declaration of his own identity: "I am French, and it grieves me to say it." Although he does "not accuse those who are not responsible," he seems to accept, if only implicitly, responsibility himself for what he saw. When he witnesses the cannibalism in Brazil, he can confidently declare his identity as a Frenchman and feel secure in the knowledge that part of being French means that he will not eat – "really" chew – human flesh. What we are witnessing in this passage is the splintering off of a Protestant identity. It is not his *national* identity that puts him beyond the reach of this fear of consuming human flesh, but rather his *religious* identity. It does not grieve him to say that he is a *Protestant* but rather to say that he is *French*. For Léry, whose primary investment is in the cause of Reformed religion, the move to distance himself from his national identity does not present the same sorts of problems that would confront English colonizers, who sought to knit national and religious identity together through colonial undertaking. Indeed, as we shall see in the final two chapters of this book, Roger Williams and John Eliot were able to gain considerable support for their projects by suggesting that the *status quo* of English colonialism threatened to sever Englishness from Protestantism.

When considered in the context of Léry's disciplined and consistent commitment to the establishment of Protestantism in the New World, Lévi-Strauss's remarks on the Léry's frivolity seem to have missed the mark. According to Lévi-Strauss, Léry and his fellow colonists, "instead of working for survival. . . spent weeks in foolish discussions" about theological matters.[15] It may indeed have been foolish for Léry's band of missionaries to engage in theological debates when they might have attended to the work of survival. But in the writing of his narrative, the debates are everything. By virtue of their ghoulish insistence on the transubstantiation of the Eucharist, Catholics would always be associated in Protestant colonial discourse with predation and slaughter. As Lestringant observes, the crisis in Sancerre gave Léry a new context in which to interpret the cannibalism he had witnessed more than a decade earlier in Brazil. According to Lestringant, it was through the description of cannibalism "that Brazil became prominent once again, and Brazil was not as alien as might have been thought to the Burgundian town in the throes of the Wars of Religion."[16] In short, the result of what Léry saw at Sancerre led to what Lestringant calls his "allegorization" of cannibalism: "Anthropophagy is not a mere fact. It can signify beyond itself: cruelty, usury, an absence of all charity."[17]

The process of allegorization that Lestringant associates specifically with Léry's descriptions of cannibalism, however, is in fact much more widespread. Indeed, a great deal of Léry's *History of a Voyage* is an allegory of the ongoing Protestant struggle within Europe. Curiously, however, Léry's allegory implicitly requires his Protestant readers both to identify with and distance themselves from the native persons portrayed therein. The result of these two contradictory operations is a profound ambivalence that will shape the Protestant colonial self-fashioning in the decades ahead. When they are not identifying with the native inhabitants as fellow victims of Catholic treachery and predation, the Protestants will be demonizing them as unconscious adherents of Roman Catholicism. But it is important to acknowledge that even when he is identifying with the Brazilian native people, the Tupinamba natives in his *History of a Voyage*, Léry does not endow them with a fully operational human subjectivity. Thus, even within the process of identification itself, there is ambivalence. Homi Bhabha has called this phenomenon "colonial mimicry," which he defines as,

the desire for a reformed, recognizable Other, *as a subject of a difference that is almost the same, but not quite.* Which is to say, that the discourse of mimicry is constructed around an *ambivalence*; in order to be effective mimicry must continually produce its slippage, its excess, its difference. The authority of that mode of colonial discourse that I have called mimicry is therefore stricken by an indeterminacy: mimicry emerges as the representation of a difference that is itself a process of disavowal.[18]

Even when Léry is encouraging his readers to see the Tupinamba as allies in the struggle against the threat of global Catholic domination, they must always function as "almost the same, but not quite."

Léry's ambivalence about his own identity as a Frenchman is of course mirrored by his response to the Tupinamba. An almost comic story he tells in the middle of his *History* gives us a sense of the ambivalence he feels toward the Tupinamba.

Not only was I kept awake by the noise that the savages made, dancing and whistling all night while eating their prisoner; but, what is more, one of them approached me with the victim's foot in hand, cooked and *boucané*, asking me (as I learned later, for I didn't understand at the time) if I wanted to eat some of it. His countenance filled me with such terror that you need hardly ask if I lost all desire to sleep. Indeed, I thought that by brandishing the human flesh he was eating, he was threatening me and wanted to make me understand that I was about to be similarly dealt with. . . At daybreak my interpreter (who had been off carousing with those rascals of savages all night long in other village houses) came to find me. Seeing me, as he said, not only ashen-faced and haggard but also feverish, he asked me whether I was sick, or if I hadn't rested well. Distraught, I answered wrathfully that they had well and truly kept me from sleeping, and that he was a scoundrel to have left me among these people whom I couldn't understand at all; still anxious as ever, I urged that we get ourselves out of there with all possible speed. Thereupon he told me that I should have no fear, and that it wasn't us they were after. When he recounted the whole business to the savages – who, rejoicing at my coming, and thinking to show me affection, had not budged from my side all night – they said that they had sensed that I had been somewhat frightened of them, for which they were very sorry.[19]

This story, which would seem to anticipate by almost three centuries the comic misunderstanding between Queequeg and Ishmael in the opening pages of *Moby Dick*, does not end in the undying friendship between Léry and his well-meaning hosts. Rather it leads to his irretrievable and irreversible horror at their barbarity. It is significant that it is precisely their "affection" that has led to his "terror." Indeed, what Léry has staked out in this passage is the ambivalence that will mark the Protestant encounter with the New World. Dissatisfied with what they have found in the Old World, Europeans in general, and Protestants in particular, will look to the New World as a means of re-imagining themselves. It would be a mistake, therefore, to suggest that only Protestants reacted with ambivalence toward the native inhabitants they encountered. As Roger Schlesinger has argued, with respect to the Catholic André Thevet, whose work Léry attempts to refute in his *History of a Voyage*, "Thevet's assessment of America and its inhabitants, moreover, reveals his ambivalence about the New World. On the one hand, he firmly believed in the innate superiority of European values and institutions and in the righteousness of the European conquest of the Indians. At the same time, he obviously respected and admired some New World rulers and considered some facets of their societies to be equal or even superior to their European equivalents."[20] If for Catholics the ambivalence derived from the conflict between their unswerving faith in their right of conquest and the recognition that individual native persons could behave nobly, for Protestants the ambivalence would be a direct function of their need to use the native inhabitants in their efforts to articulate a new sense of subjectivity, a new identity.

Léry's ambivalence toward the Brazilian native people, who almost always occupy center-stage, is palpable. He needs them, in the same way that Protestants will always need natives in their colonial narratives, but he can never fully embrace them. Early on in the text, for instance, Léry discovers in his ethnographic representations the possibility of using his descriptions of the Brazilians and their behavior as a means of commenting on the deplorable sartorial practices in his native France.

But what I have said about these savages is to show that, while we condemn them so austerely for going about shamelessly with their bodies entirely uncovered, we ourselves, in the sumptuous display, superfluity, and excess of our own costume, are hardly more laudable. And, to conclude this point, I would to God that each of us dressed modestly, and more for decency and necessity than for glory and worldliness.[21]

Articulating a theme that will sound familiar to students of English Puritanism, Léry asserts that the shamelessness with which the Indians display their bodies is more easily defended than the "sumptuous display" in dress exhibited by many Europeans, including Villegagnon, the leader of the colony. It is not that he finds the nakedness of the Indians admirable. In fact, he finds it distasteful. But, however disturbing their nakedness may be, it is without pretence. Although there was no way that he could have known it at the time, Léry is here inaugurating what would become a tradition in the Protestant representations of the native peoples of the New World: the discovery among the savages of a simplicity and honesty that serves as its own critique of the duplicity and division of Europeans. But, if the native inhabitants model for Protestant readers the simplicity and honesty that were their ideals, they embody something less than the ideal. They are almost the same but not quite.

If Léry's discovery of admirable traits among the Tupinamba differentiated his narrative from most other (Catholic) treatments of the native populations, so too did his willingness to allow them to criticize the Europeans, many of whom came to the New World only to reap economic benefits.[22] In fact, it is with great effect that Léry records the native peoples' bemusement at the colonists who risk their lives for what seem material trifles.

This nation which we consider so barbarous, charitably mocks those who cross the sea at the risk of their lives to go seek brazilwood in order to get rich; however blind this people may be in attributing more to nature and to the fertility of the earth than we do to the power and the providence of God, it will rise up in judgment against those despoilers who are as abundant over here, among those bearing the title of Christians, as they are scarce over there, among the native inhabitants. Therefore, to take up what I said elsewhere – that the Tupinamba mortally hate the avaricious – would to God that the latter might be imprisoned among them, so that they might even in this life serve as demons and furies to torment those whose maws are insatiable, who do nothing but suck the blood and marrow of others. To our great shame, and to justify our savages in the little care that they have for the things of this world, I had to make this digression in their favor.[23]

We witness in this passage the confluence of a series of strategies that would become commonplace in Protestant colonial writing by the middle of the next century. By putting critical words in the mouths of his savages, Léry constructs them as allies of the Protestant cause. Léry thus allows his Protestant readers to see the drama unfolding in the New World as merely another version of *their* drama. Although he authorizes them to articulate a critique of Catholic colonial practices, Léry stops short of embracing the Tupinamba as human beings. Indeed, they seem to function in the passage, not as human subjects, but as a means by which avaricious Europeans might be made to imagine themselves as victims, if they were to be transported to the colonial scene. To the extent that they stand opposed to the Spaniards, whose avaricious conquest of the New World was already well known in Europe, the Tupinamba share something with Léry and his fellow Protestants. In the end, however, Léry can only gaze with ambivalence upon these people who are almost the same, but not quite.

Near the end of his tract, Léry's ambivalence assumes its most poignant form, when he describes himself as a man without a place.

So that saying goodbye here to America, I confess for myself that although I have always loved my country and do even now, still, seeing the little – next to none at all – of fidelity that is left here, and, what is worse, the disloyalties of people toward each other – in short, since our whole situation is Italianized, and consists only in dissimulation and words without effect – I often regret that I am not among the savages, in whom (as I have amply shown in this narrative) I have known more frankness than in many over here, who, for their condemnation, bear the title of "Christian."[24]

Throughout his *History of a voyage*, Léry uses the first-person as a means of asserting his own authority. He constantly reminds his readers that *he* has traveled to the New World, and therefore his observations and responses are not to be doubted. Here, however, Léry uses the first person not simply to assert authority but to articulate a notion of identity. Paradoxically, it is at precisely the moment when he is ready to say who he is that Léry finds the available categories to be empty of meaning.

Michel de Certeau observed that Léry's "narrative plays on the relation between the structure which establishes the separation and the operation which overcomes it, creating effects of meaning in this fashion. The break is what is taken for granted everywhere by the text, itself a labor of suturing."[25] Although de Certeau's claims for the text as a whole seem plausible, this passage would seem to suggest that "the labor of suturing" becomes increasingly difficult for Léry to perform convincingly. He seems not to identify with France – a place that "consists only in dissimulation and words without effect." Moreover, France has become "Italianized," no doubt a reference to the influence of the papacy as well as to the increasing factionalization that greatly troubled Léry. It is clear from this passage that Léry has found in his travels some glimpse of a new subjectivity. Constantly referring to those who "bear the title of 'Christian'" throughout the *History of a Voyage*, Léry seems to have discovered in his own travels the ideal way to live as a Christian. But the mournful quality of his observation seems to place that idealized identity just out of his grasp. He does not wish to leave France, and yet he longs for a self that is actualized by the voyage away from France. He longs for something that is always just out of reach. As de Certeau observed, "his is a reverse pilgrimage: far from rejoining the referential body of an orthodoxy (the sacred city, the tomb, the basilica), his itinerary goes from the center to the borders, in searching for a space where he can find a ground."[26] As I suggested in the introduction to this book, such is the nature of the colonial adventure. It is always a voyage to the margins to find something that will have value in the metropolitan center. For Léry, that thing of value is a stable notion of Protestant identity.

FEAR AND LOVE

Although DeBry made the texts of Harriot and Léry function
together within the context of the *Great Voyages*, we should not let
that fact obscure some fundamental differences between the two.
Léry's *History of a Voyage* is a description of an attempt to establish
an explicitly Protestant colony in the New World. Harriot's *Briefe
and True Report*, on the other hand, is primarily a promotional pamphlet intended to convince his countrymen of the advantages of
the colonial enterprise. To put it another way, Léry went to the
New World as a Protestant first and as a Frenchman second, while
Harriot, on the other hand, went to Virginia as an Englishman
first, and as a Protestant only second, if at all. If Léry's text, therefore, is about the Protestant potential of the colonial undertaking,
then Harriot's is about the national potential of the same. The
crucial point here is that DeBry saw that these very different sorts
of texts could both be put to work in the service of a common goal,
namely the advancement of international Protestantism. To say
that is also to suggest that DeBry almost certainly recognized in
the early English voyages to Virginia the beginnings of what was
to become the first colony established by a Protestant nation.

Unlike Léry's text, which constructs the colonial endeavor as an
explicit allegory of the doctrinal conflict between the Catholics
and the Protestants, Harriot's *Briefe and True Report* seems to recognize, if only implicitly, the importance that the colonial project
might occupy in England's ongoing effort to fashion itself as a
nation. But just as Léry needed the Tupinamba to stage the conflict between Protestants and Catholics, Harriot needed the Indians of Virginia to demonstrate the ease with which English colonists might occupy their colonies in the New World.[27] The native
people in Harriot, however, are not explicitly functioning as actors
in a European drama. Rather they are implicitly defining the
nature and purpose of English colonialism. Writing at a point
when the Spanish atrocities in the New World have given the
English an easy way of distinguishing their own colonial
enterprises from those of the Spanish, Harriot must define England's relation to the inhabitants in distinctly different terms. As
Harriot implicitly demonstrates, the relationship with the native
people will define English colonial identity. Where Léry's narrative
requires him to identify with the Tupinamba at the same time as

he distances himself from them, Harriot's identity is not dependent on perceiving the inhabitants as participating in an analogous struggle. Rather Harriot shows that English colonial identity resides in the relationship itself. Léry ultimately arrives at an
impasse because he is left with no place to go. He cannot completely accept his identity as a Frenchman. Nor can he contentedly
live among the Tupinamba. Harriot suggests that the English will
function as protectors of the native people. In Harriot's text,
therefore, it becomes clear that the English must become the
adoptive parents of the Indians – adoptive parents who will train
and educate the Indians in European ways. But, as he must confront the possibility that the inhabitants will not always be obedi-
ent and cooperative children, Harriot must acknowledge that the
relationship of the parent to the child is ultimately an ambivalent
one.

As J. H. Elliott has observed, continental Europe had acquired
"by the early 1580s . . . the most lurid information about Spanish
conduct in the Indies." And European impressions were only
reinforced by DeBry's engravings of *Brevíssima relación* which left
"an indelible image of Spanish atrocities on the European consciousness."[28] As I suggested in the last chapter, the English were
quick to grasp the implications of the Spanish atrocities – implications that would impinge both on England's emerging colonial
operations and on England's own position within European geopolitics. Just as the translators of Las Casas, whose work we examined above, seized upon the chance to incite a xenophobic reaction
along religious lines, so too other writers saw in Las Casas the
possibility of defining England's own nascent colonial project in
contrast to the cruel and rapacious ways of the Spanish adventurers in the New World. In addition to Richard Hakluyt, whose
influential pamphlet we have already discussed, John Hooker, who
augmented *Holinshed's Chronicles of Ireland* in 1586, also suggested
that England's colonial adventures could be defined against those
of the Spanish. He accordingly opened his portion of the *Chronicles*
with an Epistle Dedicatorie to Sir Walter Ralegh in which he
praised Ralegh who had,

made a plantation of the people of your owne English nation in Virginia,
the first English colonie that ever was there planted, to the no little
derogation of the glorie of the Spaniards, & an impeach to their vaunts;
who bicause with all cruell immanitie, contrarie to all naturall

humanitie, they subdued a naked and a yeelding people, whom they sought for gaine and not for any religion or plantation of a commonwealth. . . and against the course of all humane nature did scorch and rost them to death, as by their owne histories dooth appeare.[29]

Although Hooker does not specify which of "theire own histories" he was reading, it is likely that he was using Las Casas, the very same text Hakluyt himself had mined for graphic descriptions of Spanish cruelty. In any event, Hooker's unnamed source is irrelevant. What is important is the, by now, almost obligatory figuring of English colonialism as diametrically opposed to that of the Spanish.

The English attached many words to the Spanish colonial efforts: cruel, greedy, murderous, monstrous, inhumane. They also attached many words to the native people whom the Spanish encountered: innocent, yielding, naked, peaceable, mild, gentle. But there was one emotion that the English used to characterize the mechanism by which the Spanish gained control over the native populations: fear. To understand the semantic value of the word fear in the context of colonial promotion in London during the 1580s, one need only cast a brief glance at the 1583 translation of Las Casas's *Brevíssima relación*.

the Spaniardes advised with themselves to make a massacre, or a chastise (as they speake) to the ende, to raise and plant a *dread* of their cruelties in every corner of all that countrey.

How this hath been always their customary manner of doing, in every region which they have entred into, to execute incontinent upon their first arrival, some notable cruell butcherie, to the ende, that those poore and innocent lambes should tremble for *feare*. [my italics][30]

Although DeBry's engravings based on Las Casas offered readers the most gripping visual rendition of the fear that the Spanish inspired in the native inhabitants, there is very little in them that would have been new to the English. The *Brevíssima relación* is, in fact, filled with stories of helpless native people submitting to terror. In most cases, they submit only to be brutally murdered by the Spanish, but in a few instances, the Indians are so terrorized that they take their own lives. As perceived by the English in the 1580s, to colonize as a Spaniard was to rule by fear. To colonize as a Protestant, however, was to announce one's desire to be loved by the native people.

Even Thomas Harriot, although he does not mention Las Casas

or the Spanish atrocities, shows signs of having grasped the importance of avoiding the brutality of the Spanish. But in Harriot's text, the attempt to imagine a relationship with the Virginia natives that is not governed by fear conflicts with his desire to assure potential investors that the English will be able to control both the Indians and the territory that they occupy. This is of course the conflict between fear and love – a conflict that English colonial writers would struggle to reconcile for more than a century. Harriot's articulation of it is revealing.

At resteth I speak a word or two of the natural inhabitants, their natures and manners, leaving large discourse thereof until time more convenient hereafter: nowe only so far forth, as that you may know, how that they in respect of troubling our inhabiting and planting are not to be feared; but that they shall have cause both to fear and love us, that shall inhabit with them.[31]

In this passage, which is taken from the opening paragraph of the final section of the *Briefe Report*, Harriot seems to avoid choosing between two ways of imagining the English relationship with the native people. Because the *Briefe Report* was primarily intended to reassure potential investors of, among other things, the ease with which the native inhabitants might be made to submit to English rule, Harriot had to recognize the value of fear as a tool of control. And yet, as a political creature attempting to imagine the difficulty of promoting among the English a colonial enterprise that openly sought to intimidate the native populations, Harriot perceived the importance of love. Rather than embrace the Machiavellian assertion that "it is much safer to be feared than to be loved," Harriot therefore suggests that the English colonists will be able to do what Machiavelli says is most difficult to do, namely to rule by fear *and* love.[32] Ultimately, Harriot will have to choose between fear and love, and not surprisingly, he will choose fear. Before he arrives at that moment, however, Harriot argues that there is no reason that the English cannot expect to enjoy a "loving" relationship with the native inhabitants.

According to Harriot, the fear and love of the native people will do more than function as Machiavellian tools of control. In Harriot's construction of the scene of the colonial encounter, these feelings on the part of the native inhabiitants will obviate the need for fear on the part of the English. The "natives", Harriot tells us, "are not to be feared," precisely because "*they* shall have cause both to fear and love us." Not much later in the *Brief Report*, continuing his tendency to displace the emotional burden onto the native populations, Harriot will implicitly suggest that the native inhabitants' fear and love will make it unnecessary for the English to feel desire toward them. Indeed, as I will contend in later chapters, the English displacement of desire onto the native populations will constitute a prominent feature of their colonial narratives.

In respect of us they are a people poore, and for want of skill and judgement in the knowledge and use of our things, do esteem our trifles before things of greater value: Notwithstanding in their proper manner considering the want of such means as we have, they seem very ingenious; For although they have no such tooles, nor any such crafts, sciences, and arts as we; yet in those things they do, they show excellencie of wit. And by how much they upon due consideration shall find our manner of knowledges and crafts to exceed theirs in perfection, and speed for doing or execution, by so much the more is it probable that they should desire our friendships and love, and have the greater respect for pleasing and obeying us. Whereby may bee hoped if meanes of good government bee used, that they may in short time be brought to civilitie, and the embracing of true religion.[33]

Although the passage reveals an explicit commitment to Protestantism in the concluding phrase – "the embracing of true religion" – what marks it more definitively as a piece of English Protestant colonial writing is the subtle series of moves that effectively displace the colonial desire onto the native populations. Indeed, subsequent Protestant writers, wary of the overly rapacious desires that seemed to drive Catholic colonization, would consistently attempt to represent the native peoples they encountered as "desiring" the friendship, commerce, and faith of the English.

Having transferred to the native inhabitants the desire for the love and good will of the English, Harriot buries the desires of the English in a series of passive constructions: "whereby may be hoped if meanes of good government bee used, that they may in short time be brought to civilitie, and the embracing of true religion." It is important to note that the displacement is narrated by language outlining a series of transactions in which the English always find themselves in possession of the objects of Indian desire: "skill and judgement," "things of greater value," "tools," "crafts," "sciences," "friendship and love," and last but not least, "true religion."[34] In other words, Harriot envisions an economy in which the English are conveniently in possession of the most valued commodities. Such a structure would of course have helped to reassure potential investors of the likelihood of realizing profits without having to resort to terrorizing the native inhabitants. If the natives make the mistake of valuing a trifle "before things of greater value," then that is not the problem of the colonizers.

There is yet another way to read the above passage, and that is as a passage that constructs the native people as children. Harriot is careful to defend the native inhabitants by suggesting that their failure to discern the true value of "things" is to be attributed to a lack of "skill and judgement" rather than to some congenital defect. "In those things they do," Harriot tells us, "they show excellencie of wit." The problem, in other words, is developmental. There is no reason to assume that the native people won't show that same "excellencie of wit" once they have been equipped with "the knowledge and use of our things." Harriot would seem to be constructing the situation as one in which the native inhabitants are children who need to learn "respect for pleasing and obeying" the English. As Harriot continues, it becomes clear that this is precisely how he views the native people – as children.

These their opinions I have set down the more at large that it may appear unto you that there is good hope that they may be brought through discreet dealing and government to the embracing of the truth and consequently to honour, obey, fear, and love us.[35]

The last four verbs of this sentence would seem to construct the relationship between the native people and the English as a parent–child relationship. For it is the child's duty to "honour, obey, fear, and love" the parent. The naive native inhabitants, who cannot recognize the value of the things of the English, who do not possess tools, will become the children of the English.

Harriot's attempts to define the relationship between his people and the native populations must end finally in the acknowledgement that the Indians will almost certainly need to be motivated by fear if the English are to have their way. It is at this point that Harriot's implicit treatment of the Indians as children must finally give way to a much more Machiavellian set of instincts.

And although some of our companie towards the end of the year, shewed themselves too fierce, in slaying some of the people, in some towns, upon causes that on our part, might easily enough have been borne withall: yet notwithstanding because it was on their part justly deserved, the alteration of their opinions generally and for the most part concerning us is the less to be doubted. And whatsoever else they may be, by carefulness of ourselves need nothing at all to be feared. The best nevertheless in all this as in all actions besides is to be endeavored and hoped, and of the worst that may happen to notice to be taken with consideration, and as much as may be eschewed.[36]

Harriot, who is usually so precise, chooses not to tell the readers even the most basic details of the episode: how it happened, where it happened, how many people were involved, etc. Nor does Harriot offer any answers to the more vexing questions that the mysterious slayings occasion: Why, for instance, have the Indians "justly deserved" the harsh penalty if the colonists were "too fierce" – especially if the behavior that deserved the penalty "might easily enough have been borne withall"? Instead, he chooses to refer to this lethal event only in vague terms: the colonists are said to have slain "*some* of the people in *some* of the towns." It would appear that, when confronted with recalcitrant native inhabitants, the English have had to abandon love and cling to fear. In spite of the criticism of English behavior implicit in his evasive description, Harriot reassures his readers that the outcome has not jeopardized the standing of the English among the native people. The renewed (if begrudging) respect for the English on the part of the Indians, Harriot implies, will allow the English to continue in their colonial efforts without fear. Significantly, Harriot has returned his readers to the starting point of his discussion of the native peoples and their customs. Just as at the outset he suggested that the fear and love of the native people would alleviate the need for the English to fear them, so too now Harriot concludes by asserting that, as a result of the actions of the colonizers, the native inhabitants "need nothing at all to be feared."[37]

It would be easy to dismiss Harriot's rationalization as simply another example of the coercion that lay just below the surface of the English rhetoric pertaining to their colonization of the New World. According to Stephen Greenblatt, Harriot's text presents its readers with "a strange paradox: Harriot tests and seems to confirm the most radically subversive hypothesis in his culture about the origin and function of religion by imposing his religion – with its intense claims to transcendence, unique truth, inescapable coercive force – on others." The paradox, for Greenblatt, lies in the fact that Harriot's text, in what would appear to be a dangerously subversive move, unmasks the "coercive force" necessary to promote the spread of Christianity in the New World. And yet, even after exposing the power relations, the text seems not to have damaged or discredited the project of imposing Christianity on the native populations of America. Greenblatt explains the paradox by suggesting that "the subversiveness . . . is at the same time contained by the power it would appear to threaten. . . One may go still further and suggest that the power Harriot both serves and embodies not only produces its own subversion but is actively built upon it; the project of evangelical colonialism is not set over against the skeptical critique of religious coercion but battens on the very confirmation of that critique."[38]

By suggesting that the contradictions in the discursive formations of the state ultimately increase rather than diminish the power of the state, Greenblatt pursues a Foucauldian line of argument. Accordingly, Harriot's testing of what Greenblatt calls the "Machiavellian hypothesis" is "invisible not only to those on whom the religion is supposedly imposed but also to most readers and quite possibly to Harriot himself." It would appear that the scheming prince of Machiavelli has been replaced by Foucault's pervasive notion of state power. Therefore, Harriot – who "might not have grasped fully the disturbing implications of his own text" – is not so much the author of a Machiavellian conspiracy to impose a belief system upon helpless native inhabitants as he is an unwitting participant in a much larger plan to extend the reach of England's state power. Harriot's role in this plan is to articulate the potentially subversive strand in a discourse of power that, paradoxically, requires subversion in order to ensure its ultimate success. Or, quoting Greenblatt again, this "subversiveness is the very product of that power and furthers its ends."[39]

Ultimately Greenblatt sees Harriot's text as an instance of "the process whereby Indian culture is constituted as a culture and thus brought into the light for study, discipline, correction, transformation."[40] I would argue, however, that there is something a good deal more interesting going on in Harriot's text than simply the erasure of another culture. Harriot would seem to be using the emotions of the "natural inhabitants" to describe a conflict within himself and the English. Indeed, Harriot's desire for both fear and love points to an underlying ambivalence that permeated English attitudes both toward themselves and toward native populations – an ambivalence that would become England's most easily discernible response to the native populations during the next century. Moreover, in imagining the English as eliciting both fear and love from the natives of Virginia, Harriot was presciently articulating what would become England's primary mode in its management of the native populations in its colonies. However, rather than functioning simply as strategic modalities in a Machiavellian quest for power, the fear and love of the native peoples also formed a crucial component in England's attempt to conceive of and represent itself as a colonizing nation. As the breakdown of the binary in Harriot's text would suggest, fear was ultimately more effective than love in the maintenance of order and control. And it would be this simple, incontrovertible fact that would present the English with the greatest difficulty in the years ahead as they sought, through their colonial enterprises, to construct an unambiguously Protestant national identity. While fear might serve the immediate needs of a nation attempting to extract obedience from uncooperative native inhabitants, it would always threaten to overshadow the love that, rhetorically at least, marked English colonialism as Protestant.

TRUE PICTURES AND FASHIONS

As Hugh Honour observed some time ago, the engraved images of the *Great Voyages* seem to follow the contours of the ongoing Protestant encounter with the New World. Initially, European Protestants placed the native populations at the center of the colonial encounter as a means of distinguishing their colonizing adventures from those of the Catholics. Eventually, however, the native people were "reduced to the role of 'extras' in the great drama of European expansion." DeBry's *Great Voyages* does indeed seem to develop along the lines that Honour suggests. The first volume contains no images of Europeans, save for the handful of engravings of Picts at the very end – about which I shall say more in a moment. In the next two volumes, Europeans appear only as marginal characters. And in volumes 4,

Figure 1. "A weroan or great Lorde of Virginia" from Thomas Harriot, *A briefe and true report of the New Found Land of Virginia*, Frankfurt, 1590.

On of the chieff Ladyes of Secota. IIII.

Figure 2. "On the cheiff Ladyes of Secota" from Harriot, *A briefe and true report of the New Found Land of Virginia*.

Ayounge gentill woeman doughter VI.
of Secota.

Figure 3. "A yonge and gentill woeman doughter of Secota" from Harriot, *A briefe and true report of the New Found Land of Virginia.*

Their feetheynge of their meate in XV.
earthen pottes.

Figure 4. "Their seetheynge of their meete in earthen pottes" from Harriot, *A briefe and true report of the New Found Land of Virginia.*

Figure 5. "Their sitting at meate" from Harriot, *A briefe and true report of the New Found Land of Virginia.*

Figure 6. "The true picture of one picte" from Harriot, *A briefe and true report of the New Found Land of Virginia.*

Figure 7. "The true picture of a women picte" from Harriot, *A briefe and true report of the New Found Land of Virginia*.

AMERICAE TERTIA PARS
Memorabilē prouinciæ Braſiliæ Hiſtoriam
continēs, germanico primùm ſermone ſcriptam à
Ioāne Stadio Homburgēſi Heſſo, nunc autem
latinitate donatam à Teucrio Annæo Priuato Col
chanthe Po:& Med: Addita eſt Narratio profectionis
Ioannis Lerij in eamdem Prouinciam, quā ille initio
gallicè conſcripſit, poſtea verò Latinam fecit. His ac
ceſsit Deſcriptio Morum & Ferocitatis incolarum
illius Regionis; atque Colloquium ipſorum idio-
mate conſcriptum.

Omnia recens euulgata, & eiconibus in æs inciſis
ac ad viuum expreſsis illuſtrata, ad normam exem
plaris prædictorum Autorum: ſtudio & diligentia
Theodori de Bry Leodienſis, atque ciuis.
Francofurtenſis anno M D XCII.

Venales reperiūtur in officina
Theodori de Bry.

Figure 8. Frontispiece from Theodor DeBry, *Americae Tertia Pars*, Frankfurt, 1592.

Figure 9. From Hans Staden, *Historiae Brasilianae*, liber primus, ch. 40, in DeBry, *Americae Tertia Pars*.

Figure 10. From Hans Staden, *Historiae Brasilianae*, liber secundus, ch. 29, in DeBry, *Americae Tertia Pars*.

Figure 11. From Jean de Léry, *Historia Navigationis in Brasiliam Americae Provinciam*, ch. 9, in DeBry, *Amencae Tertia Pars*.

5, and 6, the brutal Spaniards emerge larger than life as the butchers of the innocent Indians. From that point on, as Honour argues, "despite the steadily increasing interest they held for philosophers and missionaries, and the fear they continued to inspire in settlers, the Indians were steadily pushed to the back of the European picture of America. Sometimes they were almost pushed out of it altogether."[41]

In the remaining pages of this chapter, I will comment briefly on some of the images that accompanied DeBry's editions of Harriot's *Briefe and True Report* and Léry's *History of a Voyage*. Although the images in both volumes grant pre-eminence to the native populations, one can discern a less-than-subtle shift in emphasis from the first volume to the third. If DeBry's engravings for his edition of Harriot's *Briefe and True Report* seem to emphasize the love of the native inhabitants, the engravings that accompany his edition of Léry's *History* seem to be dominated by fear. It is not my intention to suggest that fear eventually governed Protestant encounters with and representations of the native inhabitants, but rather that fear and love combined to generate a complex and enduring ambivalence toward the native people. DeBry's engravings in the early volumes of the *Great Voyages*, therefore, can serve as point of departure for exploring this ambivalence.

It would be a gross overstatement to assert that DeBry transforms Harriot's text into something radically different from what it originally was. At the same time, however, one must acknowledge that the experience of reading DeBry's engraved folio edition of Harriot's *Briefe and True Report* differs significantly from that of reading the unillustrated quarto. Perhaps the best way to describe the difference is to say that DeBry's version is more expansive. He implicitly reinforces Harriot's claims by offering visual confirmation of the loving nature of the people and the material bounty of the place, but he goes further than Harriot as he attempts to construct a broader English and European context for the colonizing efforts that Harriot only narrowly situates.

The literal surface of DeBry's engravings is an ethnographic one.[42] Accordingly, one of their most striking features is the absence of any depictions of English settlers. Just as the fears and desires of the English are largely absent from Harriot's text, the English themselves are absent from DeBry's images. In this respect, DeBry seems to be following White, who does not seem to have produced any images of colonists interacting with the Indians either. Paul Hulton explains the absence in White by suggesting that his primary duty on the Virginia voyage was to document the native flora and fauna, including the inhabitants. It was not his job to represent the English, but rather to bring back as much information as possible about the land and its inhabitants. While maintaining White's exclusive focus on the native populations, DeBry subtly manipulates the ethnographic content of the images to produce a narrative that has as much to do with Protestant colonial ambitions as it does with ethnographic realism.[43]

The most noticeable way in which DeBry alters White's original images is in his tendency to Europeanize the features of the Indians. As historian J. H. Elliott wryly noted, "Readers dependent on De Bry's famous engravings for their image of the American Indian could be forgiven for assuming that the forests of America were peopled by heroic nudes, whose perfectly proportioned bodies made them first cousins of the ancient Greeks and Romans."[44] According to Mary Fuller, this process of "Europeanization" makes DeBry's engravings "more available for forms of ideological appropriation."[45] By Europeanizing the Indians, DeBry implicitly suggests that the process of transforming Indian culture is possible and that it has already begun. The Europeanization also suggests that the differences between the Indians and the English are ones of degree rather than of kind. That is, as Fuller and other critics have noted, the DeBry engravings suggest that Indian culture is simply a lesser developed version of English culture. Or, in words that I would argue apply more to DeBry than they do to Harriot, Stephen Greenblatt suggests that, "Harriot not only thought he was encountering a simplified version of his own culture but also evidently believed that he was encountering his own civilization's past."[46] I would suggest, moreover, that DeBry's Europeanization of the features of the Indians signifies that he saw in the English colonial project the possibility of transporting an idealized version of European Protestant culture to the New World.

Perhaps more than anything else, the Europeanization of the Indians' features speaks to the fears and desires of the English as they confronted the prospect of establishing colonies in the New World. The English desired to imagine themselves in possession of orderly colonies. They desired to imagine themselves as loved

by the native people. They desired also to recover through colonialism something from the past – a simplicity and honesty that
these people seemed to possess. But the English also had much to
fear. They feared losing control of themselves and their colonies.
They feared being attacked by the native inhabitants. They feared
the very strangeness of them. They feared that they would not be
able to love them. And probably most of all, the English feared
that they would arrive in the New World and become the same
monsters that the Spanish had become in their colonies. DeBry's
engravings are allegories of these fears and desires. In other words
these fears and desires of the English couldn't be articulated
openly, but they needed nonetheless to find a means of expression.
DeBry's allegorical engravings are such a means.

Several of DeBry's engravings present readers with structurally
similar images that offer representations of native people in the
foreground against a populated landscape in the background. In
each case, DeBry (or his assistant Gysbert Van Veen) constructs
the engraving by superimposing a reproduction of one of John
White's drawings of an individual Indian onto a reproduction of
one of White's landscape pictures. Each image depicts Indians
standing on an elevated foreground, with a populated landscape
in the background below, with both the foreground and the background taken from White's watercolors. The effects of DeBry's
superimposition of the foreground figures onto the background
landscape are both subtle and complicated. Standing literally
between the background and the viewers, the figures in the foreground seem to mediate between the viewers and the landscape.
Depicted in the *contrapposto* posture that was popular in the Man-
nerist painting of the period, these foreground figures seem
explicitly designed to render the strangeness and otherness of the
native inhabitants more familiar to English viewers. The position
that the foreground figures occupy within the engravings is also
significant. Apparently in control of everything they survey in the
valley below them, these foreground figures seem to function as
the arbiters of order and control in the engravings. These images
all suggest a metonymy of sorts: By mastering the savage in the
foreground the viewer will have command of all that is in the
background.

In figure 1, probably the most potentially menacing of this
group of engravings, we see a Europeanized representation of John

White's watercolor of an Indian lord. In the John White original, however, we see only the view from the front. DeBry, therefore, has fabricated from his imagination a view of this lord from the rear, the surprising effect of which is to demystify (and desexualize) entirely the suggestive tail that appears to dangle between the legs and therefore makes the lord in the John White original look like a devil. The haughty and self-conscious pose of the lord suggests to the viewer that the scene in the foreground is posed and contrasts with the spontaneity of the background.

It is also worth remarking that the background of this image depicts a group of Indians who are all engaged in the same activity – a sameness that would seem to render Indian culture in simple terms. In addition to the gestures and poses of figures, which lend a timeless quality to the engravings, the landscape seems to be peopled by "duplicates" and therefore eliminates the need to imagine Indian culture as complex or multivocal. Therefore, even in their primitive state, these Indians display a cultural unity and cohesion that would serve the English well as they attempted to transform and convert that culture. The backgrounds can also be used to counteract any impressions that the text might give the readers. After describing all of the various accoutrements of the Indians in their formal war garb (including chains, plates, quivers, tails), DeBry offers the following summary of their looks in the accompanying caption.

In this manner they go to war, or tho [sic] their solemn feasts and banquets. They take much pleasure in hunting of deer whereof there is great store in the country, for it is fruitful, pleasant, and full of Goodly woods. It hath also store of rivers full of divers sorts of fish. When they go to battle they paint their bodies in the most terrible manner that they can devise.

DeBry's suggestion that the Indians' costume is the same for war as it is for feasts is significant. In other words, this image and its caption transform what might be one of the most threatening moments in the text into one that focuses on the abundance of the land and the good nature of its inhabitants. Rather than focus on the warlike nature of the inhabitants, DeBry transforms the image into one of celebration. The organized, restrained manner of the Indians' hunting is also worth remarking. In the center and right of the engraving, we find four Indians engaged in shooting deer with bows and arrows, while on the far left another half-dozen-or-so men look on. The hunting therefore is portrayed as a social activity, and one that is pursued in a leisurely manner. But in addition to undercutting the potentially threatening message of the caption, the background communicates to the readers one of the central themes of most of the promotional literature, namely that Virginia is a land of plenty that will allow anyone to live like an aristocrat. The effect is to make the reader wonder whether the point of the final sentence isn't to say that "the most terrible manner that they can devise" is really not so terrible after all.

The next several engravings make use of a background of men fishing. Several of the captions of these engravings make mention of the pleasure that the Indian women take in watching their men fish. In figure 2 we are told that, "They are also delighted with walking in to the fields, and besides the river, to see the hunting of deers and catching of fish." And in figure 3, we are also told that the young women "delight also in seeing fish taken in the rivers." The overall effect of the background scenes depicting fishing is to communicate to the reader a sense of order and hierarchy. Just as the men fishing seem to be going about their business in an orderly way, so too the women gazing at them from the foreground behave in an appropriately respectful manner, "delighting" in watching the men. But the interplay of the foreground figures with the background scene also suggests another agenda. The engraving seems to put the viewer in the position of the foreground figures who look with love upon the men in the background. And yet the foreground contains images of women whose lack of modesty might make some readers uncomfortable. The overall effect, therefore, is to elicit discomfort from the viewer and then contain it within the structure of the image. DeBry's masterful engraving, therefore, coincidentally recalls a moment from Léry's text, where the author confronts the nudity of the Margaia with a complex mixture of embarrassment and pleasure.[47] In contrast, however, to the moment in Léry, where the tension seems less successfully resolved, DeBry, by juxtaposing the immodesty of the Virginia women to their traditional respect for a male hierarchy, allows readers to encounter the strangeness and difference in the native people and not be completely horrified by it.

In the engravings entitled, "Their seething of their meat in earthen pots," and "Their sitting at meat" (figures 4 and 5), we are encouraged by the captions to admire the craftsmanship with which they make their vessels and to take a lesson from the dietary habits of the Indians. In the first, we are told that "they are moderate in their eating whereby they avoid sickness. I would to god we would follow their example." And in the second caption, readers are reminded again that "they are very sober in their eating and drinking, and consequently very long lived because they do not oppress nature."[48] Harriot's praise of the simplicity and purity of Indian culture might at first strike us as insincere, but it seems to articulate a desire that would become ever more central to England's colonial undertaking, namely that the colonial endeavour would somehow transform those English people who participated in it. Colonial adventure, therefore, becomes a mechanism whereby the English can seek the renewal of their own culture. Far from being insincere, Harriot here gives voice to one of the most profound impulses for colonizing, namely to make England an even better version of itself. This pair of images maps out a belief that colonizing the New World would help the English to bring about not simply the cultural transformation of the native populations, but to endow their own culture with a sense of meaning and purpose that it has lacked for some time.

DeBry concludes his volume of Harriot with five engravings of Picts, and at the bottom of the title page introducing this section, he reveals to readers his source for the images:

The Painter of whom I have had the first of the inhabitants of Virginia, give me allso these 5 figures fallowing, fownd as he did assured [sic] me in a oold English chronicle, the which I wold well sett to the ende of thees first figures, for to showe how that the Inhabitants of the great Bretannie have bin in times past as Sauvage as those of Virginia.

As Mary Campell has argued with respect to DeBry's engravings of the Picts, "These engravings set up a parallel between colonists and colonized that portrays civilization as a cultural maturing process – a matter of historical development rather than a sign of absolute European difference."[49] The consequences of such an attitude are indeed significant. Rather than imagining the natives of Virginia as completely other than the Europeans, DeBry chooses to portray them as nothing more (and nothing less) than Europeans *manqués*, that is to say, human beings who have not yet had the benefit of European civilization. DeBry's engravings of the Picts, therefore, seem to be the inverse of his images of the natives of Virginia: just as he has rendered the Indians more familiar, he renders the European ancestors less so.

If the images that accompany DeBry's edition of Harriot emphasize the hope that colonial endeavor would eventually render the Indians more European and civilized, then the images he chooses to include in his edition of Léry provide an unvarnished portrait of native culture without the benefits of European intervention. Indeed, DeBry's decision to include, in his third volume, Hans Staden's much less sanguine account of life among the Brazilian native people, would only seem to reinforce the sense of urgency that he felt regarding the colonial project. Moreover, the fact that most of the engravings that illustrate the Léry volume are based on the woodcuts of Staden would also seem to suggest that DeBry was determined to demonstrate to his readers the importance of *not* leaving the native people fall victim to their own barbaric customs or to Catholic cruelty. The overwhelming pre-occupation of the engravings, therefore, is with the cannibalism that both Léry and Staden found so disturbing and fascinating. Accordingly the frontispiece of the third volume (figure 8) of the *Great Voyages* consists of menacing native inhabitants eating human limbs. On the left is a man eating what appears to be a detached human leg; and on the right is a woman eating a detached human arm as a child reaches over her shoulders and tries to grab hold of the arm. In the bottom window at the center, we have a miniature view of the native inhabitants cooking a body over open flames. At the top in each corner DeBry depicts native inhabitants who strike defiant and menacing poses.

Several engravings of the woodcuts by Hans Staden show Staden himself witnessing the horrors of cannabalism. In figure 9, Staden seems to present viewers with an imploring look as a native inhabitant is cooked and devoured before his very eyes. And in figure 10, Staden stands off to the side with his arms crossed in front of his chest, as native inhabitants cook the head and entrails of one of their victims. In figure 11, Staden stands behind all of the native inhabitants with his arms up in the air, as various body parts are roasted over an open fire. In each of these images, Staden appears static in the face of the frenzied activity of the native people.

These images give us an entirely different view of the native people. Whereas in the images accompanying the Harriot text, the Indians are presented as friendly, Europeanized savages, who seem only to lack the gentle and loving guidance of English settlers, DeBry gives us in his Léry volume a completely different picture of the native populations. Here, the native people seem beyond hope of reclamation. Within the scope of his larger work, DeBry would seem to have constructed the limits of fear and love. Indeed, as the *Great Voyages* progress, the volumes immediately following Léry bring Europeans the horrifying images of the Spanish slaughtering the innocent native people. To look at the images contained in the *Great Voyages*, is indeed to look at a pictorial record marked by ambivalence. In one volume the native inhabaitants appear almost civilized. In the next, they are ferocious. And finally they are consumed, not by their own orgies of cannibalism, but by European greed and cruelty.

The effect of DeBry's publication of Léry and Harriot is to suggest that the ideals of a purely Protestant colonialism could be embodied in a national project, such as the one that the English were about to undertake. Moreover, DeBry's tantalizing engravings render the native inhabitants as central figures in the European Protestant's quest for a coherent identity. Ultimately, English colonial writers would follow DeBry's implicit lead: by both identifying with the native people and rejecting them – by loving them and fearing them – they would be able to construct their colonial project as the means by which their own emerging national and religious identities could be most successfully articulated and woven together. Not only could the native people serve as stand-ins for the Catholic menace, but at the same time they could also function as fellow victims of Catholic cruelty, thereby allowing the English to articulate their own identity both in opposition to and in concert with the native populations. As we will see later in this study, the natives will be appropriated by Roger Williams and John Eliot to do the work of representing, not the differences between Catholics and Protestants, but rather the divisions among English Protestants themselves. In those writings, the Indians will figure centrally in the English desire to overcome self-division and internal strife through colonialism. Before we get there, however, we need to examine England's failure to make use of the native inhabitants in its attempt to bring its Irish colony under its control. Unlike DeBry, whose early engravings literally placed the native people at the center of the colonial tableau, Edmund Spenser gives us evidence of the difficulty the English encountered in imagining a positive role for the native Irish in the colonial endeavor. Not coincidentally, I would argue, this failure of imagination went hand-in-hand with Spenser's inability to recognize the importance of constructing a resolutely Protestant English identity through the colonial effort. The result, as we shall see, is nothing short of the collapse of both colonial and national identity.

CHAPTER THREE

Forgoing the nation: the Irish problem

According to Thomas Churchyard, Humphrey Gilbert justified his notoriously brutal treatment of the Irish by opining "that no conquered nacion will ever yelde willinglie their obedience for love but rather for feare."[1] If Gilbert's feeling was shared by many of his contemporaries – and a good number of the accounts from the Elizabethan period suggest that it was – then England's management of its Irish colony, would seem to have been governed by principles that ran counter to Thomas Harriot's optimistic suggestion that the English might expect to elicit obedience from the native inhabitants of America through fear and love. Ironically, England's prolonged attempt to rein in its Irish colony and establish its rule over a resistant Irish population proved considerably less successful than its analogous efforts in the New World. Although it would be too simplistic to suggest that England's lack of success in Ireland resulted from its heavy-handed and unrelentingly brutal treatment of the native Irish, such an assertion would not be entirely inaccurate. The failure I wish to examine in this chapter, however, is not simply the English failure to "love" the Irish or to convince the Irish to "love" them. More specifically, I wish to explore Edmund Spenser's refusal to imagine a positive role for the native Irish in the English colonization of Ireland. In other words, in his *A View of the Present State of Ireland* Spenser rejects the allegorical structure of colonialism and, lacking an allegorical structure, *A View* also fails to deliver a compelling logic for colonial adventure.

In focusing on *A View*, I want to acknowledge that I am examining a text which, after centuries of relative neglect, has emerged in the past two decades as the focal point of a vigorous debate that has brought attention to a range of questions that had hitherto been studiously avoided by Spenserians: To what extent did

68

Spenser himself personally endorse (or even participate in) the brutality of the Elizabethan colonial regime in Ireland? Should *The Faerie Queene* continue to be read as somehow separate from (and hence uninfluenced by) Spenser's problematic colonial politics?[2] And more generally, should we as literary critics make distinctions between a given writer's "literary" productions and his or her "non-literary" productions?[3] These questions have in turn led to a good deal of speculation on the status of *A View* as a text: Do the characters in *A View* speak for Spenser? Did Spenser speak for or against Elizabeth's Irish policy? Was *A View* suppressed or censored?[4] In this chapter, I hope to push the discussion of Spenser's infamous text in another direction: I want to ask what his text might tell us about one of the more general problems that confronted the English on the eve of their ambitious attempts to construct their own colonial empire. My specific interest in Spenser's text lies less in the brutality that it can be interpreted to promote than in the problems that arise from the most extreme positions one of its speakers takes. In short, it will be my argument in this chapter that Spenser's *View* offers us a significant counter-example to the other Protestant colonial texts we will examine. Rather than hoping that England's colonial engagement in Ireland might help to generate a coherent English Protestant identity, Spenser articulates the fear that colonial activity will inevitably lead to the degradation of that identity.

While scholars have recognized for some time the ways in which *The Faerie Queene* participates in an attempt to define and promote a sense of national identity, *A View's* critics have only recently begun to explore the important connections between Spenser's experiences in Ireland and his doubts about the durability of English national identity in the colonial scene.[5] This chapter suggests that beneath the inflammatory propositions for the solution of the so-called Irish problem, lie in fact some of the same concerns that critics have recently argued preoccupy Spenser in his composition of *The Faerie Queene*. Finally, at the end of this chapter, I shall suggest that *A View* can help us to reformulate some long held assumptions regarding the relationship between England's involvement in Ireland and its subsequent colonial undertakings.

Written in 1596, against the backdrop of the Munster rebellion, Spenser's *View* seems to suggest that the prospects of achieving control in a colonial setting – or at least of achieving control through peaceful, non-invasive means – were, at best, bleak. *A View* presents its readers with an alarming picture of a colony whose native population, instead of embracing English ways and customs, has actually subverted the English who have been sent there to colonize them. In fact, *A View* suggests not only that the tools of English colonial management have proven ineffectual in the struggle to bring Ireland under English control, but that those very tools, namely England's attempts to reform Irish legal, cultural, and religious institutions, have helped the Irish to undermine the English effort to establish an effective and stable colonial government. As a result of this gloomy analysis, *A View* seems to assert that the native Irish will respond not to gentle treatment but to brutality and violence. And *A View's* draconian pronouncements (of which there are many) have lead many readers to conclude, as C. S. Lewis did, that Spenser himself "was the instrument of a detestable policy in Ireland."[6]

A View does not put forth an argument monologically.[7] Instead it presents us with a dialogue between two characters who, like most Englishmen, agree from the outset that the goal of establishing order in the unruly colony should be England's first priority. Eudoxius, whose name translates as "good opinion," is possessed of the notion that England can achieve the political submission of Ireland, without recourse to violence, by pursuing the reform of Ireland's Laws, Customs, and Religion, not coincidentally the three topics that he and his partner in the dialogue, Irenius, agree to discuss. For his part, Irenius, whose name evokes both his connection with Ireland and the anger or "ire" that seems to motivate his most extreme responses, is determined to convince Eudoxius that the situation in Ireland is so dire as to require the harshest measures. In the position taken by Eudoxius, we can discern many of the assumptions that will inform England's subsequent colonization of the New World. Eudoxius speaks for those who promoted – or at least hoped for – a bloodless colonialism, while Irenius gives voice to the more severe view that colonial endeavor would require forceful measures in order to bring potentially unruly and uncooperative native populations into line.

In insisting that we take *A View's* dialogic structure seriously, I am not suggesting that we ignore its apparent advocacy of terror and intimidation as legitimate means of extracting obedience from uncooperative native people. But I am suggesting that Spenser's analysis in *A View* can offer us a glimpse of the difficulties of constructing a colonial ideology in the absence of a coherent national identity. In fact, it is only by reading a colonial text in which national identity fails to function that we can get a sense of its absolute indispensability in the colonial undertaking. Spenser's *View* implicitly suggests that the construction of a national identity is the most urgent concern facing those who would bring the Irish colony under English control once and for all. And to achieve that goal, Irenius embraces the dubious strategy of erasing Irish identity altogether. By eradicating Irish identity, Irenius incorrectly supposes that the English colonization could be completed.[8]

FULL OF HER OWN NATION

It is to some instances of Irenius's use of the word "nation" in *A View* that I will turn first, as I attempt to argue for the significance of the concept in this text. Although Irenius uses the word "nation" inconsistently – at times, almost archaically, to connote nothing more than a specific ethnic grouping – he sometimes uses it in a distinctly modern sense, to connote Benedict Anderson's evocative notion of "an imagined political community."[9] In recent years, a number of scholars have argued persuasively for the emergence during the Elizabethan period of "a specifically national sense of self."[10] Read in this light, Spenser's *View* offers readers a fascinating glimpse of an English national identity that, on the one hand, presents itself as an ideal and, on the other, refuses to operate in practice.

Significantly, in Spenser's text, it is the Irish and not the English who seem to exemplify Anderson's notion of "nation-ness." Irenius therefore constructs Irish national identity as an object to be examined, understood, and ultimately eradicated if England's colonization of Ireland is to be satisfactorily completed. In other words, Irenius must acknowledge that the Irishman's concept of himself as part of a nation is the most difficult obstacle confronting the English in their efforts to colonize the island. Conversely it is the English lack of a strong national self-concept that renders their colonizers ineffectual in their conquest of the island. In his attempts to understand the origins of the Irish national self-concept, Irenius reminds Eudoxius of the heterogenous origins of the Irish people.

> Before we enter into the treatise of their customs it is first needful to consider from whence they first sprung, for the sundry manners of the nations from whence that people which are now called Irish were derived... For *not of one nation* was it peopled as it is, but of sundry people.[11]

It is important to remember that Irenius's assertion of the heterogenous origins of Irish customs does not function in *A View* as part of an attempt to undermine the legitimacy of Irish culture or Irish national identity, but rather as part of a genuine attempt to understand the ways in which the Irish have been able to constitute themselves successfully as a nation.[12] As Irenius will later remark, Ireland is not alone in being constituted of many nations: "I think there is no nation now in Christendom, nor much further, but is mingled and compounded with others."[13]

If Ireland is no different from the rest of Europe, in terms of its origins, it certainly functions quite differently from England. Although the Irish may have derived their own identity from many nations, they seem far more capable of acting like a nation than do the English. Indeed, Ireland's ability to constitute itself as a nation – and England's inability to do so – would seem to constitute the most confounding problem that confronts Irenius, as he contemplates the state of Ireland. Late in *A View*, Irenius offers this assessment of the nature of the task that confronts the English:

> And therefore, since Ireland is *full of her own nation* that may not be rooted out, and somewhat stored with English already and more to be, I think it best by an union of manners and conformity of minds, to bring them *to be one people*, and to put away the dislikeful concept both of the one and the other, which will be by no means better than by this intermingling of them, that neither all the Irish may dwell together, nor all the English, but by translating of them, and scattering them in small numbers amongst the English, not only to bring them by daily conversation unto better liking of each other, but also to make both of them less able to hurt.[14]

Although in the above passage Irenius almost certainly means, quite literally, that the problem with Ireland is that it is too full of Irish people, his words lend themselves to another, more figural, meaning, namely that the Irish are full of their own sense of nation-ness. Such a reading seems more plausible, when one reads the rest of the passage, which is essentially about constructing a new colonial identity for Ireland. When Irenius argues for the necessity of bringing all of those residing in Ireland "to be one people," he disingenuously suggests that this is to be done by bringing together the "manners" and "minds" of those who live there. As is abundantly clear in the rest of *A View*, when Irenius suggests the making of one people out of Ireland, he is really arguing for the transplanting of English identity in Ireland. What is ironic about this pronouncement of Irenius's is the fact that the Irish are already capable of acting like "one people." And the English are not. Irish national identity is constituted as plenitude. English national identity is constituted as lack. If we see in this passage the same structure of desire that I outlined in the first chapter, then we must also acknowledge that, at least as far as Irenius is concerned, the colonial undertaking offers very little hope of ever satisfying England's desire of formulating and articulating a coherent national identity.

Indeed, what Irenius suggests just a few pages later would almost certainly seem to demonstrate his acknowledgment that the Irish are operating with a fully functional sense of national identity. The real purpose of the English in Ireland, therefore, is first to eradicate the national identity of the Irish and then to get the Irishman to accept a new identity:

Moreover for the breaking of these heads and septs which I told you was one of the greatest strengths of the Irish, methinks it should do very well to renew that old statute that was made in the reign of Edward the Fourth in England, by which it was commanded that whereas all men then used to be called by the name of their septs according to their several nations, and had no surnames at all, that from thenceforth each one should take unto himself a several surname, either of his trade or faculty or of some quality of his body or mind, or of the place where he dwelt, so as every one should be distinguished from other or from the most part; whereby they shall not only not depend upon the head of their sept as now they do, but also shall in short time learn quite to *forget his Irish nation*.[15]

As I will suggest later, it is ultimately not the Irishman who will "forget his Irish nation." The problem is that the English who have been sent over to colonize have forgotten their own sense of nation, and the Irish have tenaciously clung to theirs. Irenius therefore constructs this sense of nation-ness as both the object to be desired by the English and that which must be destroyed in the Irish at all costs. His discussion of the laws and the customs of Ireland is really only an examination of the extent to which these discourses have enabled the Irish to nurture their own sense of nation-ness without the English realizing it. By destroying Irish identity, therefore, Irenius hopes he will create a durable and functional English identity.[16]

A great deal of *A View*, therefore, concerns the process whereby the Irish have managed to continue to function as a group without being detected by the English. This is because of allegory, the trope by which people are able to say one thing and mean another. To have recognized oneself as the member of a nation in the colonial setting is to have embraced a notion of allegory. For the colonizer, it is allegory that enables him to see that what he is doing is participating in the national narrative. For the colonized, it is allegory that enables him to retain his own sense of identity by nurturing an invisible bond with his colonized compatriots. Although allegory defined in this way would seem to be reduced to a form of lying, I would suggest that the construction of an allegory is no closer to lying than the construction of any fiction. And in the specific instance at hand, we are finally talking about the construction of fictions that enable individuals to see themselves as adhering to a particular group. With respect to the colonizers, the task is to render that fiction open and obvious, whereas colonized populations must make their defining fictions invisible to the colonizers. Thus, Irenius is mistaken insofar as he believes that, by forcing the Irish to forget their own nation, he will enable (or coerce) the English to remember theirs.

FORGETTING NATURE AND FORGOING NATION

As disturbing as are the powers of the Irish to remember their own nation, Irenius and Eudoxius must confront the more threatening and horrifying phenomenon of Englishmen forsaking their own national identity for that of the Irish. It is to this vexing fact that Irenius alludes early on in *A View* when he describes the descendants of that "great store of gentlemen" that Henry II brought with him to Ireland. They "abide still," Irenius tells Eudoxius, "a mighty people of so many as remain English of them." Reacting with surprise as he so dependably does, Eudoxius wonders how it has come to pass that the English settlers have taken up an identity that they were sent over to eradicate. The exchange is revealing.

EUDOX: What is this that ye say of so many as remain English of them? Why are not they that were once English abiding English still?
IREN: No, for the most part of them are degenerated and grown almost mere Irish, yea and more malicious to the English than the very Irish themselves.
EUDOX: What hear I? And is it possible that an Englishman brought up naturally in such sweet civility as England affords should find such liking in that barbarous rudeness that he should *forget his own nature and forgo his own nation?* How may this be, or what, I pray you, may be the cause hereof?[17]

Although Eudoxius expresses shock upon hearing that Englishmen have failed to maintain their own sense of national identity in the colony, Irenius merely describes what most English observers of Ireland during the waning years of the sixteenth century knew as the problem of "degeneracy."[18] By far the most interesting feature of Eudoxius's outraged response, however, is the question he asks at the end: How can an English settler "forget his own nature and forgo his own nation?" By constructing the failure of national identity as a violation of nature, Eudoxius reveals that he has assumed that national identity is unalterable, immutable. If in the post-modern moment, it is a generally accepted truth, as Linda Colley has asserted, that nations are "problematic, protean and artificial constructs," it is also probably true that we are prepared to take a question such as the one Eudoxius asks at face value.[19] That is, we assume that his assertion that national identity represents a natural rather than an artifical distinction is indeed what we might expect from someone writing in the early modern era. But the most unsettling conclusion of *A View* will be its contention that the national identity of the English proves to be an unreliable vehicle for the transformation of Irish culture.

Before *A View* can arrive at the surprisingly modern realization that national identity seems not to function with the same reliability as nature, Eudoxius will continue to link nature and nation. He finds it, for instance, "very strange . . . that men should so much degenerate from their *first natures* as to grow wild." And when Irenius tells him that some of the English settlers have "shaken off their English names and put on Irish," Eudoxius asks, "Is it possible that any should so *far grow out of frame* that they should in so short space quite forget their *country* and their own names?" Irenius responds by observing that it is "for hatred of the English," that these settlers have "so disguised their own names." Rather than clarifying the matter for Eudoxius, however, Irenius's explanation seems only to prompt another question. Eudoxius asks, "Could they ever conceive any such devilish dislike of their own *natural country* as that they would be ashamed of her name, and bite off her dug from which they sucked life?"[20] Once again, Eudoxius implicitly defines national identity as a function of nature.

By far, the most upsetting (and fascinating) aspect of English degeneracy had to do not with names but with language. Asserting the same connection between nature and nation as Eudoxius, Irenius says, "I have to find fault with the abuse of language, that is, for the speaking of Irish amongst the English, which, as it is *unnatural* that any people should love another's language more than their own, so it is very inconvenient and the cause of many other evils."[21] Spenser was of course not the first commentator on Ireland to express his dismay over the survival and success of the Irish language. Richard Stanyhurst, who continued Holinshed's account of the history of Ireland, had in 1586 attributed a whole range of problems to the stubborn survival of the Irish language. Among these was the degradation of the English language in Ireland which Stanyhurst claimed, in an observation that has obvious and interesting ramifications for students of Spenser, had retained "the dregs of the old ancient Chaucer English."[22]

Ultimately, the relationship between nature and identity in *A View* is muddled. Near the end of *A View*, in his last attempt to grasp the disturbing altering of allegiances that seems to have taken place in Ireland, Eudoxius suggests that the fault lies with the country itself:

EUDOX: In truth, Irenius, this is more than ever I heard, that the English Irish there should be worse than the wild Irish. Lord, how quickly doth that country alter men's natures![23]

As it turns out, Irenius cannot endorse Eudoxius's formulation. He seems, in other words, to be forced to recognize that there is something in the Englishmen who go to Ireland that predisposes them to embrace Irish customs. Irenius must therefore modify Eudoxius's assertion:

> IREN: ... neither is the nature of the country to alter a man's manners, but the bad minds of them who, having been brought up at home under a strait rule of duty and obedience, being always restrained by sharp penalties from lewd behaviour, so soon as they come thither, where they see law so slackly tended, they grow more loose and careless of their duty, as it is the nature of all men to love liberty; so they become flat libertines and fall to flat licentiousness, more boldly daring to disobey the law through presumption of favour and friendship than any Irish dare.[24]

As Irenius constructs it, "the nature of all men is to love liberty." In other words, it is not the nature of men to be English: what renders them English therefore is artificial. And it is the artificiality of English identity that makes it so difficult to transport successfully to the colony. It would appear that for the Englishman to forgo his nation is not to forget nature, but simply to do what comes "naturally" to him. But rather than support English identity with ideological machinery, Irenius turns to the crude tools of repression. As we shall see in the next chapter, the ultimate path that English colonialism took was to accept the challenge of forging a national identity through a colonial ideology. Rather than regard colonial adventure as a threat to national identity, subsequent writers would find in colonial activity an opportunity to construct a national identity.

SEEMING TO ACKNOWLEDGE SUBJECTION

Irenius surprises Eudoxius – and presumably the English readers for whom Eudoxius stands – when he suggests that the laws are one of "the evils which seem to be most hurtful to the common weale of that land." Eudoxius, who cannot immediately accept Irenius's assertion that the English laws have actually done harm to the English cause in Ireland, asks Irenius the questions that I would argue Spenser wanted his readers to ask: "Why Irenius can there be any evil in the laws? Can the things which are ordained for the safety and good of all: turn to the evil and hurt of them?"[25] In Irenius's analysis, the laws have functioned in Ireland by giving the Irish a means of behaving in unison. Or, to use his language, the laws seem to allow the Irish "to be one people." And it doesn't matter whether the laws are of the making of the Irish. Or whether they are English laws. The result is the same. In each case, the Irish function as a nation while giving the impression that they are in fact submitting to English rule.

Irenius answers Eudoxius's question with the disturbing assertion that the imposition of English law, contrary to all reasonable expectations, has presented the native Irish with a powerful means of subverting English attempts to exert control over the island. Invoking a medical analogy, Irenius contends that law has lost its power to effect positive change in the colony: "But it falleth out in laws no otherwise, then it doth in physic." In medicine, one treatment may work on a patient for a while, but through "unseasonableness of the time . . . instead of good it worketh hurt." Such is the case with laws:

So the laws were at first intended for the formation of abuses, and peaceable continuance of the subjects: but are since either disannulled or quite prevaricated through change and alteration of times, yet are they good still in them selves.[26]

So frequently is medicine invoked in *A View,* that it emerges as the most powerful discourse for describing the paradigmatic relationship between the imperial nation and its well-managed colony. And yet, by suggesting that "law" operates according to the same rules as "physic," Irenius elides two competing models for the management and implementation of colonial designs. Unlike the doctor, who independently prescribes medicines for his patients, colonial administrators in Ireland were not free to decide which legal "remedies" to "prescribe" and which to abandon. And unlike medicines, whose effects on the body are direct and immediate, laws require, as Irenius will painstakingly show, the intervention and involvement of many potentially unreliable agents.[27]

In other words, the fantasy of the colonialist-as-physician is a response to the failure of the English to be able to conduct surveillance successfully in the colony. In the end, "law" and "physic" are driven by deeply antithetical notions, but Irenius must embrace the idea of treating the colony like a sick patient because it implies a degree of control and surveillance that the legal discourse can scarcely match. Just as the doctor is always present to manage the patient's regimen and oversee the implementation of the cure, so too Irenius imagines the colonial scene as one that should be overseen by one man, who responds directly and immediately (and sometimes ruthlessly) to problems as they arise. By constructing the colony as an ailing body and the colonizer as a doctor, Irenius is able to eliminate the threat posed by the nation-ness of the colonized. In Irenius's fantasy of the doctor-patient relationship, the doctor is able to eradicate the Irish desire to function as a nation. As a model of colonial interaction, therefore, the doctor-patient relationship suggests that the national identity of the Irish is something that can be removed with the appropriate course of treatment.

From Irenius's perspective, the attempts to gain control of the colony through legal reform will inevitably fail because laws allow the colonized Irish both to express and to conceal their desires to behave as a nation. When Irenius begins his discussion of laws in earnest by describing the laws of the Irish, namely Brehon Laws, Eudoxius is shocked to hear of the extent to which the native law is still practiced in Ireland. Irenius's description of the current situation in Ireland reveals the extent to which Brehon Law functions as an expression of national will and desire.

IREN. Yes, truly, for there are many wide countries in Ireland in which the laws of England were never established, nor any acknowledgement of subjection made, and also even in those which are subdued, and *seem to acknowledge subjection*, yet the same Brehon law is *privily practised* amongst themselves, by reason that *dwelling as they do whole nations and septs of the Irish together without any Englishman amongst them*, they may do what they list, and compound or altogether *conceal amongst themselves* their own crimes, of which *no notice can be had* by them which would and might might amend the same by the rule of the laws of England.[28]

Brehon Law functions in the above passage as an expression of Irishness. It does not really matter whether it is openly or "privily practised." For the Irish to subject themselves to English law would mean that they have relinquished their sense of national identity and accepted another. All of Irenius's tales of the perversions of law in Ireland follow the same basic pattern: What is privily practised ends up controlling the scene.

With respect to Brehon Law, Irenius really describes two distinct problems that confront the English who would impose their own legal system upon the Irish. On the one hand, there are parts of Ireland where the Irish still practice Brehon Law simply because the English have never established their own laws. On the other hand, the more disturbing fact is that Brehon Law is still "privily practised" in many of those areas which "seem to acknowledge subjection." Irenius constructs this indigenous version of law as capable of concealment. True, the Brehon Laws enable the Irish to conceal their crimes from the English, but perhaps more crucially, they enable the Irish both to nurture and to conceal their own desires. If the point of the imposition of English law on the colony was to ensure the subjection of the Irish to the English, then the existence of this other discourse enables the Irish to "seem to acknowledge subjection" while in reality only fulfilling their own national desires.

The bulk of Irenius's critique of the legal situation in Ireland is taken up precisely with this problem of the Irish appearing to embrace English law while in reality only doing as they please. We might keep in mind here the simplest definition of allegory that I mentioned at the outset: to say one thing and mean another. In other words, the Irish are saying that they are accepting the subjection of the English, while in fact they are intending quite the opposite. The laws have merely given them a discourse with which to express their own desires as a nation. As I suggested earlier, we should not confuse this allegorizing of the Irish with lying. While the intent of the Irish is of course to deceive the colonizing English, the ultimate result of their manipulation of the legal discourse is to give them a language through which they can continue to constitute themselves as a distinct group. It is precisely that narrative of the failure of English legal institutions to bring about a change in the behavior of the Irish that vexes Irenius. Irenius complains, for instance, about what happens in jury trials in Ireland "when the cause shall fall between an Irish man and an English":

... but now that the Irish have stepped into the realms of the English, who are now become so heedful and provident to keep them forth from henceforth, that they make no scruple of conscience to pass against them, it is good reason that either that course of the law for trials be altered, or other provision for juries be made.

In other words, now that the Irish are sitting on juries, they are passing judgment against the English whenever they come before them. That is to say, the Irish have constructed themselves as Irish to such an extent that their identity as Irishmen functions as the highest value. They will always find in favor of the Irishman whenever there is a question.

But the treachery and deception of the Irish goes beyond their service on juries. Irenius continues his complaint by suggesting that the Irish are even able to display their national desires when serving as witnesses:

Not only so in their verdicts but also in all other their dealings. Specially with the English they are most willfully bent, for though *they will not seem manifestly* to do it, yet will some one or other subtle headed fellow amongst them pick some quirk, devise some subtle evasion, whereof the rest will lightly take hold, and suffer themselves easily *to be led by him to that them selves desired*.[29]

Irenius's description of the process by which the Irish have confounded the English judicial system is really quite stunning. In this instance, Irenius describes a subtle means of communication. The result is that the Irish are able to constitute themselves as a group and somehow appoint one of their number to evade the law. In turn, the Irish are able to "be led by him to that themselves desired." In every case, what is desired is to thwart the English judicial system – in other words to remain Irish. And the English judicial system presents the Irish with no obstacle to expressing and fulfilling their own desires as a people.

OFFENSIVE AND REPUGNANT CUSTOMS

If, in Irenius's analysis, laws – whether they be English or Irish – have afforded the Irish with the means of expressing a corporate identity, the same is also true for Irish customs. Indeed, it is to the extent that they provide the Irish with a vehicle for self-expression that Irenius finds Irish customs objectionable. I should here acknowledge that Spenser's analysis of Irish customs has generated in recent years a lively debate among critics from the fields of history and literary studies. On the one hand, there is the historian Brendan Bradshaw who suggests that Spenser constructed a "spurious ethnography of the native race," in order to justify "his stark final solution of the Irish problem."[30] And on the other hand, there is the literary critic Sheila T. Cavanagh, who argues that Spenser's *View* "demonstrates dramatically more compassion and understanding for the native inhabitants than most of the comparable treatises composed by his fellow English authors."[31] The debate, in other words, consists of an attempt to position Spenser with respect to his contemporaries and to answer the question of whether he was articulating what, even in the late sixteenth century, would have been recognized as extreme views. Although this is an important question, it will not be my primary concern here. Instead, I propose to interrogate the structure that Irenius attributes to Irish customs. For it is in that structure that we can discern the outlines of Spenser's two-fold fear regarding culture: the customs of the Irish demonstrate first the persistent ability of the Irish to act as a nation, and second the corresponding inability of the English either to act as a nation or to unravel Ireland's cohesion as a nation.

When Irenius opens his discussion of Irish customs, Eudoxius mistakenly believes that he is about to hear a learned disquisition on what he calls the "sweet remembrances of antiquities" of Ireland. What he hears instead is Irenius's extremely focused discussion of those "customs of the Irish as seem offensive and repugnant to the good government of that realm."[32] All of the customs Irenius singles out for scrutiny involve concealment. Each custom, rather than revealing something specific about Irish identity, reveals the limits of, and poses new challenges to, English surveillance of the Irish. Rather than suggesting that the customs themselves are symbolic of Irish identity, Irenius seems to argue that the customs allow the Irish to mask their identity. Irenius, therefore, is determined to strip away the surfaces to lay bare what lies beneath. The customs that Irenius attacks all allow the construction of some sort of unpoliced space. Whether, as in the case of the mantles and glibs, that space is personal or, as in the case of the bollies and folkmotes, that space is social, the customs allow for the construction of a space in which an Irish identity might survive and flourish. And by constructing the space for an Irish identity, these customs allow the Irish to function as a group or, more specifically, as a nation. The customs, in other words, allow the Irish not to forget their nation.

Irenius opens his litany of offensive Irish customs by describing and decrying the Irish practice of "Bollying." Eudoxius, quite understandably, wants to know what is wrong with this apparently harmless habit of grazing cattle on the outskirts of the towns.

IREN: But by this custom of Bollying there grow in the meantime many great enormities unto that commonwealth. For, first, if there be any outlawes or loose people, as they are never without some which live upon *stealths* and spoils, they are even more succoured and find relief only in these Bollies being *upon the waste places*; where else they should be driven shortly to starve, or to come down to the towns to seek relief, where by one means or another they would soon be caught. Besides, such *stealths* of cattle as they make they bring commonly to those Bollies where they are received readily, and the thief harboured from *danger of law or such officers* as might light upon him.[33]

Whatever else the bolly does, it offers the Irish a ready place to conceal criminals and stolen cattle. In their bollies, the Irish have managed to construct a space that cannot be penetrated by English law. It is of course ironic to note that the custom of bollying makes use of the "waste places," because in subsequent colonial discourse, the English would justify their conquests by virtue of their own making use of what was otherwise a "waste land."[34] For the bollies to work in the way that Irenius suggests they do, there must be cooperation between those who put their cattle out to graze in the "waste places," and those who seek refuge from the law. In other words, the bollies create a space that is friendly to the Irish outlaws. But there is more here. The bollies literally operate in the most open spaces. Rather than locating the illicit activities of the Irish in the nooks and crannies of the realm, Irenius acknowledges that Irish subversion takes place out in the open. The bolly reveals the power of the Irish to fashion a functional custom in a place deemed a "waste place" by the English. But it also reveals the English inability to interpret the landscape. It is the English who have deemed the bollies "waste places". In so doing, they have obviously miscalculated. The bolly is a place that helps the Irish to generate refuge, economic gain, not to mention some sort of identity. The bolly is therefore an allegorical space for the Irish, where they may appear to be submitting to English rule while in reality doing as they please. One of the goals of the English occupation of Ireland was of course to achieve the literal control of the space, and the bolly demonstrates how successful the Irish have been in maintaining their control over the countryside.

Like the bolly, an open space in which the Irish are able to hide criminals, the folkmote functions as a public meeting where the Irish are able to transact their nefarious business out in the open.

IREN: There is a great use among the Irish to make great assemblies
together upon a Rath or hill, there to parly (as they say) about
matters and wrongs between township and township, or one private
person and another, but well I wot and true it hath been oftentimes
approved, that in these meetings many mischiefs have been both
practised and wrought. For to them do commonly resort all the scum
of loose people, where they may freely meet and confer of what they
list, which else they could not do without suspicion or knowledge of
others. Besides at these parlies I have diverse times known that
many Englishmen and other good Irish subjects have been villain-
ously murdered, by moving one quarrel or another amongst them,
for the Irish never come to those raths but armed whether on horse-
back or on foot, which the English nothing suspecting, are then commonly taken at tag like sheep in the pinfold.[35]

The folkmote is a custom that allows the Irish to practice mischief
under the seemingly harmless guise of a public assembly.[36] Irenius,
by drawing our attention to the fate of the unsuspecting English
who are "taken at tag like sheep," constructs the folkmote as a
space that the English can neither interpret nor control. The folkmote, therefore, presents the English with yet another instance of
the power of Irish identity, and the corresponding inability of the
English to eradicate that identity. Indeed, the folkmote, by providing a cover for the Irish who wish to murder the English, literally
destroys English identity.

The most colorful customs that Irenius wishes to outlaw, the
wearing of mantles and glibs, were also probably the ones that
would have been most widely known in England. And like the bollies and folkmotes that Eudoxius considers so harmless, mantles
and glibs would hardly have struck most readers as threatening.[37]
As in his attack on bollies and folkmotes, though, Irenius suggests
that the real harm of mantles and glibs lies in their power to
conceal the nefarious schemes and designs of the Irish. Unlike
bollies and folkmotes, however, which allow the Irish to devise and
practice villainy in public spaces, the wearing of mantles and glibs
concerns the individual Irishman's construction of his own personal space. I quote Irenius's description of the mantle at some
length because the hyperbole would be difficult to convey using
only short excerpts:

IREN: Because the commodity doth not countervail the discommodity.
For the inconveniences which thereby do arise are much more many,
for it is a fit house for an outlaw, a meet bed for a rebel, and an apt

cloak for a thief. First the outlaw being for his many crimes and villainies banished from the towns and houses of honest men, and wandering in waste places far from danger of law, maketh his mantle his house, and under it covereth himself from the wrath of heaven, from the offence of the earth, and from the sight of men: when it raineth it is his pentice, when it bloweth it is his tent, when it freezeth it is his tabernacle; in summer he can wear it loose, in winter he can wrap it close; at all times he can use it, never heavy, never cumbersome. Likewise for a rebel it is as serviceable: for in his war that he maketh (if at least it deserve the name of war) when he still flyeth from his foe and lurketh in the thick woods and straight passages waiting for advantages, it is his bed, yea and almost all his household stuff. For the wood is his house against all weathers, and his mantle is his cave to sleep in. There he wrappeth his self round and ensconceth himself more strongly against the gnats which in the country do more annoy the naked rebels whilst they keep the woods, and do more sharply wound them than all their enemies's swords or spears which can seldom come nigh them; yea and often times their mantle serveth them when they are near driven, being wrapped about their left arm instead of a target, for it is hard to cut through it with a sword; besides it is light to bear, light to throw away, and being as they are commonly naked, it is to them all in all. Lastly, for a thief it is so handsomely in his way. . .[38]

Readers should here remember that we are talking about a *coat* – a coat that does literally *everything*. In a subsequent part of the description that I did not quote, Irenius even suggests that the coat can function as a woman's birthing room, where she may both conceive and deliver a child without anyone ever knowing. The mantle literally constructs an impenetrable space in which the Irish man or woman can live without interference from anyone. Curiously, it is not so much what the mantle *is* as what it *conceals* that renders it so troubling to Irenius. The mantle, rather than representing something repulsively Irish that must be eradicated, instead provides the individual the space wherein he (or she!) might define and defend his own identity as an Irishman.

Like the mantle, the glib also functions as a means of constructing a personal space, and Irenius argues that its use must be banned.

IREN: I fear not the blame of any undeserved mislikes, but for the Irish glibs I say that besides their savage brutishness and loathly filthiness, which is not to be named, they are fit masks as a mantle is for a thief, for whensoever he hath run himself into that peril of the

law that he will not be known, he either cutteth off his glib quite,
by which he becometh nothing like himself, or pulleth it so low down
over his eyes that it is very hard to discern his thievish countenance,
and therefore fit to be trussed up with the mantle.[39]

The most surprising assertion about the glib is that it allows the
Irishman to become "nothing like himself." The point isn't that
identity is located in the custom of wearing the glib, but rather
that the glib allows the Irishman's interior to deviate from his
exterior. What lies behind the glib is "nothing like" the face that
the glib presents to the world outside. The glib, in other words,
allows the Irishman to present to the world a literal exterior that
does not correspond to his figurative interior. The glib, in short,
is an allegorical device.

All of the customs that Irenius would eradicate in fact assume
the status of allegorical devices – that is, they allow the Irish to
carry on the fiction that they are submitting to English rule, when
in fact they are continuing to construct themselves as Irish. Just
as the Irish have been able to find within the English legal system
a language with which to maintain and express their own identity
as a nation, so too has the survival of these apparently benign
customs given the Irish a means of remaining Irish. To be sure,
Irenius's urge to eliminate these customs would seem to form part
of a larger program of terror and repression, but as I shall argue
in the next section, it is not at all clear whether Spenser believed
such a program would work. In fact, the question that should confront us when we read *A View* is not whether Spenser "virtuously
contemplate[s] the perpetration of carnage," as Brendan Bradshaw suggests.[40] Rather, we must ask ourselves whether Spenser
really believed that Irenius's plans for an unprecedented military
campaign would finally bring Ireland under English control.

THE AWE OF PRESENCE

The real challenge facing Spenser in *A View* was a simple and, as
it turns out, insurmountable one: How could colonizers who don't
behave like a nation colonize a people who *do* behave like a nation?
We can therefore read Irenius's solution to the problem of Irish
intransigence as an attempt to overcome England's fundamental
lack of a reliable and stable concept of national identity within the
colony. In place of what he considers the premature and misguided

attempts to reform Ireland through its legal system, its culture, or its religion, Irenius offers Eudoxius the idea of strategically placed garrisons as a means of keeping the Irish in check. Early in *A View*, Irenius draws on historical precedent to justify his plan. Explaining the success of the Norman conquest of England, for instance, Irenius reminds Eudoxius of the willingness of William the conqueror to be

> *present in person* to overlook the magistrates, and to *overawe* the subjects with the *terror* of his sword and countenance of the majesty. . .The like regard and moderation ought to be had in tempering and managing of this stubborn nation of the Irish, to bring them from their delight of licentious barbarism unto the love of goodness and civility.

Irenius continues by reminding Eudoxius of all the "brawls" and "rebellions" that the Normans had to suppress in their conquest of England, "all [of] which they nevertheless fairly overcame by reason of the *continual presence of the king*, whose only person is oftentimes instead of an army to contain the unruly from a thousand evil occasions."[41] Uttered practically at the outset of *A View*, these lines articulate probably the *only* thing that would have been absolutely inconceivable in the Elizabethan management of the colony. Ireland was not about to be graced by the presence of the monarch. Even if Elizabeth were in the habit of leading armies to foreign territories, she would probably have thought twice before venturing to Ireland.[42]

We should not fail to note that the presence of the king did more than simply terrorize the natives. It provided the colonizers with a constant reminder of where their allegiances should lie. In Irenius's analysis, it was this presence that anchored the identity of those sent over to colonize. As long as the king was "*present in person* to overlook the magistrates," the English colonizer would not be tempted to "forget his own nature and forgo his nation." Irenius's wistful longing for monarchical presence calls to mind Benedict Anderson's "idea of [the nation as] a sociological organism moving calendrically through homogenous, empty time" that we discussed earlier. The failure of the English to function as a nation in Ireland was a failure of imagination. Literally removed from the gaze of the "countenance of the majesty," the English have been unable to perceive the invisible bonds that might tie them to one another and forge them into a nation. To put it another way, the English have failed to recognize that *they* could function, in the *absence* of the monarch, as an allegorical reminder of the monarch's continued figural *presence* in Ireland.

Because, in Irenius's formulation, the presence of the king is inextricably linked to fear, and because the English governors and magistrates have failed to compensate in any meaningful way for the *absence* of the monarch, Irenius puts forth terror as the only possible way of projecting English *presence* into Ireland. Later in *A View*, for instance, arguing against the notion of seating the Lord Deputy in Dublin, Irenius describes Dublin as "least needing the *awe* of his *presence* for the Irishman, I assure you, *fears* the government no longer than he is within sight or reach."[43] The problem of course is that this thing called presence is a scarce commodity. Given the English predisposition to turn Irish, it is clear that not every English person could project awe with his presence. But Irenius is left with no other option than that of suggesting that the English settlers be dispersed among the Irish.

For that is the evil which I now find in all Ireland, that the Irish dwell altogether by their septs and several nations so as they may practice or conspire what they will, whereas if there were Englishe shed amongst them and placed over them they should not be able once to stir or murmure, but that it should be known, and they shortened according to their demerits.[44]

Significantly, Irenius has earlier ruled out the idea of placing the English among the Irish, because that practice has only led to the so-called "degeneracy" of the English. Eudoxius recalls Irenius's earlier reluctance and questions the wisdom of Irenius's proposal:

me thinks your late advisement was verie evil, whereby you wished the Irish to be sowed and sprinkled with the English in all the Irish countries, to have English planted amongst them, for to bring them to English fashions. Since the English be sooner drawn to the Irish, than the Irish to the English. . . better to part the Irish and English, than to mingle them together. [45]

Eudoxius's question forces Irenius to modify his earlier proposal. Instead of randomly "sprinkling" the Irish counties with English settlers, Irenius suggests that the Irish population should be divided into "hundreds." Over each one of these "hundreds" Irenius would place an "alderman," who would be what he calls "an Englishman of special regard."

Quite correctly, Eudoxius realizes that this solution poses the same risks as the earlier practice of allowing the Irish to live by themselves. Under the new arrangement the Irish would so far outnumber the English "alderman" that they would be able once again to evade English control. Therefore, Eudoxius challenges Irenius again:

> Now, methinks, Irenius, ye are to be warned to take good heed, lest unawares ye fall into the inconvenience which you formerly found fault with in others; namely that by this booking of them you do not gather them into a new head, and having broken their former strength, doe not again unite them more strongly... lest ye also give them occasion and means to practise any harm in any conspiracy.[46]

Spenser himself could hardly have been unaware of the fundamental contradiction that Eudoxius and Irenius here struggle to resolve. If one leaves the Irish to their own devices, then they may plot insurrections, disturbances, and rebellions where and when they please. If, on the other hand, one distributes the English settlers among the Irish, then one will almost inevitably witness the disturbing spectacle of degeneracy. It is my belief that Spenser perceived this problem and that he realized that neither solution was workable.[47]

Without a stable national identity, to which the English might be presumed to cling, the best solution that Irenius can devise is that of a "provost marshal," who will essentially terrorize the native Irish:

> I would wish that there were a provost marshal appointed in every shire which should *continually walk through the country* with half dozen or half a score horsemen to take up such loose persons as they should find thus wandering, whom he should punish by his own authority with such pains as the persons should seem to deserve, for if he be but once so taken idly roguing he may punish him more lightly as with stocks or such like, but if he be found again so loitering he may scourge him with whips or rods, after which, if he be again taken, let him have the bitterness of the martial law.[48]

Eudoxius wonders why this sort of work can't be done by the sherriffs, but Irenius asserts that a mere sherriff does not have the power to "work that terror in the hearts of them," that a marshal does. What seems to distinguish the marshal, however, from the sherriff, is not the nature of his work, but rather a set of personal qualities that enable him to penetrate the Irish community without being contaminated by it. The marshal, in other words, is very much like Talus, the brutally efficient instrument of justice from Book 5 of the *Faerie Queene,* who performs his duties with an inhuman consistency and regularity.

In the end, Irenius's solution to the failure of English identity in Ireland does not exclusively reside in the fantasy of a machine-like marshal meting out "the bitterness of the martial law." In addition, he proposes the creation of a new position, namely that of a "lord lieutenant," who would reside, not in Ireland, but in England. Moreover, he would greatly expand the powers of the current office of the lord deputy so that his authority would "be more ample and absolute than it is." Such changes are necessary, he says, because "it is not possible for the council here to direct a governor there, who shall be forced oftentimes to follow necessity of present occasions and to take the sudden advantage of time, which being once left will not be recovered."[49] History has shown that Elizabeth eventually embraced Irenius's proposed solution, but history has also shown that such a solution was less than satisfactory. The Earl of Essex, to whom Irenius seems to point, was tried and executed for treason as a result of his tenure in Ireland.

Irenius's proposed solution for the Irish problem differs dramatically from the methods that England ultimately employed in its colonization of the New World. Rather than deploying an ideology, Irenius deploys an army. And rather than recognizing that colonialism could only operate successfully with a fully developed national ideology, Irenius proposes a structural change that seems woefully inadequate to the task at hand. I shall conclude this chapter by arguing that the most crucial component missing from Irenius's analysis is a recognition of the centrality of the Protestant religion to any English colonial undertaking.

RELIGION NEEDETH QUIET TIMES

One of the more surprising features of *A View* is the absence of any serious discussion of the role of religion in the colonial endeavor. This absence is of course all the more remarkable when considered in the context of England's subsequent colonial efforts, which placed religion at the center. Irenius justifies this omission by arguing that there was little point in preaching to a people who remained politically and militarily opposed to English rule:

For instruction in religion needeth quiet times, and ere we seek to settle a sound discipline in the clergy, we must purchase peace unto the laity; for it is ill time to preach amongst swords, and most hard or rather impossible it is to settle a good opinion in the minds of men, for matters of religion doubtful, which have a doubtless evil opinion of ourselves; for ere a new be brought in, the old must be removed.

Elaborating on his point, Irenius suggests that the colonial context was not one that would allow for religious idealism. Instead, one had to be pragmatic.

The care of the soul and soul matters are to be preferred before the care of the body, in consideration of the worthiness thereof, but not in the time of reformation. For if you should know a wicked person dangerously sick, having now both soul and body greatly diseased, yet both recoverable, would ye not think it ill advisement to bring the preacher before the physician?[50]

Later colonists would of course prefer the care of the soul before the care of the body – at least rhetorically. Irenius refused to acknowledge that religion might serve as a practical tool for either the development of an ideology or the administration of a colony. By forgoing religion, Irenius was forgoing the possibility of conducting colonialism with a fully functioning national identity. To read Spenser's *View*, therefore, is to understand, by virtue of their absence, the crucial role that Protestantism and national identity might play in the colonial enterprise.

Among other things, Spenser's text should force us to reconsider the relationship that historians have long assumed existed between England's colonization of Ireland and its subsequent colonization of the New World. To be sure, in the most basic sense, Nicholas Canny's assertion that England's "years in Ireland were years of apprenticeship," is correct.[51] But it would be a mistake to conclude, as Robert Williams does, that the discourses that governed England's involvement in Ireland were identical to "the colonizing discourse later carried by Elizabeth's Protestant crusaders to the New World."[52] In fact, the colonial ideology that would later emerge as England established colonies in the New World, although it justified and smoothed over its share of atrocities, was markedly different from the one that was operating in Ireland during Spenser's time. By itself, Spenser's *View* cannot tell us of course what happened in England's subsequent colonial endeavors. But it can offer us a powerful demonstration of what happens when a thinker as smart and sophisticated as Spenser attempts to resolve complicated colonial problems without faith in the existence or efficacy of a transportable and reliable English national identity. As England's subsequent experience in its American colonies shows, English colonial promoters eventually realized that Protestantism and the English nation could both achieve their fullest articulation through the colonial project. If Spenser's *View* demonstrates that colonial-ness needs nation-ness, then in the next chapter we shall discover that the relationship between the nation and the colony was not uni-directional. That is to say, we will witness the powerful discovery by a group of English divines that nation-ness needs colonial-ness.

CHAPTER FOUR

Preaching the nation: the sermon as promotion

Some fifty years ago, quite against the grain of the historiographical orthodoxy of the moment, Perry Miller argued that the significance of religion in the development of the Virginia colony needed to be reassessed. Challenging as too simplistic the widely held view that figured the Virginia colony as primarily or exclusively a commercial endeavor, Miller argued that the commercialism of the Virginia undertaking was, from very early on, articulated within an explicitly Protestant frame.[1] For his evidence, Miller pointed to a group of early seventeenth-century sermons that explicitly extolled the Christian virtues of participation in the Virginia colony. The divines who wrote these sermons skillfully wove together the themes of financial gain and spiritual salvation as they attempted to convince their listeners and readers that England's colonial adventures were the perfect way to serve God. "The Virginia Company," Miller wrote, "being an English enterprise, was not only Christian but specifically Protestant . . . the quality of their piety, their sense of their relation to God, was so thoroughly Protestant as to be virtually indistinguishable from the Puritan."[2] These Virginia sermons do indeed reveal a determination on the part of their authors to cast England's earliest colonial efforts in explicitly Protestant terms. And Miller is also correct to argue that the "the quality of their piety" is difficult to distinguish from that of the better known Puritan divines who later migrated to New England. Indeed, as John Parker has argued in reference to the same sermons, "This was the voice of Puritanism, giving English colonization literature a strong, clear purpose in an appeal made directly to the people. Although the Virginia Company was by no means an exclusively Puritan enterprise, they were making the most of it as a vehicle for carrying their faith to the New World."[3] In this chapter, I will argue that these sermons do much

93

more than reveal the extent to which the Virginia enterprise was constructed as a Protestant undertaking, although to be sure they do that. In their sermons, these divines contend that the English lack both a coherent sense of national identity and an explicit commitment to Protestantism. In the colonial undertaking, therefore, this handful of divines attempts to discover a means by which the English can re-imagine themselves as a Protestant nation. In this sense, colonialism becomes not only a vehicle for carrying Englishness and Protestantism to the new world, as Miller and Parker suggest, but also the very means by which the English can re-affirm their identity as Protestants and as a nation.

In the Virginia sermons, colonial discourse serves the complex and important function of rationalizing one of the central paradoxes of colonialism, namely that the survival of the nation can only be ensured by a marginal activity that occurs by and large outside of its borders. In other words, the Virginia divines deploy colonial discourse allegorically by presenting it as the most effective means of articulating a Protestant English identity, of narrating the losses and desires of the Protestant nation. These sermons bring together two discourses, therefore, that are inherently fraught with contradictions: The discourse of nation and the discourse of colony. These ministers realize that by bringing the two discourses together, they can resolve the tensions that existed between a Protestant English identity and the colonial undertaking itself – tensions largely derived from the injunctions against cruelty to the native populations and against caring too much for things of this world. Not only do these sermons suggest that colonial behavior is consistent with an English Protestant identity, but that in fact colonialism is the only way to ensure the survival of that identity. The sermons proceed by showing that beneath a surface of contradictions lay a deep affinity between the colonial enterprise and England's ongoing struggle to define itself as a nation. England's story as a Protestant nation, in other words, can be narrated through its colonies.

By asserting that colonial activity will ensure the eventual triumph of England and Protestantism, the Virginia sermons reveal quite startlingly their participation in an allegorical structure of desire. The literal text of the sermons is the colonial project itself, but the figurative text toward which the sermons all point is England's ongoing quest for a national identity. By the beginning of the seventeenth century, many in England could only look with regret upon their country's failure to build a colonial empire that would contest Spanish domination in the New World. Such an empire, the Virginia ministers contend in their sermons, would simultaneously relieve England of its crippling social and economic problems and give Protestantism a vital presence in the New World. Moreover, the Virginia sermons, mourning the lost colonial opportunities of the past, figure the Virginia colony as a means of recovering something from the past that has been lost. Colonialism becomes the most effective means of investing a nostalgic yearning for national coherence with tangibility and "palpableness." The vision which these sermons articulate is one in which the past is integrated with the present, the self with the other, and the nation with the colony.

The colonial project offers England not only a means of achieving a set of national desires, but also a language for describing those desires. By giving a shape to the desires of the nation in a way that no other undertaking can, the colonial project itself becomes the way that the nation can express its desires. Ironically, however, the deepest desires of the colonial undertaking itself – the desire for profit and power – must never be articulated openly.[4] Unlike the Spanish, whose colonial project was figured by the English as an expression of naked desires, the English structured their colonial project in such a way as to avoid having to confront their own desires. These sermons employ the concept of the nation as a means of deferring and displacing desire. Therefore, rather than articulating the desire to subjugate the native populations or the desire to achieve a profitable colonial operation, these ministers present the colonial undertaking as an allegory for the building of the nation. It is important to remember here that implicit in these allegories of nation-building are multiple other narratives and desires. In other words, the allegorical structure implied by these sermons is not simply bipartite, gesturing only at the nation and its colony. Rather, the structure of these sermons allows readers to see that what is being explicitly offered through colonial activity – a coherent religious and national identity – will be supplemented by other gains as well, namely economic benefit from colonial resources and political control of the native populations.

Borrowing a term from Benedict Anderson, whom I discussed

earlier, I would argue that these ministers discover in colonialism a new way of narrating "nation-ness." If, as Anderson suggests, the notion of an organism traveling horizontally through space and vertically through time is a precise analogue of the nation, then colonialism would seem to offer the ideal way of achieving this sense of "nation-ness." The sermons I discuss in the pages ahead share four crucial characteristics that confirm their participation in the discourse of "nation-ness." First, all offer their listeners a narrative of loss as a means of describing the current state of the nation, and as I suggested in the first chapter, such loss forms one of bases of colonial desire. Second, all of them refer to a general antipathy, or even hostility, to the colonial project within England. Third, all confront the need to defer or regulate desire. Fourth, all confirm that the conversion of native populations will be the central signifying feature of the colonial endeavor – the task that, more than any other one, will mark this colonial project as both English and Protestant. Ultimately, the distinguishing feature of these sermons is not simply their commitment to a Protestant colonial identity but to that identity articulated in explicitly national terms.

THE IMPUDENCIE OF OUR NATION

It is not surprising that Robert Gray opens his 1609 sermon, *A Good Speed to Virginia*, by asserting that England's nascent colonial project would serve as a means of redressing specific ills faced by the English nation. As I have suggested in previous chapters, colonial promoters often claimed that colonial endeavor would remedy problems as diverse as overpopulation, religious division, and economic stagnation. What is striking about Gray's formulation, though, is the barely disguised note of desperation that would seem to suggest that it is Gray's contention that his nation's survival depends on the success of the colonial undertaking. Colonialism emerges in Gray's sermon as the defining activity in his nation's pursuit of a coherent identity.

Bemoaning the almost insoluble problems that have arisen as a result of enclosures and the steady migration of idle persons into England's urban centers, Gray likens England to a beehive, in which the drones have failed to follow nature's call to venture out into the world. In order to prevent England from degenerating into such a dysfunctional hive, therefore, Gray urges the nation's less productive members to remove themselves to a place where they might be employed in activities that will benefit the entire social unit. Comparing the average man to an unambitious bee, Gray argues that,

> so improvident and irrespective is man, that he had rather live like a drone, and feede uppon the fruites of other mens labors, wherunto God hath not entituled him, then looke out and flie abroad, like the Bee to gather the pleasures and riches of the earth, which God hath given him to enjoy.[5]

By comparing the colonial migration of the English to the bees' "natural" urge to "flie abroad," Gray would seem to be suggesting that the antidote to England's social chaos was to be discovered in the hitherto overlooked ability of laborers to exert agency in an economy that, on the surface at least, defied their control. As Karen Kupperman has argued, the image of the hive figured prominently in attempts to depict the colonial project as a means of achieving "a society in which workers willingly engaged in productive activity rather than being compelled to orderly labor."[6] The hive, in other words, functioned as the quintessential image of order, and the bees as the quintessential creatures of obedience. One need only recall Shakespeare's memorable deployment of the image in *Henry V* to see the hive operating as the model of the ordered society:

> Therefore doth heaven divide
> The state of man in diverse functions,
> Setting endeavor in continual motion,
> To which is fixed, as an aim or butt,
> Obedience; for so work the honey-bees,
> Creatures that by a rule in nature teach
> The act of order to a peopled kingdom.[7]

The Archbishop of Canterbury utters these words to reassure the young King Henry that his kingdom will remain secure as he engages in a military campaign in France. Because his subjects will behave like bees, Henry need not fear for the integrity of the social structure he temporarily leaves behind him.

Although the hive functioned for Gray and others as an exemplary instance of internal social cohesion, I would contend that its appeal as a model for colonial endeavor also lay in its ability to depict a social group whose population was dynamic. In this sense, Gray's use of the image is quite different from that of the Archbishop of Canterbury in Shakespeare's play. Unlike Canterbury, who marvels at the ability of the individual bee to retain his sense of place in the absence of the monarch, Gray praises the industrious bee who actually makes himself more valuable to the hive as a whole by vacating his place. Indeed, whereas the Archbishop deploys the image of the hive to convince Henry that he will find the same statically ordered kingdom upon his return from France, Gray uses the image to encourage his countrymen to respond dynamically to profound social changes. All of this is of course to suggest that Gray's use of the hive speaks to that paradox of colonialism I mentioned at the outset of this chapter. Like the hive, the nation ensures its survival by encouraging some of its members to leave and engage in productive labor on the margins. Resolving this paradox was important to Gray whose intention it was to cultivate a perception of colonization, not as a marginal past-time conducted on the fringes of the known world, but as the central activity of a nation preoccupied with its own survival.

The image of the hive constructs the nation's most pressing problems as social and economic in nature. Gray does not wait long, however, to suggest that colonial activity will afford his nation an opportunity to confront and resolve an even more profound, albeit less tangible, set of problems. Turning momentarily from England's ongoing effort to colonize Virginia, Gray recalls with some pain England's earlier refusal to support Columbus' voyage to the New World.

When Christopher Columbus made proffer to the Kings of England, Portugall, and Spaine, to invest them with the most precious and richest veynes of the whole earth ... this offer was not only rejected, but the man himself, who deserves ever to be renowned, was (of us English specially) scorned and accounted for an idle novellist. Some think it was because of his poore apparell, and simple lookes, but surely it is rather to be imputed to the improvidency and impudencie of our nation, which hath alwayes bred such diffidence in us, that we conceit no new report, bee it ever so likely, nor believe any thing best never so probable, before we see the effects.[8]

By attributing the decision to reject Columbus's offer to "the improvidency and impudencie of our nation," Gray forces all of his readers to accept part of the blame. Rather than allowing this fateful misjudgment to remain part of an almost forgotten past, Gray chooses to construct it as part of the active memory of the nation. As such, the current colonial project in Virginia functions as a means of reworking and redeeming a moment of failure from England's past. The effect of Gray's anecdote is to suggest to his readers that the Virginia enterprise functions as an analogue for Columbus's voyage. To reject Gray, therefore, is to reject Columbus all over again. And to reject Virginia is to reject the success of Spain. As long as Gray's readers refuse to redeem the past, England's national self-image will have to be constructed in terms of loss, in terms of the colonies it doesn't possess, in terms of the riches it hasn't gained, in terms of the heroes it has rejected. Thus, colonial adventure promises to repair that foundational loss that has occurred with the rejection of Columbus. Moreover, implicit in Gray's honorific treatment of Columbus would seem to be the suggestion that, at least in some respects, the Spanish colonial experience has become an object deserving of imitation, not scorn.

Gray's figuring of the nation as hive and as body and his invocation of Columbus point to an attempt, on his part, to constitute England as an organism whose existence can only be completely described with reference to temporality or history.[9] After appealing to nature in the image of the hive, and to history in the person of Columbus, Gray returns to nature to emphasize the salubrious effects of colonialism. Using language that offers readers an unvarnished depiction of England's plight, Gray suggests that his nation's

> multitudes like too much bloud in the body, do infect our countrey with plague and povertie, our land hath brought forth, but it hath not milke sufficient in the breast thereof to nourish all those children which it hath brought forth, it affordeth neither employment nor preferment for those that depend upon it and hereupon it is, that many serviceable men give themselves to lewd courses, as to robbing by the highway, theft, cosoning, sharking upon the land, piracie upon the sea...[10]

England is both a body with too much blood and a mother with insufficient milk. At first glance, Gray's simultaneous deployment of these two physiological images would seem contradictory, as each image constitutes England's problems in starkly contrasting terms: surplus and scarcity. And yet colonial activity was defined, in some very real sense, by the flow of men and commodities back and forth across the ocean. By forcing the blood to flow out into the colonies, colonialism would make the milk flow back into the land. The colony, therefore, is a powerful imaginary place that will rid the imperial country of its most bilious elements and simultaneously replenish it with valuable commodities.

What's missing, of course, from Gray's depiction of his nation as a body with too much blood is any mention of desire. In fact, it would seem to be the case that England's lack of achievement in the colonial arena could be attributed to a distinct lack of desire. The "diffident" nation who refused Columbus's offer lacked the desire necessary to accept the challenges of colonialism. The images of the hive and of the body would seem to suggest that Gray is trying to replace desire with necessity. By "naturalizing" the desire to colonize, however, Gray does more than supply an essential element that is missing. He profoundly shapes the identity of the English. To be an English colonist is to lack desire. Gray turns this apparent defect into a strength. All of this begins to make more sense, when he finally turns to a description of the role of the native populations in the English colonial scheme. He relates a no doubt apocryphal story of an African people who actually invite outsiders to colonize them.

And surely so desirous is man of civill societie by nature, that he easily yields to discipline and government if he see any reasonable motive to induce him to the same. For we reade of certaine people in Affrica, inhabiting the mountaine Magnan, which oftentimes do constraine straungers which travell that way, to take the government of them, and to impose lawes unto them, whereby they may be justly and orderly governed: and many Nations willingly submitted themselves to the subjection of the Romanes, being allured thereunto by Justice, equitie, clemencie, and upright dealing of the Romaine captaines: for it is not the nature of men, but the education of men, which make them barbarous and uncivill, and therefore chaunge the education of men, and you shall see that their nature will be greatly rectified and corrected.[11]

Gray's anecdote, the most striking feature of which is the displacement of colonial desire, subtly shifts the terms of the colonial engagement: it is not the colonizers who desire what the native people have, but rather the native people who desire to acquire the knowledge of the strangers. Accordingly, it is the natives who "constraine" the strangers. Likewise, Gray attributes agency to the "Nations [who] willingly submitted themselves to the subjection of the Romanes." In both of these examples, Gray finds evidence that men have an innate desire for laws and good government.

When Gray goes on to describe what he knows about the native people of Virginia, whom the English presumably will colonize, he assumes that the English will find in the native inhabitants, if not a desire, at least a willingness to be subjugated.

> The report goeth, that in Virginia the people are savage and incredibly rude, they worship the divell, offer their young children in sacrifice unto him, wander by and downe like beastes, and in manners and conditions, differ very little from beasts, having no Art, no science, no trade, to employ themselves, or give themselves unto, yet by nature loving and gentle, and desirous to imbrace a better condition. Oh how happy were that man which could reduce this people from brutishnesse, to civilitie, to religion, to Christianitie, to the saving of their soules; happy is that man and blest of God, whom God hath endued, either with meanes or will to attempt this business, but farre be it from the nature of the English to exercise any bloudie crueltie amongst these people: farre be it from the hearts of the English, to give them occasion, that the holy name of God, should be dishonoured among the Infidels, or that in the plantation of that continent, they should give any cause to the world, to say that they sought the wealth of that countrie above or before the glorie of God, and the propagation of his kingdome.[12]

Gray's "report" tells him that the native inhabitants of Virginia are completely lacking in what the English will have to offer them: they have "no Art, no science, no trade." The native inhabitants do, however, possess an abundance of desire – the desire to acquire knowledge, the desire to change, the desire to embrace a better condition. Gray defines the English, on the other hand, as possessing only one desire, namely the desire to give glory to God and to propagate his kingdom. The native inhabitants' desire for self-improvement and the English desire to do God's work notwithstanding, Gray does not anticipate the encounter between native people and English to proceed without conflict. Thus, the man who will attempt the task of converting them must be somebody with "meanes or will." Gray explicitly warns the English, however, against exercising cruelty or doing anything that will allow the world to say that England desires wealth "above or before the glorie of God." It is the nature of Gray's injunction against cruelty that points readers to Gray's awareness of the symbolic function of the colonial enterprise. Ultimately, it is Gray's fear of the words of other nations that shapes his vision of the encounter. In their colonizing, the English must not give the world any reason to speak ill of them. To signify to the world that one had desires other than to convert the native people would be anathema to the English. Their colonial project must speak other things.

Gray then goes on to recall (approvingly) the famous story of Christopher Columbus's use of the lunar eclipse to convince the West Indians of his power. Gray suggests that the English should follow his example:

I remember the practice of Christopher Columbus, which he used amongst the west Indians, to perswade them to receive his Spaniardes to societie and commerce, which was, he observed that they were super-stitiously given to worship the moone, and by the skill he had in Astrono-mie, he foresaw that within three daies the moone should be eclipsed; whereupon he called them together, and told them, that he had often used his best meanes, to bring them to a civill, and friendly converse with strangers, but they would not harken unto him, and therefore in the presence of them all, he called upon the moone to revenge such a barbarous people, which denied strangers to converse and commerce with them: within three dayes after the moone was much darkened by reason of the Eclipse, which when the Indians saw, they thought the moone to be angrie with them, and fearing some plague would proceed from her displeasure they were easily induced to do whatsoever Columbus would have them.[13]

This well-known story stands of course as a classic example of one of the Europeans' primary assumptions in their colonization of the New World, namely that their superior knowledge of science and technology would enable them to persuade the Indians to do their bidding. Only words, not force, would be necessary to convince the Indians to submit to European rule. Gray's own confidence in the power of words as a means of persuasion mirrors his fear of the words that might be spoken about the English and their colonial enterprises.

If Gray's optimism in the above passage strikes one as unlikely to be believed even by his most naive readers, it does not last for long. Soon enough, he has to concede the possible necessity of violence. But violence, as it turns out, is not necessarily the sure sign of failure that his cautions against cruelty might lead us to believe. Rather, violence can be described in words that make it look other than what it might at first appear.

In like maner should all men use their wits in the first place, and weapons should alwayes be the last meanes in all our projects. And therefore
although the children of Joseph have an expresse commaundement here
in this place to destroy those Idolaters, and possesse their land, yet foras-
much as we have no precept but by example, we must first trie all means
before weapons, and when we take them into our hands, necessitie of
preserving our owne lives, must rather move us to destroy the enemyes
of God, then either ambition as greedinesse of gaine, or crueltie, or anie
private respect whatsoever.[14]

The scriptural text for Gray's sermon is the seventeenth chapter
of Joshua, in which the children of Joseph complain about having
only "one lot." Joshua responds by urging them to take the land
of the Canaanites by force: "Thou art a great people, and hast
great power: thou shalt not have one lot only ... for thou shalt
drive out the Canaanites ... though they be strong." For Gray,
who finds himself in the position of promoting a milder form of
colonial engagement, the scriptural passage might at first seem to
cast a different light upon the English colonial efforts. But his
point seems clear. Wits must be tried before weapons. But if wits
cannot produce the desired results, then the English may resort
to force in order to achieve their goals. But the goal for Gray is
not the commercial profit. Instead, it is the propagation of the
Christian faith. What is shared, however, is the refusal to express
the political subjugation of the native populations as a desire or
end in itself. That desire must always be deferred, either by
emphasizing the inherently humane and moral nature of the
means of colonialism, or by emphasizing the explicitly good and
noble nature of the ultimate ends of the colonial endeavor.

Therefore, one doesn't read Gray's ultimate endorsement of
England's right to engage militarily with the natives of Virginia
as a contradiction. He has shifted the terms of the discussion.
Instead of simply evaluating the colonial project on the basis of
the means used, we now see that some goals demand exceptional
means:

all Polititians doe with one consent, holde and maintaine, that a Christian king may lawfullie make warre upon barbarous and Savage people,
and such as live under no lawfull or warrantable government, and may
make a conquest of them, so that the warre be undertaken to this ende,
to reclaime and reduce those Savages from their barbarous kinds of life,
and from their brutish and ferine manners, to humanitie, pietie, and
honestie.

Just a few lines later, Gray calls upon the "judgement of Augustine himselfe," whose writing, he suggests, has supported the claim that "we might lawfully make warre upon the Savages of Virginia our project, having the endes aforesaid."[15] By initially asserting that the English will not need to resort to violence, Gray points to the most dramatic way in which the English hoped to distinguish their colonial program from that of the Spanish. But he is not completely unrealistic about England's chances of prosecuting a peaceful colonial occupation. Thus he must also prepare his readers for the possibility of violence. In Gray's rhetoric, however, the threat of force is always accompanied by an implicit or explicit disclaimer. For instance, at one moment, he argues that the English do have the right to use force, but he simultaneously suggests that their chances of exercising that right are remote. In a reversal of this position, he seems to concede that war will be almost inevitable but that the war will be for the noble end of bringing the savages "to humanitie, pietie, and honestie." By coupling the right to use violence with promises of moderation, Gray attempts to assert the primary means by which the English will distinguish themselves in their colonial endeavors. But he also attempts to shift the focus of the colonial discussion from the means to the ends. For it is the ends, finally, which not only will justify the project, but also garner crucial support at home.

Although Gray would seem to be arguing in the above passage that even petty criminals could be rendered of service in the colonial undertaking, he will later urge caution in the selection of colonists: "that for this present business of plantation in Virginia, there must bee speciall choice and care had of such persons as shall be sent thither."[16] Gray is quick, however, to assert that even mediocre men can be brought to do good things by a "Prince" who is willing to exercise his authority:

Thus in conscience towards God, and in affection towards his subjects ought a Prince to stand affected. And if he stand so affected he will punish such as are wild and vitious, and he will advance such as are vertuous and well disposed; he will incourage the painfull and industrious, and he will correct the idle and dissolute; he will establish true religion, and he will repress heresies and schismes; he will releeve the weake and impotent, and he will suppress the mutinous and insolent; so that God will give a blessing and all things will prosper under his government.[17]

Ultimately, people in Gray's position had no choice but to put forth the figure of the stern magistrate as the solution to the double bind in which they inevitably found themselves. If the colonial project did not promise to remove "the idle and dissolute" from England, it would lose a significant part of its appeal. And yet the inclusion of potentially disruptive elements in the colonial project threatened to derail one of the other promised benefits of colonialism, namely the exportation of civility and Christianity.

A SHAME UPON YOUR NATION

In a sermon published in the same year as that of Robert Gray, William Symonds also undertakes to defend and promote England's colonial efforts in Virginia. In the scriptural text for Symonds's sermon, *Genesis* 12:1–3, God says to Abram, "Get thee out of thy Countrey." And in return God promises Abram, "I will make of thee a great nation." It is significant that the promise God makes implies that Abram's status as a great nation will not be realized until he gets out of the country. In the same way, Symonds implies that England will not become a great nation until at least some of its people leave the country. In other words, deploying a typological framework similar to the one that would be used by subsequent Puritan colonial writers, Symonds compares the colonial project to the foundational act of the Israelite nation. Symonds's sermon attempts to show that the colonial enterprise, rather than challenging the discourse of nation-ness, in fact, renders it much more highly rational. In Symonds's sermon, the colonial discourse appears as the most effective means of restoring the coherence and integrity to the idea of the Protestant English nation, which is figured as fractured and incomplete.

In the biblical text, Abram's departure from the country enables Israel subsequently to constitute itself as a great nation. Similarly, in order for England to undergo the same transformation into a great nation, some of its citizens will need to leave the country. They will need to colonize.

But further if you will have *Abram's* blessing, you must doe your diligence to walke in those wayes, by which the Lord doeth give his blessings – And as we are in continuall expectation of some honourable effect, if you continue in the faith: so will you bring a confusion upon your selves and a shame upon your Nation, if you sticke not fast to God, and his blessed commandments.[18]

As Symonds constructs it, the failure of the few will lead to the disgrace of the many. The failure to colonize, in other words, will inevitably "bring – a shame upon your Nation." Colonial activity is not the private act of private individuals pursuing their own private gains. Rather, to colonize is to represent and constitute the nation.

Like Gray, Symonds presents his listeners with a dismal picture of the current state of England and offers the colonial undertaking as the only means for England to solve its problems as a nation. In fact, using the image of the hive to represent the alarming deterioration of English society, Symonds presents listeners with a picture that closely resembles that of Gray.

But look seriously into the land, and see whether there bee not just cause, if not a necessity to seek abroad. The people blessed be God, doe swarme in the land, as yong bees in a hive in June; insomuch that there is very hardly room for one man to live by another. The mightier like old strong bees thrust the weaker, as younger, out of their hives: Lords of Manors convert towneships, in which were a hundreth or two hundreth communicants, to a shepheard and his dog. The true labouring husband-man, that susteineth the prince by the plow, who was wont to feede manie poore, to set many people on worke, and pay twice as much subsidie and fifteenes to the king, for his proportion of earth, as his Landlord did for tenne times as much; that was wont to furnish the church with Saints, the musters with able persons to fighte for their soveraigne, is now in many places turned labourer, and can hardly scape the statute of rogues and vagrants... The rich shop-keeper hath the good honest poore labourer at such advantage, that he can grind his face when he pleaseth. The poore mettall man worketh his bones out, and swelteth himselfe in the fire, yet for all his labour, having charge of wife and children, hee can hardly keepe himselfe from the almes box... Many such sweets are in *England*, which I know not how better to interpret then to say the strong olde bees doe beate out the younger, to swarme and hive them-selves elsewhere. Take the opportunity, good honest labourers which indeede bring all the hony to the hive, God may so blesse you, that the proverbe may be true of you that *A May swarme, is worth a kings ransome*.[19]

Symonds's usage of the image is differently inflected to that of Gray. Where Gray at first lays the blame at the feet of the lazy drone who refuses to leave the hive, Symonds constructs all of the bees as victims of a society whose means to provide for its members has been outstripped by its growth in population. Moreover, the topical allusion to the process of enclosure, whereby "towne-ships" are converted from "a hundreth or two hundreth communi-cants, to a shepheard and his dog," serves to reinforce the notion that people displaced by social and economic progress are in fact victims rather than culprits. Despite the subtle difference in tone, however, Symonds' usage of the image functions almost identically to that of Gray. Just as the well-being of the hive is ensured only by the willingness of some of the bees to venture abroad, the social and economic integrity of the nation can only be guaranteed by the formation of colonies.

Deploying the same language of surplus and scarcity as Gray to describe the problems of the nation, Symonds makes a remarkable discovery. Like Gray, who figures England as a body with too much blood, Symonds also attributes the causes of England's plight to an abundance of an otherwise desirable commodity, namely virtue. According to Symonds, therefore, colonial undertaking will allow its participants to display their virtue more visibly than if they were to stay at home.

Sure it is verie true, that manie a man, while he staieth at home, liveth in obscuritie, as in the darkest night, though his vertues and worth deserve better respect. For at home what can bee a mans regarde, where there be millions of his rank, though not better deserving, yet better favoured. Get abroad where vertue is skant, and there, by the advancing of thy wisdome and vertue, thou shalt bee more eminent and famous in a yeare, then at home halfe of thy ranke shall bee all their daies: hidden vertue is neglected, but abroade is magnified. . .When a man of worth is among many men of like worth, he is accounted rather a curse then a blessing, such is the corruption of flesh and bloud, infected with envy and with pride.[20]

By suggesting that virtue is subject to the laws of supply and demand, Symonds implies that England's fundamental problems really are nothing more than problems of appearance. Paradoxi-cally, because of a surplus of virtue at home, ordinary English men and women appear less virtuous than they really are. Thus, rather than lacking virtue altogether, society's apparently idle and dissol-ute members will discover that their virtue is merely hidden by their unfortunate circumstances. As he constructs it, virtue is really nothing more than a commodity, whose value will inevitably be determined by its scarcity. Hence, he urges potential colonists to regard the colonial experience as an investment opportunity. By transporting their virtue abroad, they will enhance the value of a commodity which, if left at home, would hardly fetch any notice at all.

According to Symonds, colonialism will do more than correct the problem of undervalued virtue. It will offer England the opportunity to reconfirm its identity as a Protestant nation and to assert that identity with greater vigor on the international stage. In Symonds's view, nothing reveals this potential of colonialism more clearly than the presence of "enemies" who attempt to thwart England's colonial efforts. Referring again to Genesis, Symonds retells the story of Abram's rescue of his brother Lot from his captivity among the Sodomites. The lesson of this story, he tells us is, "that in a strange Countrey, we must looke for enemies." From John, he recalls the words of Christ to the Apostles: "In this world you shall have trouble." In other words, anticipating the Jeremiads that would become popular in the American colonies later in the century, Symonds asserts that the enemies of the colonial enterprise are merely a sign of its blessedness. And just as Abram and the Apostles overcame their enemies, so too will the Virginia colony. Moreover, the biblical examples will give the English a means of defending their enterprise in explicitly Protestant terms: "I hope out of these words thus generally delivered, every true hearted Protestant, can frame out an answere unto the objection, that is thought much to impeach this Plantation in VIRGINIA." Connecting biblical history to the present, Symonds suggests that the enemies of the Protestants are not unlike the enemies of the Israelites.

For they find in the totall, how many Kingdomes they have lost, and doe daily lose; how many battailes they have fought, in all which to the Protestants, as the Cananites, would prove to the Israelites in Caleb's judgement, so have they bene, even Bread for us... Ask what is become of the many shippes that came into the Narrow seas in the yeere 1588?

In the English imagination, the symbolic value of the defeat of the Armada in 1588 was unmatched. This decisive military victory that ended the threat of invasion by the Spanish signified England's coming of age as a Protestant nation. By associating England's colonial efforts in Virginia with this proud moment in his nation's history, Symonds implicitly suggests that the Virginia colony will acquire a similar symbolic importance not just for those directly involved in the colony, but for the nation as a whole.

When confronting the basic moral question of whether England can justify the use of force to achieve its colonial goals, Symonds demonstrates the intimate connections that link the idea of the colony to the idea of the nation. Repeating what we must presume was one of the principal objections raised against England's colonial efforts, Symonds strenuously rejects the notion that the term "invasion" might apply to what the English were undertaking. Calling upon unnamed "objectors", Symonds challenges critics of colonialism to find a context in which force, as exercised by the righteous nation, would not be permissible.

> The countrey, they say, is possessed by owners, that rule, and governe it in their owne right: then with what consience, and equitie can we offer to thrust them, by violence, out of their inheritances? For answere to this objection: first it is plaine, that the objector supposeth it is not lawfull to invade the territories of other princes, by force of sword.

Symonds then offers a catalogue of irreproachable biblical figures who have seen fit to invade another country at some point or other. His list includes such Old Testament notables as Joshua, David, and Solomon. Accusing the objector of forming his ideas "in the fantasticall shop of his addle imagination," Symonds suggests that his objector would even refuse to allow princes to "make offensive warres, if it were to gaine the whole world to Christ." By accusing the Virginia colony's unnamed critics of refusing to see the greater good to be gained through colonial activity, Symonds reveals his own criteria for judging the morality of such ventures to be inextricably linked to England's rights as a nation.[21]

Symonds's next move in his defense of the Virginia colony is to point out the absurdity of questioning the right of the sovereign, under any circumstances, to take the land of another "prince." To object to colonizing on these grounds, Symonds asserts, is to object to the very means by which England's sovereign can claim his title. He asks,

> whether (if it be unlawfull to conquere) the crowne fit well on the head of our most sacred soveraigne? (whose dayes be as the dayes of heaven O Lord) For by this objection they shew, that had they power to untwist what, which in so many ages hath beene well spunne, they would write him crownlesse, as farre as hee hath his title from the conqueror.[22]

By implying that the right to colonize is as fundamental as the English king's right to sit on the throne, Symonds attempts to neutralize all objections to England's colonial efforts. According to Symonds, all objections of this sort undermine all hierarchical arrangements of power including the monarchy and nation.[23] By asserting that the propriety of colonialism is linked to the propriety of the monarchy itself, Symonds reveals a shrewdness that goes beyond associating his opponents with illicit thoughts. Indeed, Symonds's argument implicitly recognizes that, if it was to survive, the Virginia colony needed to be regarded by the public as essential to the survival and well-being of the nation as the monarchy itself.

Having established England's fundamental right as a nation to colonize, Symonds makes quick work of dismissing the suggestion that the English would simply repeat the atrocities of the Spanish in their colonial undertakings. Without identifying the Spanish by name, Symonds recites a litany of colonial excesses that no listener or reader would have failed to associate with the Spanish colonization of the New World.

O but, in entring of other countries, there must needes be much lamentable effusion of bloud. Certainly our objector was hatched of some popish egge; and it may be in a JESUIT's vault, where they feede themselves fat, with tormenting innocents. Why is there no remedie, but assoone as we come on land, like Wolves, and Lyons, and Tygres, long famished, we must teare in peeces, murther, and torment the naturall inhabitants, with cruelties never read, nor heard before? must we needs burne millions of them, and cast millions into the sea? must we baite them with dogges, that shall eate up the mothers with their children? let such be the practices of the divell, of Abaddon the sonne of perdition, of Antichrist and his frie, that is of purple Rome.[24]

Symonds is of course wrong to suggest that such acts were "never read, nor heard before." As I suggested earlier, with the translation and publication of Las Casas in English in 1583, the English were able to read all about the brutality and cruelty of the Spanish.[25] In fact, it is precisely because the atrocities were known by the English that Symonds must reassure his audience that an English colony would behave in a dramatically different fashion from a Spanish one. In the end, Symonds's most compelling reassurance rests in the assertion that the righteousness of England's colonial undertaking will be ensured by the doctrinal purity of the English nation.

THE STAINE THAT STICKES UPON OUR NATION

In the year following the publication of the sermons of Robert Gray and William Symonds, William Crashaw published *A Sermon Preached in London before the right honorable the Lord Lawarre, Lord Governor and Captaine Generall of Virginea, and others of his Maiesties Counsell for that Kingdome, and the rest of the Adventurers in that Plantation.* Like Gray and Symonds, Crashaw suggests that the fate of England will rest on its success in colonial adventures. Near the end of his sermon, in a move that recalls Gray, Crashaw asserts that the Virginia colony will help England to overcome the humiliation it has suffered for having rejected the offer of Christopher Columbus.

And to add one word more, (but it is of much moment), we shall hereby wipe off the staine that stickes upon our nation since, (either for idleness or some other base feares, or foolish conceits) we refused the offer of the west Indies, made unto us by that famous Christopher Columbus, who upon Englands refusall, tendred it to the Prince that now enjoieth them.[26]

Just as the stain resulting from England's refusal of Columbus's offer "stickes upon our nation," so too will the success of the Virginia colony contribute to the well-being of the nation. Just as the colonial effort represented for Gray and Symonds a means of writing and rewriting England's history as a nation, so too Crashaw will offer his readers the discourse of colonialism as the best means of narrating the successes and failures of the English nation. To be a Protestant nation is to colonize, and to tell the story of that nation is to tell the story of its colonies.

The most significant difference between Crashaw's sermon and those of his fellow divines who also promoted the Virginia colony is his willingness to use the language of exchange to describe the project. Like the others, Crashaw displaces the desire for colonialism onto the native inhabitants, asserting that the English colonists have found "favor in the eyes of the savages, who rather invite us then resist us."[27] But Crashaw takes the displacement of colonial desire one step further, suggesting that desires can be regulated in a formal system of exchange. His model is Abraham who, wanted a place to burie in, and liked a peece of land: and being a great man, and therefore loved of the heathen, they bad him chuse where hee would, and take it: No, saith Abraham, but I will buie it, and so he paide the price of it: so must all the children of Abraham doe. Thirdly, it is most lawfull to exchange with other Nations, for that which they may spare, and it is lawfull for a Christian to have commerce in civill things even with the heathen. . .[28]

By engaging in exchange instead of dispossession, Abraham thus serves as an irreproachable model of colonial virtue. In the neutral territory of the economic marketplace, Christians and Heathens alike may coexist and engage in mutually beneficial transactions. With his suggestion that the heathen nations may have commodities to "spare," Crashaw implicitly defines the English as lacking. Colonialism, therefore, is figured as an activity that will bring with it plenitude and fulfillment.

Although Crashaw's sermon still depicts his nation in terms of lack or need, his language of the marketplace constructs the colonial encounter in terms that are much more highly rationalized than those of either Gray or Symonds. Rather than deploying the socially cataclysmic images of the overcrowded hive or the overly sanguineous body, Crashaw argues that colonial endeavor is simply the most rational way for England to acquire the commodities that it lacks. Moreover, by describing the colonial endeavor in economic terms, Crashaw is able to answer critics who argue that the English will simply reproduce the atrocities of the Spanish.

Upon these grounds, which I hope are undeniable, I answere more particularly to the present occasion: that first we will take nothing from the Savages by power nor pillage, by craft nor violence, neither goods, lands nor libertie, much lesse life (as some other Christian nations have done, to the dishonour of religion.) We will offer them no wrong, but rather defend them from it: and this is not my bare speech, but order is so taken both in our Pattents and Instructions, and such is the resolution of our Governours.[29]

In stark contrast to the Spanish (no doubt one of the "other Christian nations" alluded to) who took goods, lands, and libertie from the native people by power, pillage and craft, the English will take nothing from the natives without simultaneously giving something (presumably of equal value) in return. And to lend weight to his claim, Crashaw points to the "Pattents and Instructions" of the colony which have the effect of making the mandate of exchange legally binding upon the English colonists.

By emphasizing this code of economic justice which is built into the English colonial program, Crashaw is able to distinguish England's colonial efforts from those of the Spanish. But he is quick to disabuse his listeners of the impression that England's colonial program exists solely for the benefit of any natives the colonists might encounter.

> Secondly, we will exchange with them for that which they may spare, and we doe neede, and they shall have that which we may spare, and they doe much more need. But what they may spare first, land and roome for us to plant in... Againe, they may spare us Timber, Masts, Crystall (if not better stones) Wine, Copper, Iron, Pitch, Tar, Sassafras, Sope-ashes (for all these and more, we are sure the Countrey yeeldes in great abundance) and who knowes not we want these, and are beholden to some for them, with whom it were better for us if we had lesse to doe.[30]

It is probably no accident that Crashaw begins his inventory of commodities "which they may spare" with two items of commercial and military significance. And the ominously pointed warning that immediately follows the list serves to remind his audience of England's vulnerability so long as it must rely on others (including potential adversaries) for raw materials of strategic importance. Colonialism therefore will not simply line the purses of those individuals who invest in the various ventures. By suggesting that colonialism will help England provide for its own national security, Crashaw insists that England's colonial interests are also national interests.

The rhetorical climax of Crashaw's sermon coincides with his description of the precise nature of the exchange that will form the basis of the English relationship with the natives. In a dazzling display of verbal virtuosity, Crashaw suggests that England will offer the natives conversion in return for the precious commodities of the New World.

> These things they have, these they may spare, these we neede, these we will take of them. But what will we give them: first, we will give them such things as they greatly desire, and doe holde such things as they greatly desire, and doe holde a sufficient recompence for any of the fore-saide commodities we take of them: but we holde it not so: and therefore out of our humanitie and conscience, we will give them more, namely such things as they want and neede, and are infinitely more excellent then all wee take from them:
>
> and that is:

1. Civilitie for their bodies.

2. Christianitie for their soules:

The first to make them men: the second happy men; the first to cover their bodies from the shame of the world: the second to cover their soules from the wrath of God: the lesse of these two (being that for the bodie) will make them richer then we finde them.[31]

Although the anaphora of the first sentence lends rhetorical force to Crashaw's description of the transaction that will take place between colonizers and native people, it also renders in no uncertain terms the coercive nature of the marketplace in which the native inhabitants will find themselves. Everything about the "exchange" will be determined in advance by the English: the commodities to be traded, their quantities, and their prices. It is also important to observe that, once again, desire is projected onto the native populations: the English "neede," while the native inhabitants "desire". But, economically speaking, the colonial project promises to do much more than satisfy England's needs for scarce commodities. Indeed, if we are to believe Crashaw and the other promoters, colonial adventure will bring about a complete socio-economic renewal in England, solving such troubling problems as overpopulation, unemployment, and crime. The colonial encounter, therefore, becomes the perfect way for England to satisfy its needs and thereby make itself complete as a nation.

As appealing as are these promises of economic prosperity and social harmony, they introduce a new set of tensions and contradictions into the colonial discourse. Promoters like Crashaw are faced with the problem of explaining how England's least productive members are to be removed to the colonies and there transformed into diligent, productive and law abiding subjects. In other words, the removal of idlers might solve a domestic problem for England, but it will ultimately raise the potentially more complicated question of how one might govern and control a group of independent-minded colonists from a distance of several thousand miles. And if those colonists are not inclined to behave in the most orderly and productive fashion while under the surveillance of the English state, one might reasonably wonder why they will suddenly modify their behavior once they find themselves beyond the reach of English law. This question relates directly, of course, to the matter of England's promise to produce a colonial operation that will provide the native populations with "civilitie for their bodies" and "christianitie for their soules."

Crashaw's answer to the potentially debilitating problem of colonial disorder is to suggest that the colonial undertaking will possess its own inherent discipline. In contrast to Gray and Symonds who suggest that the entire social organism is in a state of disarray because of fundamental scarcities, Crashaw argues that England suffers from an unhealthy surfeit of luxury. And whereas Gray and Symonds construct the colonial project as a way of augmenting overtaxed resources, Crashaw suggests that the colonial project will reform its participants by exposing them to the hardships caused by scarcity.

> Let us not deceive our selves. Stately houses, costly apparell, rich furniture, soft beds, daintie fare, dalliance and pleasures, huntings and horseraces, sports and pastimes, feasts and banquets [were] not the meanes whereby our forefathers conquered kingdomes, subdued their enemies, converted heathen, civilized the Barbarians, and setled their commonwealths: nay they exposed themselves to frost and colde, snow and heate, rane and tempests, hunger and thirst, and cared not what hardnesse, what extremitie, what pinching miseries they endured, so they might achieve the ends they aimed at: and shall wee thinke to bring to passe a matter of this honour and excellencie, which the ages to come shall stand amazed to beholde, and not to endure much corporall hardnesse?[32]

We should, of course, not forget either that Crashaw was himself a Puritan, nor that he delivered his sermon before a predominantly aristocratic audience. And since the kinds of vices he denounces here are not those of the lower classes, this part of the sermon could certainly be read as Crashaw's attempt to take advantage of his captive audience and play the part of the puritan minister inveighing against aristocratic frivolity.

Although one may assume that Crashaw is critical of the materialism of the aristocrats (and other adventurers), it is important to recognize that Crashaw does not reject the material success of "our forefathers." To be sure, he promotes colonialism as a vehicle for introducing discipline to the privileged classes. But if the colonial project is initially to serve as a kind of "boot-camp" for young aristocratic adventurers, Crashaw implicitly suggests that it will ultimately bring its participants the same sorts of material rewards that "our forefathers" gained through their exploits. It is thus important to note that in the above passage

Crashaw objects not to the forefathers' acquisition of material wealth but to the material ease of the descendants whose leisurely lifestyles have been acquired without the necessary hardships. After all, as Crashaw describes it, the forefathers only acquired their wealth in the pursuit of other, more worthy objectives: the conquering of kingdoms, the conversion of heathen, the civilizing of barbarians, etc. The "stately houses" then were merely the outward, worldly symbols of a series of monumental spiritual undertakings.

Unlike Gray and Symonds who portray the colonial enterprise as a way of achieving material, social and spiritual progress, Crashaw would seem to be saying that the chief advantage of the colonial endeavor is precisely its potential for creating initial hardship. Hence, in Crashaw's scheme, the participants will achieve a spiritual renewal commensurate with the hardships they endure as a part of their colonial experience. Ultimately, however, Crashaw's colonial vision converges with that of Gray and Symonds. By beginning the above passage with "stately houses" and ending it with a "matter" that "the ages to come shall stand amazed to beholde," Crashaw seems to suggest to his listeners that, with the appropriate amount of sacrifice, they too will be able to leave this world with the same kinds of material accumulations as their forefathers. If this is the case, then the problem that Crashaw describes is bound to repeat itself. As the members of one generation inherit the "stately houses, costly apparell, rich furniture, soft beds, daintie fare," etc., from their predecessors, they will need to find a means of divesting themselves of these distractions so that they can acquire the discipline and desire to build their own monuments. Colonialism, according to Crashaw, is precisely that means.

Ultimately, for Crashaw, the colonization of Virginia represents a chance for England as a nation to continue the work of the Protestant reformation. Recalling the numerous times that prominent Protestants have been cursed by various Popes, Crashaw attempts to reassure his audience that the Virginia undertaking, like Protestantism itself, will succeed in confounding all adherents of Roman Catholicism, especially the Pope himself:

. . .for what Protestant or any other did he [i.e. the Pope] ever curse but God blest them the more: Leo the 10. cursed Luther, and all men expected when he should have died some horrible death: but he lived to

die in his bed, and proved the confounder of the Pope in his life and
death. Paul the 3. cursed Henry the 8. but after that he rooted the Pope
out of England. Impious Pius the 5. cursed noble Elizabeth of England,
and all the poore Papists of the world lookt when some terrible confusion
should have fallen on her and her kingdome: but she lived to see the
death of that Pope, and six or seven more; and more than thirtie years
after lived in that glorie, as never Queene on earth. . .[33]

There is at least one significant feature that differentiates the
Virginia undertaking from Luther, Henry, and Elizabeth. The Virginia undertaking is a national enterprise, while these others are
simply personal. The Virginia undertaking offers the English the
opportunity to act as a nation of Protestants. With its emphasis
on individual faith and the individual's relationship with God,
Protestantism would seem to discourage the strong institutional
identity possessed by Catholics. And yet, colonial adventure,
because it demands, before all else, an individual investment
(corporeal or financial), would seem to present English Protestants with the ideal way to overcome their antipathy toward
corporate endeavors. Colonialism, therefore, offers the English
people not only the chance to act as individual Protestants but
also as a nation of Protestants.

A LAUGHING STOCK AMONG OUR NEIGHBOUR NATIONS

Near the end of his 1613 sermon, *Good newes from Virginia*, Alexander Whitaker warns his countrymen against abandoning its colonial endeavors in Virginia. Recalling for his readers the losses
that Spain and Portugal incurred on the way to establishing their
profitable colonies, Whitaker suggests that by abandoning the project at this point, England will only leave the way open for other
nations to benefit from England's efforts. But the economic
reasons form only one aspect of Whitaker's rationale. He also
argues in favor of the colony on the grounds that the English
nation needs the colonies in order to preserve its stature among
other nations.

Remember, I beseech you, how many lives were lost, how many years
were spent, what discouragements, what great losses the Adventurers of
Spaine and Portugale suffered and under-went, before they could be
setled in the West Indies, or receive any profitable returne from thence:
and now behold what rich loads, what profitable returnes are yearely

shipped from thence. Shall our Nation, hitherto famous for noble attempts, and the honorable finishing of what they have undertaken, be now taxed for inconstancie, and blamed by the enemies of our prot-estation, for uncharitableness? Yea, shall we be a scorne among Princes, and a laughing stock among our neighbor Nations, for basely leaving what we honorably began; yea, for beginning a Discoverie, whose riches other men shall gather, so soone as wee have forsaken it? Awake you true hearted English men, you servants of Jesus Christ, remember that the Plantation is Gods, and the reward your Countries.[34]

Whitaker here outlines two separate lines of reasoning that are intended to keep England in the business of sponsoring colonies. The first is economic. The second ideological. It is important to note how different these lines of reason are. The investment in colonial endeavors of England was never the same as that of Spain. England's investment was conducted, by and large, by private indi-viduals who invested their private funds in the colonial companies. The losses, therefore, are not, strictly speaking, England's. And yet the assumption that the private activity of these investors and colonizers will lead to the increased prestige of the nation is clear. One need only scrutinize the final sentence of the above passage to grasp the subtle connections he asserts between colony, God, and country. The colony in Virginia is the best way for the individ-ual Englishman to imagine himself as participating in an activity that will be conceived in terms of Protestantism and Englishness.

Whitaker's sermon, like the others promoting the Virginia colony, suggests that the ultimate goal of the colony is not the financial enrichment of the individual investors but rather the saving of the souls of the natives of Virginia.

This is the doctrine, and I beseech God to stirre up your minds to the practise of liberalitie in all things towards all men. And remember the poore estate of the ignorant inhabitants of *Virginia*. Cast forth your almes (my brethren of England) and extend your liberality on these charitable works, which God hath called you to performe. Let not the servants of superstition, that think to merit by their good works (as they term them) goe beyond us in well doing; neither let them be able to open their mouths against us, and to condemne the religion of our Protestation, for want of charitable deeds. Those that cannot help in monies by reason of their poverty, may venture their persons hither, &heere not only serve God, but helpe also these poore Indians, and build a sure foundation for themselves, but if you can do neither of these, then send your earnest prayers to God for the prosperity of this worke.[35]

Whitaker's plea goes out to all Englishmen: "my brethren of England." This project of converting the "poore Indians" presents itself to the English as the means of imagining themselves as a nation of Protestants. In contrast to the Catholics, whose doctrine of good works lends itself readily to the notion of "well doing," the Protestants, "for want of charitable deeds," might appear to be lacking. The colony in Virginia therefore gives the English the ideal means of expressing their identity as a Protestant nation.

Like his predecessors in the promotional pulpit, Whitaker encourages his audience to look within England's borders to see the disarray that will be cured by the successful colony.

The commandement of God is, that there should be no beggers in Israel. But look into the streets of our cities, and pass from them into all the quarters of England, and you shall find neither Court nor Countrey, Citie or Village, withoute the importunate cravings of those that crie, *Give, Give*. From hence it is that so many base theeves, and pettie robbers, lurke in every corner, until the common trees of execution hang them up.[36]

Whitaker's frame of reference is the nation. It may be within the cities and villages that one sees the devastating effects of poverty: the petty crimes and the brutal punishments. But it is the responsibility of the nation to correct these problems. Colonialism offers the nation just such an opportunity to re-imagine itself.

OUR *DOCTRINALL*, NOT *NATIONALL* ENEMIES

Almost a decade after Alexander Whitaker's sermon, poet and Anglican divine John Donne, delivered his own sermon to the members of the Virginia Company, in which he issued an appeal to all Englishmen to support the colonial enterprise, especially the work of converting the natives to Christianity. The lines along which Donne suggests that these conversions will proceed are generally similar to those preached by the other ministers whose sermons we have examined here.

Further and hasten you this blessed, this joyfull, this glorious consummation of all, and happie reunion of all bodies to their Soules, by preaching the *Gospell* to those men. Preach to them Doctrinally, preach to them Practically; Enamore them with your *Justice*, and, (as farre as may consist with your security) your *Civilitie*; but inflame them with your *godlinesse*, and your *Religion*. Bring them to *love* and *Reverence* the name of that *King*,

that sends men to teach them the wayes of *Civilitie* in this world, but to
fear and *adore* the Name of that *King of Kings*, that sends men to teach
them the waies of Religion, for the next world.[37]

With his use of words like "enamore," "love," "reverence," "fear,"
and "adore," Donne clearly indicates that he has embraced a colonial ideology that emphasizes the importance of love without
ruling out the usefulness of fear. Although there is nothing overtly
menacing in Donne's enthusiastic forecast of missionary success,
the terms of his "gospel" engagement would seem to leave very
little room for the native people to say no. Moreover, the ultimate
role that the native populations seem destined to play in Donne's
vision is that of vassals, ultimately to God, but first to the King of
England who has been kind enough to send "men to teach them
the wayes of civilitie."

In Donne's sermon, therefore, we see that, in his attitude
toward the native populations, he has effectively reproduced the
positions taken by those who had ascended to the pulpit to preach
for Virginia some ten years before him. But the similarities
between Donne and his predecessors do not stop there. Like Gray
and Symonds and the others, Donne asserts that England's colonial activity in Virginia will help to solve social and economic
woes at home:

It [the colonial enterprise] shall redeeme many a wretch from the Jawes
of death, from the hands of the Executioner, upon whom, perchaunce a
small fault, or perchance a first fault, or perchance a fault heartily and
sincerely repented, perchance no fault, but malice, had otherwise cast a
present, ignominious death. It shall sweep your streets, and wash your
dores, from idle persons, and the children of idle persons, and imploy
them: and truely, if the whole Countrey were but such a *Bridewell*, to
force idle persons to work, it had a good use.[38]

Donne's apparent sympathy for the wretch who, through colonialism, will be able to escape from the executioner's grasp seems
to identify him more closely with William Symonds than with any
of the other Virginia ministers. After all, it was Symonds who was
able to discern that idleness was not necessarily the fault of the
idle person, but rather a function of significant, systemic problems
that were the responsibility of all members of society. But, as I
suggested in my reading of Symonds' sermon, the question of
where one locates the source of the problem of idleness is less
significant than where one proposes to find the solution. And like

the rest of the Virginia ministers, Donne asserts that colonial endeavor will be good for what ails English society.

While Donne's Virginia sermon eloquently echoes both the logic and the rhetoric of earlier promotional literature, it does introduce his audience to a new, potentially troubling, strain in the ediface of English colonial ideology. In a passage immediately following the one quoted above, Donne urges his listeners to regard their rivals for colonial territories as "Doctrinall" ones rather than as "National" ones:

> already it is a marke for the Envy, and for the ambition of our Enemies; I speake but of our *Doctrinall*, not *Nationall* Enemies; as they are *Papists*, they are sory we have this Countrey; and surely, twenty Lectures in matter of Controversie, doe not so much vexe them, as one Ship that goes, and strengthens that Plantation.[39]

Whatever else Donne's distinction between these two sorts of enemies might represent, it almost surely does not mean that he sees the colonial project as inevitably pitting England's "Nationall" interests against its "Doctrinall" ones. Indeed, it is important to say that nowhere else in his sermon does Donne suggest that England's colonial efforts will do anything other than promote the well-being of *both* the nation and its Protestant faith. More generally, it is unlikely that Donne could have perceived the particular path that England's own doctrinal conflicts would take in the decades following his Virginia sermon. For instance, Donne could hardly have anticipated that England's religious and political struggles would have become so bitter that they would lead to a decade-long civil war and culminate in the execution of the English king. And it is even more unlikely that Donne could have forecasted the shifting political and religious context, within which England would situate its colonial efforts. And yet, his deliberate attempt to distinguish between the two would seem to indicate an awareness that England's religious and national identity are not necessarily – or at least not always – coterminous. Donne presciently, if perhaps unwittingly, pointed to the very lines along which colonial conflict would develop in the decades ahead.

If the colonial enterprise, therefore, as imagined during the first decade of the seventeenth century by the Virginia ministers, was one that would project a unified and coherent English Protestant identity into the New World, it would not be long before England's colonies themselves would be transformed into sites of doctrinal and political conflict. Rather than providing the means by which Englishness and Protestantism could be seemlessly woven together, the colonial project ultimately gave voice to the same doctrinal differences that threatened to sunder the English state. In other words, only as long as the colonial enterprise remained more imaginary than real, could it provide the English with the hope of discovering a discourse that might serve to unite the nation against its Catholic rivals. Indeed, as John Donne seems to have realized – perhaps because of his own painful journey from Roman Catholicism to Anglicanism – not all doctrinal differences could, in the end, be easily mapped out along national lines. In the next chapter, I propose to examine a text that demonstrates the ease with which colonial conflict could be made to tell the story, not of a Protestant nation's struggle for survival within a Catholic Europe, but of England's struggle to overcome the political and religious divisions that threatened its very survival as a nation.

CHAPTER FIVE

Love and shame: Roger Williams and A Key into the Language of America

I suggested in the last chapter that there was, during the early years of English colonization, a discernable tendency to construct the colonial venture as a means of projecting a vital Protestant presence into the New World and thereby challenging the perceived threat of Catholic hegemony in the region. England's colonies could, therefore, give substance to a national and religious identity that seemed ever in danger of dissolving. In this sense, the Virginia divines, as I have called them, seem to have discovered a way of overcoming the difficulty that confronted Edmund Spenser as he tried to imagine the successful colonization of Ireland in the absence of a coherent English national identity. Moreover, these divines also seem to have realized the promise implicit in Théodore DeBry's monumental work, namely that national and religious aspirations could be neatly combined under the umbrella of colonial activity. Indeed, in the preaching of these divines, colonial activity is effectively and persuasively represented as absolutely central to England's struggle to construct itself as a Protestant nation.

If one senses during the early colonial period the desire to imagine the colonies as pure expressions of an unconflicted national identity, one discovers that such a desire was not easily attainable, as England's colonial culture soon became as divided as the nation that spawned it. In this chapter, we will explore the ways in which Roger Williams's 1643 text, *A Key into the Language of America*, exploits those divisions in order to advance his own colony of Providence Plantations over the already established and much admired Massachusetts Bay Colony. If anything, Williams's *Key* shows us that the emergence of conflict in the colonies intensified England's desire to make its colonial ventures speak, in some concrete way, for the nation as a whole. Therefore, rather than spelling the end of England's dependence on the allegorical mode to narrate the crucial connections between its colonies and its status as a Protestant nation, colonial conflict only rendered the task of writing colonial allegory all the more urgent. In these last two chapters, therefore, we get a glimpse both of the limits of colonial discourse in providing a coherent identity for the English nation and of the ever-present hope that colonial adventure would furnish just such a discourse.

I should say something at this point about my choice of the writings of Roger Williams and John Eliot as the focus of the final two chapters of this book. Few scholars would disagree with the assertion that these two writers were the most important voices on Indian affairs in the seventeenth century.[1] Even so, their writings on native Americans have not, in recent years, received the critical attention they deserve.[2] Most anthologies of early American literature include no selections from Eliot's work, and Williams fares only marginally better, represented usually by a chapter from his *A Key into the Language of America* and a couple of passages from his *Bloudy Tenent of Persecution*. There are probably many reasons for this relative neglect, including the expansion of the literary canon, which has necessarily meant that some writers have disappeared, either partially or altogether, from our view. In the cases of Williams and Eliot, however, I would suggest that there has been another force at work as well. Each of these writers has, in a sense, fallen victim to his own success. Lionized by critics for their work championing Indian rights, both Williams and Eliot have provided fodder for hagiographical appreciations as often as they have been the subjects of serious scholarly examination.[3]

As scholars have undertaken the revision of the history of the colonial period, they have tended to regard Williams and Eliot with skepticism, if not outright derision. Although these two men showed more compassion toward the Indians than most of their Puritan brethren, historians have often emphasized the role that each played in the ultimate destruction of indigenous society and culture.[4] In a sense, Williams and Eliot have found themselves without a constituency among scholars. Their writings on the Indians have not generally been regarded as sophisticated enough to warrant the kinds of rhetorical analysis that literary scholars perform, and as the field of colonial history has moved away from the study of the Puritan mind and into "Ethnohistory," neither one of these men has seemed to present a very compelling subject for intensive study.[5]

Besides their obvious importance in any study of Anglo-Indian relations in the seventeenth century, Roger Williams and John Eliot deserve our attention in *this* study because they illustrate the ways in which the inhabitants could emerge as crucial figures, not in allegories of England's attempts to promote its own interests against those of its Catholic rivals, but rather in England's ongoing struggle to conceive of itself as a Protestant nation in the face of potentially ruinous religious and political strife. As I suggested in the last chapter, colonial discourse could be used to good effect to forge a bond between Protestantism and English national identity. Both Eliot and Williams implicitly accept this premise, advanced by the Virginia divines, but they recognize that colonial discourse in general, and their writings about the native people in particular, can be put to work in England's search for a solution to its seemingly intractable internal disputes about faith, ideology, and governance.

My argument in this chapter will consist of an exploration of three basic moves that I perceive Williams performing in his *Key*. First I will show the ways that Williams strategically attempts to sever Protestantism from Englishness, as he undertakes to answer the very basic question of what it might mean for a nation to proclaim, through colonialism, its commitment to Christianity or to Protestantism. This operation, which is necessitated by the fact that his immediate rivals are not Spanish or French but other English colonists, anticipates Williams's next move, namely that of undoing the binary distinctions that would have governed his English readers' perceptions of the Indians. Finally, once he has managed to disrupt the expectations of his readers, Williams can then undertake to demonstrate how his own colonial practices eschew the use of fear and intimidation in favor of the cultivation of the love and respect that the Indians seem all too ready to extend to their colonizing neighbors. In short, Williams is able in his *Key* to level the same critique at his Massachusetts adversaries that earlier English colonial writers wielded in their condemnation of the cruelty and inhumanity of the Spanish.

Before turning to Williams's writings themselves, however, I will offer some background to the publication of the *Key*. For Williams, who had been banished from the Massachusetts Bay colony in 1636, for "opinions [that] were adjudged by all, magistrates and ministers . . . to be erroneous, and very dangerous," the mission of promoting and defending his own colony of Providence Plantations was an urgent one.[6] Without a patent from Parliament to legitimate the new colony, Williams would have no legal recourse to the constant meddling of the Massachusetts Puritans. So, in the spring of 1643, thirteen years after he had fled to the New World to avoid persecution, Roger Williams returned to England to petition Parliament for a patent for his colony. Williams knew that John Winthrop and the leaders of the Bay colony, who had accused him of spreading sick opinions throughout their colony and of intending "to erect a plantation about the Naragansett Bay, from whence the infection would easily spread," would instruct their influential London agents to wage a vigorous campaign against his efforts to obtain a patent.[7] Williams recognized that his petition for a patent put the puritans in Parliament in an awkward position. In effect, he was asking them to choose between his own barely established and struggling colony and the well-financed and much respected Massachusetts Bay colony.

Fortunately Williams arrived in London with the manuscript of what was shortly to become *A Key into the Language of America,* a book that was to win him the respect and admiration of his countrymen for years to come.[8] Unique among all of the books published in London during the seventeenth century, the *Key* was the only one devoted exclusively to the study of the Algonquin language.[9] But the *Key* was more than a phrasebook. Each of the thirty-two chapters, in addition to providing readers with the basic Algonquin phrases and vocabulary necessary for dozens of occasions and activities, also undertook to educate readers in the cultural and social practices of the Indians. A brief survey of some of the chapter topics gives an indication of the book's scope. Chapters on eating, greeting, the family, parts of the body, weather, fishing, hunting, trading, religion, marriage, death, and burial (among others) comprised this eclectic volume.

The form of Williams's book defies easy description. Each of the thirty-two chapters contains columns of words and expressions, with the Algonquin on the left and the English on the right. Punctuating the vocabulary lists are Williams's "Observations." And concluding each chapter is a poem, usually pertaining to the subject matter of the chapter. In his "Directions for the Use of the Language," Williams claims that he originally intended to write a dialogue, but that he has had to modify that plan:

> *A Dialogue also I had thoughts of, but avoided for brevities sake, and yet (with no small paines) I have so framed every Chapter and the matter of it, as I may call it an Implicite Dialogue.*[10]

A dialogue indeed it is, and in several ways. Each of the thirty-two chapters alternates dialogically between the Indian words and phrases and their English translations on the one hand, and Williams's "observations" on the other. The translation sections themselves frequently read like dialogues, alternating between question and response. But in yet another sense, as Ivy Schweitzer has pointed out, the text functions as a "cultural dialogue" between Indian and Anglo, as Williams attempts to relate Indian cultural phenomena to his native England.[11]

Also contained within the pages of the *Key* was a thinly disguised polemic against the Massachusetts Puritans – a polemic that appealed to the same sense of nation-ness that the Virginia ministers in the last chapter found so useful. But unlike those ministers, who merely argued for the essentialness of colonial endeavor, Williams had to argue that his own colonial undertaking was the only legitimately English one in the New World. In other words, Williams's goal was not to enlist support for England's colonial efforts in general, but rather to draw a distinction between different colonial regimes. Williams's success was in large part due to the extent to which he was able to convince his readers that more was at stake than simply the fate of a Puritan colony. By framing the colonial issues in such a way that his readers could not help but see them as *their* issues, Williams implicitly suggested to his readers that the narrative of the colony was indeed an allegory of the narrative of the nation. Williams brilliantly and relentlessly frames his representations of Indians by allowing his readers to see the extent to which they functioned as versions of themselves and their struggles. While appearing to bring home linguistic *exotica*, Williams in fact tacitly forces his readers to situate issues of colonial rule in a domestic context. Williams subtly suggests that the Massachusetts colonists, much like the King and the clerical hierarchy within England, have succumbed to their own desire for power. By portraying the Massachusetts colonists as enemies of liberty of conscience and perpetrators of colonial cruelties, Williams tapped into powerful feelings that would continue to preserve and protect his own colony of Providence Plantations.

The stature and position Williams enjoyed as a direct result of his own self-fashioning as an expert on Native American culture should not be underestimated. Not only could Williams number among his friends such influential figures as Henry Vane, John Milton, and Sir Robert Rich, Earl of Warwick, but he could boast of being invited by Cromwell to share with him his extensive knowledge and opinions on Indian affairs.[12] In fact, some have argued that Williams was better known in his own day in London as the author of the *Key* than he was as a Massachusetts dissident or as the founder of a colony.[13] In short, Williams managed the impressive feat of converting his linguistic ability into considerable cultural and political capital, upon which he could draw not only in his successful fight for his colonial patent but also in his subsequent labors to protect his colony from Massachusetts incursions.

Perhaps the greatest irony of Williams's achievement was that he succeeded in stigmatizing the Massachusetts colonists for failing to fulfill the terms of one of the prime directives of their charter, namely that they institute organized attempts to convert the Indians. Not only did Williams himself not engage in any such attempts, but he categorically rejected their validity. Williams's position on Indian conversions is a matter to which I will return at some length later. For now, it will suffice to point out the power that the Indian discourse held over parliamentarians and others who occupied themselves with the fashioning of an English Protestant colonial policy.

NATIONS PROFESSING TO BE CHRISTIAN

Critics generally acknowledge, as Ivy Schweitzer puts it, that "Williams rejected the notions of national election and of New England as the antitype of Israel."[14] The idea, in other words, that a person's association with a particular nation or group could somehow translate into redemption or election was anathema to Williams. For this reason, Williams consistently argued that there was no necessary connection between Protestantism and Englishness. As we shall see, this move was crucial to the force of his polemic because Williams's immediate adversaries were not Spanish or French, but English. He could not easily claim that the Massachusetts Bay colonists had ceased to be Englishmen, but he could plausibly claim – especially in the highly polemicized print culture of London in the 1640s – that they had ceased to behave like true Protestants.

As strenuously as Williams resisted the notion of England as an inherently elect nation, however, we need to keep in mind that he almost certainly recognized that the vast majority of his readers believed or – more to the point – wanted to believe that Englishness and Protestantism went hand in hand. Williams, therefore, shrewdly encouraged his readers to identify with *him* as the embodiment of Protestant and English ideals, even as he insinuated that the English settlers in Massachusetts, in their zeal for order and conformity, had failed to live as true Protestants. And herein lay the real genius of his polemic against the Massachusetts Bay Puritans: Williams realized that he could, on the one hand, categorically reject the idea that the English, by virtue of their national identity, could lay claim to membership in the community of God's elect and, on the other hand, put himself (and his colony) forward as his nation's best hope of uniting Englishness and true Protestantism.

We should situate Williams's pronouncements on the relationship between religious and national identity within the context of the writings we have been considering thus far. Unlike Jean de Léry, whose experiences during the St Bartholomew's Day massacres, led him to confess, "I am French, and it grieves me to say it," Williams would not let the behavior of the Massachusetts colonists challenge his own identity as an Englishman.[15] But neither could Williams enthusiastically embrace the ambitious pronouncements of the Virginia divines, whose sermons suggested that England's colonial adventures would be more pleasing to God than those of the Spanish, simply because they were English. Instead, Williams suggested that what would mark the English colonial project as both English and Protestant was, paradoxically, its refusal to assert a necessary connection between religious and national identity. Nowhere does Williams make his position clearer than in his consistent refusal to proselytize the native inhabitants. To do so, he argued, would render the English colonies indistinguishable from those of England's Catholic rivals.

In order to articulate his case in the strongest possible terms, Williams furnished a powerful counter-example from England's own history. In *Christenings Make not Christians*, a tract he wrote shortly after he wrote the *Key*, Williams dramatized the illegitimacy of any conversion that was based solely on a change of outward form. Williams did this by providing his readers with a humbling lesson from their own *national* history.

When *England* was all *Popish* under Henry the seventh, how easie is conversion wrought to half Papist halfe-Protestant under *Henry* the eighth?

From halfe-Protestantisme halfe Popery under *Henry* the eight, to absolute Protestantisme under Edward, the sixth: from absoluer [sic] Protestation under *Edward* the sixt to absalute popery under Quegne *Mary*, and from absolute Popery under Queene *Mary*, (just like the Weathercocke, with the breath of every Prince) to absolute Protestantisme under Queene *Elizabeth* &c.[16]

In this extraordinary reprise of the religious history of England over the previous two centuries, Williams impresses upon his readers the absurdity (and danger even!) of a conformity to Protestantism that relies on merely outward displays. This was precisely the sort of conformity that he accused the Massachusetts Puritans of exacting from the settlers in their colony, and it was precisely the sort of conformity that most Puritans in England found so reprehensible about the Laudian church. Writing at a moment when many in England may indeed have wondered whether their nation was doomed to behave perpetually like a "weathercocke" in matters of religion, Williams here exploits that anxiety to defend his own refusal to proselytize. The best way to ensure England's own religious integrity, Williams shrewdly implies, is to avoid too unbridled a zeal for native conversions.

Williams's ultimate point, however, is not to scrutinize the rapidity or thoroughness of the English nation's apparent conversion to Protestantism but to establish a link between the successive re-conversions of the English people and the potential conversion to true Christianity of the native populations of America. He embarks on this digression into English history as a way of answering the question of why he has not brought more of the Indians to see the light. His answer is consistent with his position in the *Key*.

I answer, woe be to me, if I call light darknesse, or darknesse light; sweet bitter, or bitter sweet; woe be to me if I call that conversion unto God, which is indeed subversion of the soules of Millions in *Christendome*, from one false worship to another, and the prophanation of the holy name of God, his holy Son and blessed Ordinances.[17]

The English regarded the Spanish conversions of the Indians as "the subversions of the soules of Millions." And thus, by using the English fear of false conversion, Williams was able to oppose the organized efforts to convert the Indians and still harness the considerable power of such a discourse for his own agenda.

By rendering the prospect of Indian conversions in the same terms that the English thought of their own attempts to construct a holy commonwealth, Williams forced his readers to recognize the extent of their investment in the colonial project. True conversion, insisted Williams "is not a forme, nor the change of one forme into another."[18] It is instead something internal, something that cannot be brought about by "earthly weapons" nor "maintained by civill weapons." And in defending himself against the charge that he had failed to make the most of his knowledge of the Algonquin language, Williams once again reminded his readers in *Christenings Make not Christians* of the connections between their work at home and the work of the colonists abroad: Lest he be like David who wanted so badly to build the temple that he would "attempt this worke without a *Word* ... from GOD," Williams would resist the temptation to use his linguistic skills to produce insincere conversions among the Indians. The building of the temple, an image regularly deployed by Puritan writers to refer to the reconstruction of the English state, was thus easily appropriated to describe the proper work of the English colonial enterprise.

Like *Christenings make not Christians,* the *Key* warns against the dangers of indiscriminate conversions, lest the English colonies come to represent the same beliefs as those of the Catholics. In chapter 21 of the *Key,* where he discusses native religious beliefs and practices, Williams recounts his refusal to avail himself of an opportunity to encourage a number of Indians to keep the sabbath. Paraphrasing and augmenting a passage from Paul's letter to the Hebrews, Williams says,

The said *Sachim,* and the chiefe of his people, discoursed by themselves, of keeping the Englishman's day of worship, which I could easily have brought the Countrey to, but that I was perswaded ... that the two first

Principles and Foundations of true Religion or worship of the true God in Christ, are Repentance from dead workes, and Faith towards God, before the Doctrine of Baptisme, or washing and laying on of hands, which containe the Ordinances and Practices of worship; the want of which, I conceive, is the bane of millions of soules in England, and all other Nations professing to be Christian Nations, who are brought by publique authority to Baptisme and fellowship with God in Ordinances of worship, before saving worke of Repentance, and a true turning to God, *Heb. 6. 2.*

Williams once again insists on phrasing his admonition in terms that remind his English readers of just how far short their own nation falls of the ideal. When he claims that England itself is plagued by millions of false conversions, he no doubt realizes that many in England would agree with him. This was because the nature of the religious controversies that divided England in the 1640s was such that one sect might deem the beliefs and practices of other sects to be completely unfounded.[19] The North American colonies, it would seem, present England with the chance to construct an ideal Protestant community, where those who have not experienced "the saving worke of Repentance, and a true turning to God," do not compound their misfortunes by undergoing false conversions. In addition to functioning as an idealized version of England, the colonies would, by preventing the "bane" of false conversions, readily distinguish themselves from "all other Nations professing to be Christian." Implicit throughout the *Key* is the argument that Williams himself offered the English nation the best hope of securing a colonial project that would set it apart from other nations. And Williams promised to do this, not by relying on a hollow notion of national identity to guarantee the Englishness of the colonial undertaking, but rather by suggesting that a stringent adherence to the core of Protestant belief would allow England to integrate its religious and national identities through its colonial enterprises.

It is in the context of Williams's refusal to emphasize the national character of the colonial undertaking that we should read his use of the word "English" in his *Key*. Even as he suggests that their Englishness cannot prevent the Massachusetts colonists from betraying their Protestant values, Williams constantly reminds his readers that it is as Englishmen that these colonists will be known to the natives, and indeed to the rest of the world. By referring to the Massachusetts Puritans as "Englishmen," therefore, Williams forces his English readers *in England* to wonder whether they want *their* nation to be represented by this group.

By way of comparison, we might consider Thomas Morton's attack on the Massachusetts and Plymouth settlers in his *New English Canaan*, which was published in Amsterdam in 1637. In his polemic, which was at least as caustic as that of Williams, Morton describes the failings of the Plymouth colonists in almost exactly the same terms that Williams would use six years later in his *Key*. Chiding the colonists for their treacherous slaughter of peaceful Indians, for instance, Morton held that he "found the Massachusets Indian more full of humanity, then the Christians, and have had much better quarter with them."[20] And again sounding a theme that Williams would introduce in his *Key*, Morton observed that "the uncivilized people are more just than the civilized."[21] One of the most significant differences, however, between Morton and Williams was the way that they identified the targets of their respective polemics.[22] Unlike Williams, who consistently refers to the Massachusetts colonists as "Englishmen," Morton derisively refers to the Plymouth colonists as the "precise separatists." The effect of this subtle difference in appellation, I would suggest, is immeasurable. Where Morton allows his English readers to disavow responsibility for the cruelty and pettiness of *these* colonists, Williams constantly reminds his readers, by referring to the Puritans as "Englishmen," that they in some way are functioning as England's representatives in the New World. Williams, in other words, forces his readers to recognize that the deeds of these English colonists speak for England as he constructs the New England colonies as an allegory for England.[23]

EMBLEMS OF PERSECUTION

One way to describe the effects of Williams's attempts to divorce Englishness from Protestantism is to say that they forced his readers to re-align the allegorical framework within which they perceived England's colonial exploits. The world that Williams occupies is no longer the simple one projected by the Virginia ministers. Rather than consisting of native inhabitants and English, the world that Williams attempts to describe is tripartite: native inhabitants, Massachusetts settlers, and himself. He therefore systematically disrupts the binary distinctions that drove the English colonial effort in order to make room for a third term, which is his own colonial project. In other words, the *Key* seems to serve the function not of situating England's colonial projects within the context of a European competition for military and political power – which was DeBry's intention in his work – but rather within the context of an England divided. Indeed, even in his choice of printers, Williams seems to have signaled his intention to participate in the polemical battles that dominated print culture in London during the 1640s.[24]

Insofar as he claims that the actions and deeds of the Puritans and the Indians possessed signifying power, therefore, Williams can be said to have constructed his ethnography of the native people along lines similar to those of Jean de Léry. Ultimately, however, Williams would not find in his own interactions with the native inhabitants and Puritans an allegory of Protestantism's struggle for survival in Europe, but rather an allegory of true Protestantism's struggle for survival within England itself. Before he can do this, Williams must dismantle the binary oppositions that would have structured English perceptions of the native peoples and the New World. Indeed, the *Key*, by offering evidence that the natives possessed more civility than the Puritans, consistently disrupts the connections that English readers might have made between themselves and the Puritan settlers.

In a verbal description that recalls Theodor DeBry's visual representations of Indians in the process of becoming English, Williams presents readers with a picture of the Indians that produces exactly the sort of disruption I am describing. When he observes in chapter 7 of the *Key*, therefore, that some of the Indians wear their hair in the Puritan fashion, Williams encourages his English Puritan readers to see in the Indians an idealized embodiment of their own values.

Obs. Ye some cut their haire round, and some as low and as short as the sober *English*; yet I never saw any so to forget nature it selfe in such excessive length and monstrous fashion, as to the shame of the *English* Nation, I now (with griefe) see my Countrey-men in *England* are degenerated unto.[25]

This is the only moment in the entire *Key* where Williams offers explicit commentary on what he saw in London in 1643.[26]

Although it is not surprising that Williams would have been disturbed by the "monstrous fashion" that he observed, it is significant that he chooses to link the hairstyles of the Indians with the English concept of national identity. It serves Williams's purpose to cast the Indians as "roundheads" in the struggle – that is, as sober and decorous, according to the Puritan standard. Williams is not accusing his Massachusetts neighbors of wearing their hair long, but it is his intention to suggest that the Massachusetts Puritans are in some sense the "shame of the English nation." Williams's strategy in the *Key* is to encourage and allow his English readers to identify with the Indians, and then, in the course of the *Key*, he will present his readers with a subtle argument that he is a better representative of the Indians' interests, and therefore of the *national* interests of England. By suggesting that the Massachusetts puritans have mistreated the Indians, Williams suggests that *they* are the "shame of the English Nation."

In contrast to their sober hairstyle, which easily allowed readers to perceive the Indians as versions of themselves, the nakedness of the Indians would seem to present readers with an irreducible sign of their lack of civility. The Massachusetts Bay Colony seal, for instance, depicted an Indian with a bow in hand, standing naked, except for the leaves covering what Williams would call his "secret parts." Coming out of the Indian's mouth are the words, "Come over here and help us."[27] The centrality of the nakedness of the Indian in this iconographic representation of the colonial mission of the Massachusetts settlers is no coincidence. In addition to religion, the Puritans felt compelled to bring the Indians more "decent" sartorial habits. It is thus surprising that Williams, in chapter 20 of the *Key*, "Of *their nakednesse* and *clothing*," is able to transform this seemingly unambiguous sign of savagery into a sign of the humanity of the Indians. This transformation or reversal, however, would only be one of many that Williams would perform in the course of his remarkable book.

We must see Williams's chapter on clothing in the context of Puritan attitudes toward dress, in which ostentation was objectionable, whether it took the form of the elaborate vestments of the clergy or the foppery of court attire. Williams's critique of the Puritan obsession with clothing, however, seeks to point out that concern for simplicity of appearance is concern for appearance nonetheless. And Williams plays with this obsession of the

Puritans in his attempt to show that nakedness and clothedness are not stable categories. As in the chapter on hunting, which we will examine in a moment, Williams's discussion of nakedness slips easily from the literal to the figurative in his attempt to demonstrate that the Indians are less naked in a figurative (or spiritual) sense than many English. But before he makes that move, Williams will argue that their literal nakedness is less prurient than the European clothedness.

Custome hath used their minds and bodies to it [nakedness], and in such a freedom from any wantonnesse, that I have never seen that wantonnesse amongst them, as, (with griefe) I have heard of in *Europe*.[28]

This chapter, beginning as it does with the Indian word *Paúskesu*, or naked, follows the same pattern as the others we will examine. In other words, Williams starts with a word that would have signified to his English readers one of the "key" differences between their culture and that of the Indians. Not surprisingly, that difference is coded: it is not simply the case that one culture is naked and the other clothed, but that nakedness and clothedness serve to mark one of the cultures as superior.[29]

If Williams's first move is to insist that nakedness bears no necessary connection to "wantonnesse" his next move will be to strip away the veneer of sartorial superiority of the English, and the final two stanzas of the closing poem do this work:

> Many thousand proper Men and Women,
> I have seen met in one place:
> Almost all naked, yet not one,
> Thought want of clothes disgrace.

> Isreall was naked, wearing cloathes!
> The best clad English-man,
> Not cloth'd with Christ, more naked is:
> Then naked Indian.[30]

By deftly moving between figurative and literal usages of nakedness, Williams is able to play out one of his favorite themes: the English should hesitate to take refuge in their outward appearance because it means nothing. Just as civility can mask true wildness, so too can "clothedness" mask true nakedness.

Williams therefore consistently undermines the binary oppositions upon which the English colonists of Massachusetts rested their identity. In the "General Observation" near the end of chap-

ter 17, "Of beasts," for instance, in a move that seems to anticipate Jonathan Edwards's attribution of spiritual significance to
natural phenomena, Williams offers a "reading" of the natural
world that accounts for his own persecution at the hands of the
Massachusetts colonists.

The Wildernesse is a cleere resemblance of the world, where greedie and
furious men persecute and devoure the harmlesse and innocent as the
wilde beasts pursue and devoure the Hindes and Roes.[31]

From the Puritan perspective, the wilderness did not resemble the
"world" – at least not the world they hoped to create in New
England. Indeed, the Puritans hoped that their own presence in
the New World would help to tame the wilderness. Typically, Indians were included in descriptions of the natural world. And also
most of the justifications for taking away the Indian lands were
based upon the use that the Indians had made of the land. To the
extent that the Puritans discovered a wilderness, they were free
to occupy the land. As Roderick Nash has suggested, "civilized
man faced the danger of succumbing to the wildness of his sur-
roundings" in the wilderness.[32] Therefore, by suggesting that the
wilderness resembled the civilized world, Williams was undermin-
ing one of the most fiercely clung to distinctions.

Once he has established a resemblence between the wilderness
and the world, Williams then proceeds to move the Indians from
wilderness to civilization. In the "More Particular" poem, Williams suggests that while the Indians may at first appear wild, they
are indeed not nearly so fierce as the Puritans who, conversely,
appear quite tame.

> The Indians, *Wolves, yea, Dogs and Swine,*
> *I have knowne the Deere devoure;*
> *Gods Children are sweet prey to all,*
> *But the end proves sowre.*
>
> *For though Gods children lose their lives,*
> *They shall not loose an haire;*
> *But shall arise, and judge all those,*
> *That now their Judges are.*
>
> New-England's *wilde beasts are not fierce,*
> *As other wild beasts are:*
> *Some men are not so fierce, and yet*
> *from mildnesse are they farre.*[33]

The poem, which begins by placing the Indians in the same group as the beasts, performs a number of surprising reversals. In a literal sense, because the Indians did eat deer, the assertion that they are predators is true. But by the last stanza, Williams has demonstrated that appearances can be deceiving. Just as "New England's wilde beasts are not fierce, as other wild beasts are," the Puritans who persecuted him are far from mild. In effect, Williams has constructed a portrait of the colonial world in which the Indians and Englishmen have traded places. The binary distinctions that support the Puritan assertions of superiority seem to dissolve under Williams's scrutiny. The chapter on beasts therefore functions as a thinly veiled fable illustrating the aggression and cruelty of the Puritans.

Williams's attempts to dismantle the binary distinctions upon which Puritan colonial identity was established culminate in his rhetorically stunning chapter 17, "Of *their Hunting*, &c." The chapter, proceeding by means of subtle and surprising modulations, juxtaposes Indian diligence to Puritan treachery. By perceiving in Indian hunting practices the traces of a highly developed notion of property that serves the collective rather than the individual interest, Williams provides a convincing counter-argument to Puritan justifications for taking away Indian lands – justifications which in part rested on the belief that the Indians had no notion of property and therefore could not own land. Moreover, through the skillful manipulation of his text, Williams is able to discern royalist tendencies in the Puritan attitude toward native lands.

As a first move to this portion of his polemic, Williams describes how he has found in the beasts of the forest an emblematic narrative of his own persecution. In a curious account of the difficulties that the wolves pose for the Indians in their trapping of deer, Williams shifts his discussion from the specific observation of the tendency of wolves to raid the Indians' traps to the more general problem of predatory relationships.

And that wee may see how true it is, that all wild creatures, and many tame, prey upon the poore Deere (which are there in a right Embleme of Gods persecuted, that is, hunted people, as I observed in the Chapter of the Beasts according to the old and true saying:

> *Imbelles Damae quid nisi praeda sumus?*

> *To harmlesse Roes* and *Does*,
> Both wilde and tame are foes).[34]

At first, by constructing the deer as the universal symbol of prey, it would seem that Williams is decrying the predatory nature of hunting, whether it be performed by men or by other animals. But very quickly Williams transforms his narrative of hunting into one of survival by equating the deer with "God's persecuted, that is, hunted people." And after beginning the narrative from the perspective of a disinterested onlooker, Williams delivers his next observation from the point of view of the deer. The central problem of this fable becomes then that of how the "harmlesse roes and does" can distinguish between danger and safety when "both wilde and tame are foes."

The parallel between this assertion and Williams's own experience at the hands of the Massachusetts elders should by now be plain, for Williams himself, who knew what it was like to be hunted, had discovered the barbarity of the apparently civilized Puritans. Although they professed moderation, they were capable of extremism. This little fable of course forms part of the more general insistence in the *Key* that appearances are not to be trusted. In case any should miss this point, Williams abandons his general observation about the plight of deer and offers a specific example. "I remember how a poore Deere was long hunted and chased by a Wolfe," he begins. Eventually the wolf catches the deer, and while the wolf is devouring the deer, two "*English* Swine, big with Pig" pass by and drive the wolf away. The swine then eat "so much of that poore Deere, as they both surfeted and dyed that night." Williams glosses his story as follows:

The Wolfe is an Emblem of a fierce bloodsucking persecutor.
The Swine of a covetous rooting worldling, both make a prey of the Lord Jesus in his poore servants.[35]

Williams continues by observing that if the Indians do not come to their trap soon enough the wolf will devour all of the deer leaving the Indian hunter with "nothing but the bones, and the torne Deere-skins, especially if he call some of his greedy Companions to his bloody banquet." Just as Williams insists that deer must regard everyone and everything as a potential predator, no matter what their appearance, he seems to feel it important to distinguish between different forms of predation. The wolf seems to represent the Roman Catholic persecutor, whose liturgy, with its insistence on transubstantiation, was literally a "bloody banquet." The swine, on the other hand, which Williams specifi-cally designates as *English*, represents those colonists who have come to New England only to prey on the labors of the Indians.

The emblematic – one might even say allegorical – narrative of the deer, the wolf, and the swine not only serves to reinforce the crucial distinction between labor and predation but also plays a pivotal role in Williams's attempt to convince his readers of the validity and respectability of Indian forms of labor. Indeed, this chapter emphasizes both the organization and skill involved in hunting, lest any of Williams's readers equate the hunting of the Indians with that of the nobility in England. For what in England was the leisure activity of a small minority, in America, among the Indians, constituted a socially acceptable (and valuable) form of work. Providing food and clothing for all of their people, the hunting of the Indians was also a critical component of their system of territorial land claims.

Obs. When a Deere (hunted by the Indians, or Wolves) is Kild in the water. This skin is carried to the *Sachim* or Prince, within whose territory the Deere was slaine.[36]

Rather than being a disorganized, informal activity that involved the negation or outright violation of territorial claims, hunting was a social institution that respected and reinforced tribal claims to territory. The picture that Williams generates, in other words, calls to mind Théodore DeBry's engravings of John White's watercolors, which seemed to construct Indian hunting as a highly developed and organized social activity.

Moreover, Williams points out in his "General Observation" that hunting was not an individual activity, but rather an organized activity that served the needs of the social collective.

There is a blessing upon endeavour, even to the wildest *Indians*; the slug-gard rosts not that which he took in hunting, but the substance of the diligent (either in earthly or heavenly affairs) is precious, *Prov.* 25.[37]

The most "diligent" people here, at least by the way Williams has constructed the scene, are those that hunt. Typically, Puritans would have assumed "wildness" and "sluggardliness" went hand-in-hand in Indians. Here, however, Williams suggests that the "wild" work of hunting is respected by the Indians, and that within the context of their own culture, diligence is rewarded. In contrast to his fellow colonists, who did not consider hunting to be labor, and who criticized the Indians for failing to bring the land under their yoke, Williams discerns among the Indians highly developed notions of labor and social responsibility.

In another context, Williams launched a similar argument. He contended that

the Natives, though they did not, nor could subdue the Countrey, (but left it *vacuum Domicilium*) yet they hunted all the Countrey over, and for the expedition of their hunting voyages, they burnt up all the underwoods in the Countrey, once or twice a year, and therefore as Noble men in *England* possessed greate parkes, and the King, great Forrests, in *England* onely for their game, and no man might lawfully invade their Propriety: So might the natives challenge the like Propriety of the Countrey here.[38]

Williams makes the point that in England one's property rights are not based on what use one makes of the land, the game-parks of the nobles and the king being the prime example. Even if property rights were derived from one's use of the land, however, the Indians would be entitled to their land on the basis of their efforts to maintain it. Through his reference to the "controlled" fires the Indians started each year in the forests, Williams demonstrated that he recognized in their apparently destructive behavior the signs of a thoughtful and calculated form of land management.[39] Moreover, Williams distinguishes the Indians' stewardship of the land from that of the nobles who keep the land "onely for their game."

There is more to Williams's chapter on hunting than simply his attempt to question certain stereotypes. By the time the *Key* was published in 1643, the royal forests had emerged as a site of conflict between King Charles and the Puritans. In 1630, Charles had reintroduced the notorious Forest Laws, and four years later, he began extending the boundaries of the Royal Forests in an attempt to raise revenue.[40] Such a move, if politically risky, was lucrative. By 1640, in Essex alone, the king is said to have raised £300,000 through payments as punishment for violating the Forest Laws. But in that same year, after he encountered strong opposition from the Long Parliament, the king was forced to back down from the enforcement of these laws.[41] By then, it was probably too late for Charles. As one historian notes, "this abuse was one step on his road to the scaffold."[42]

Williams does not mention the Forest Laws in his chapter on hunting, but I want to suggest, nonetheless, that most London readers would have read a discussion on hunting in this context. The links, of course, are not specific. Williams's intention, I would argue, is not to write a polemic against the king, but to identify the Massachusetts Puritans with royal policies that had met with widespread public disapproval. On the one hand, Williams indicates that his chapter on hunting is not really about hunting at all, but about the persecution of the weak by the strong. But by choosing hunting as the pretext for a discussion of religious persecution, Williams has not chosen a realm of discourse that would be viewed neutrally by the majority of his English readers. Rather he has chosen a topic that was itself an "embleme" – or allegory – of abuse of power for the English of the period.

To conclude his attempt to reverse the terms that structured his readers' perceptions of colonists and Indians, Williams offers his "More Particular" poem at the end of the chapter.

> Great pains in hunting th'Indians *Wild*,
> And eke the English *tame*,
> Both take, in woods and forrests thicke,
> To get their precious game.
>
> Pleasure and Profit, Honour false,
> (The world's great Trinitie)
> Drive all men through all wayes, all times,
> All weathers, wet and drie.
>
> Pleasure and Profits, Honour sweet,
> Eternal, sure and true
> Laid up in God, with equall paines;
> Who seekes, who doth pursue?[43]

In this final poem, Williams emphasizes yet again how difficult it is to distinguish between "th'Indians wild" and "the English tame." Both hunt, and both are driven by "Pleasure, and Profit, Honour false, the world's great Trinitie." What really matters, however, is not the outward manifestation of this "trinitie" but the rewards that are not visible, the ones that are "laid up in God." By relying so heavily on outward signs for their sense of their own cultural superiority, the Puritans have committed a grave error. Williams renders this error all the more serious by demonstrating that the Puritans are outwardly no different from the Indians after all.

NATURE'S DISTINCTIONS AND NATURE'S AFFECTIONS

I have argued thus far that Williams's move to divorce Englishness from Protestantism served as the basis for his attempt to dismantle the binary oppositions that informed English perceptions of the colonial undertaking. There is, however, yet another component to Williams's brilliant and complicated polemic against his Massachusetts neighbors, and that consists of his attempt to recover and represent the cultural complexity of the native populations. But his book did more than provide incontrovertible proof of the sophistication of native culture. By endowing the Indians with a full range of human emotions and virtues, Williams portrays them as open to any attempts to convert them, should the English be interested in doing such a thing. Moreover, Williams's linguistic and cultural analysis also has the effect of portraying the English as lacking the basic emotions and virtues that the Indians possess. Williams has therefore transformed a colonial discourse predicated on limiting the emotions available to the colonized subjects into one that emphasizes the usefulness of those emotions in the colonial enterprise. Not only does he suggest that love and fear signify different things *to the English* who would colonize the Indians, but he also demonstrates that these emotions do indeed signify radically different things *to the Indians*. And in the end, he argues that fear and love produce dramatically different results. If Thomas Harriot suggested that fear would accomplish what love could not, then Williams seems to be offering his readers ethnographic proof of the efficacy of love in the management of the native populations in the colony. The effect of this analysis is to present the English as less than fully human by showing them to suffer from a poverty of emotion and virtue. The brilliance of Williams's critique, therefore, consists in his reappropriation of the conceptual framework that has structured English colonialism from the start, namely fear and love.[44]

In deploying the categories of fear and love as he attempts to put forth his colony as the only representative of true religion in the new world, Williams has, in essence, reproduced Théodore DeBry's position: On the one hand he suggests that the native inhabitants are ready to be civilized, and on the other, he shows that they cannot be left to their own devices. But, unlike DeBry, whose European context was the international religious conflict between Protestants and Catholics, Williams writes for one nation divided among itself. In other words, the proper allegorical context for Williams is not Europe's religious wars, but rather England's own poltical and religious conflicts. The genius Williams demonstrates is in his ability to situate the Massachusetts colonists on ground that no adherent to the bitter partisan debates of the 1640s would have wanted to occupy. In short, Williams manages, through his ethnographic observations, to portray the Massachusetts settlers as cruel oppressors of the native people, enemies of liberty of conscience, and proto-Catholic tyrants.

Perhaps Williams's most detailed description of the native propensity to display love comes in chapter 1, "Of *salutation.*" Remarking on the Indians' habit of inviting strangers into their homes, Williams marvels at their hospitality and generosity.

In this respect they are remarkably free and courteous, to invite all Strangers in; and if any come to them upon any occasion, they request them to *come in*, if they come not in of themselves.

Asassis.	*Warme you.*
Mattapsh yoteg.	*Sit by the fire.*
Tocketunnawem?	*What say you?*
Keen netop?	*Is it you friend?*
Peeyaush netop.	*Come hither friend.*
Petitees.	*Come in.*
Kunnunni?	*Have you seene me?*
Kunnunnous.	*I have seen you.*
Taubot mequaunnamean.	*I thank you for your kind remembrance.*
Taubot neanawayen.	*I thank you.*
Taubot neaunanamean.	*I thank you for your love.*

Observ.

I have acknowledged amongst them an heart sensible of kindnesses, and have reaped kindenesse again from many, seaven yeares after, when I my selfe had forgotten, &c. hence the Lord Jesus exhorts his followers to doe good for evill; for otherwise, sinners will do good for good, kindnesse, for kindnesse, &c.

Cowammaunsh.	*I love you.*
Cowammaunuck.	*He loves you.*
Cowammaus.	*You are loving.*
Cowautam?	*Understand you?*
Nowautam.	*I understand.*[45]

It is significant that the first chapter of Williams's *Key* is ultimately about love and understanding, two things that the Massachusetts

Puritans have failed to cultivate. Williams's story of his own for-
getfulness merely serves to reinforce the profound native commitment to a life of kindness and compassion. The final implicit dialogue, in which expressions of love are followed by expressions
of understanding serves to underscore the fact that the native
inhabitants not only practice love, but understand it as well. In
other words, when they are treated kindly by the English, they
will interpret that as a sign of favor. And they will remember
it. Conversely, when they are treated with cruelty, they will also
interpret that as a sign of the treachery of the Puritans.

Echoing Thomas Morton's earlier criticism of the "precise separatists," Williams's closing poem of the first chapter explicitly
compares the love the Indians have shown him to the utter lack
of generosity of the Puritans.

From these courteous *Salutations* Observe in generall: There is a
savour of *civility* and *courtesie* even amongst these wild *Americans*, both
amongst *themselves* and towards *strangers*.

More particular:

> The Courteous Pagan shall condemne
> Uncourteous Englishmen,
> *Who live like Foxes, Beares and Wolves,*
> *Or Lyon in his Den*

> *Let none sing* blessings *to their soules,*
> *For that they Courteous are:*
> The wild Barbarians *with no more*
> *Then Nature, goe so farre:*

> *If Natures Sons both* wild *and* tame,
> *Humane and Courteous be:*
> How ill becomes it Sonnes of God
> To want Humanity?[246]

Significantly, Williams links the kindness of the native inhabitants
to their nature. The fact that the natives derive their "humanity"
only from nature renders the lack of "humanity" of the Puritans
all the more disgraceful. When he describes the Englishmen as
living in dens "like Foxes, Beares and Wolves," Williams articulates a theme we will explore in more detail in a moment, namely
that of predation.

In chapter 5, "*Of their* relations *of* consanguinitie *and* affinitie,
or, Blood *and* Marriage," Williams elaborates on the "natural"

disposition of the native inhabitants. Implying that fear has not been necessary to bring them under control, Williams again describes the Indians in terms of love.

In the *ruines* of depraved *mankinde*, are yet to be founde *Natures distinctions,* and *Natures affections.*[47]

As Williams constructs them, the native inhabitants of America are more prone to affection than to hostility, more likely to respond to love than to fear. Williams, therefore goes to great pains to document the extent to which their lives are regulated not by fear and intimidation, but by love and generosity. Toward the end of chapter 6, *"Of the Family and business of the House,"* Williams observes their innate love of "sociableness."

The sociableness of the nature of man appears in the wildest of them, who love societie; Families, cohabitation, and consociation of houses and townes together.[48]

Because of the way he has, throughout the *Key*, defined the concept of "wildness" as depending on its binary opposite for its meaning, it is difficult for the reader not to imagine that the "tamest" Puritans in fact loathe society. Unable to allow Williams the privileges of cohabitation and consociation, the Massachusetts Puritans always seem to be looming in the background of his descriptions of the loving natives.

There is perhaps no more dramatic indication of the Indian willingness to feel love and respect for the English than in Williams's relation of their tendency to call him "Manittoo." In chapter 8 of the *Key*, entitled "Of *Discourse* and *Newes*," Williams observes that "a stranger that can relate newes in their owne language, they will stile him *Manittoo*, a God."[49] In one sense Williams here indulges in what by 1643 would have been a familiar trope to English readers of colonial literature. Accounts of first encounters of Europeans and native people abounded with descriptions of the awe the Indians expressed at the ships, the firearms, and the household goods that this first wave of settlers brought with them. In the native vocabulary and conceptual framework, it seemed, there was only one word that could describe the European colonizers and their dazzling technology: "Manittoo," or God. But Williams's variation on this old theme is shrewd and significant. English readers could perceive in Williams's tale of being called a

"Manittoo" the irrepressible desire of the native inhabitants to become more like the English – to become Manittoo themselves. In other words, this quaint and condescending anecdote reveals a group of native inhabitants ready to submit to the self-evident cultural superiority of the English. By the end of the chapter, Williams will show how this native "love" for things and people English has been undermined by the native inhabitants' "fear" of English treachery and faithlessness.

As part of Williams's attack on the Massachusetts elders, the chapter on "discourse and newes" moves quickly from a description of the Indians' attempt to style Williams a "Mannittoo," to an elaboration on the Indian desire for and pursuit of truth. To begin with, however, Williams dialogically demonstrates the workings of truth within Indian culture. Williams then modulates the dialogue onto a different level by introducing the concept of belief. But it is not until the "observation" that we realize that Williams has shifted the terms of the dialogue from quotidian and mundane truths to the one single truth of Christianity.

Cuppannawautous.	*I do not believe you.*
Cuppannawauti.	*Doe you not believe?*
Nippannawautunck ewo.	*He doth not believe me.*
Micheme nippannowautam.	*I shall never believe it.*

Obs. As one answered me when I had discoursed about many points of God, of the creation, of the soule, of the danger of it, and of the saving of it, he assented; but when I spake of the rising of the body, he cryed out, I shall never believe this.[50]

What starts out as an "implicit dialogue" between a Prince and his followers, turns into a dialogue between Williams and his Indian listeners, with Williams trying to explain some of the more difficult points of Christianity.

The dialogue does not stop there. It moves back to more earthly matters, namely the trustworthiness of the English. In a powerful anecdote, Williams allows an Indian "sachim" to deliver a devastating critique of the "faithfulness" of the Massachusetts settlers.

Obs. Canounicus, the old high *Sachim* of the *Nariganset Bay* (a wise and peacable Prince) once in a solemne Oration to my self, in a solemne assembly, using this word, said, I have never suffered any wrong to be offered to the *English* since they landed; nor never will: he often repeated this word, *Wunnaumwayean*, *Englishman*; If the *Englishman* speake true, if hee meane truly, then shall I goe to my grave in peace, and hope that the *English* and my posteritie shall live in love and peace together. I replied, that he had no cause (as I hoped) to question *Englishmans, Wunnaumwauonck*, that is, faithfulnesse, he having had long experience of their friendlinesse and trustiness. He tooke a sticke, and broke it into ten pieces, and related ten instances (laying downe a sticke to every instance) which gave him cause thus to feare and say; I satisfied him in some presently, and presented the rest to the Governours of the *English*, who, I hope, will be far from giving just cause to have *Barbarians* to question their *Wunnaumwauonck*, or faithfulnesse.[51]

What begins as a chapter on the news, turns into a discussion of Anglo-Indian relations. Williams' "observation" on the word, *Wunnaumwauonck*, which he translates as faithfulness, is pointed by virtue of what he does not say: Williams will not contradict the fundamental truth of the Indians' charge that the English have demonstrated a fundamental lack of faithfulness. He only says that he hopes it is not true. Moreover, by having Canounicus refer to the culprits as "Englishmen," Williams suggests that the Indians themselves did not make distinctions between different groups of Englishmen. Therefore, the faithfulness of the Massachusetts colonists represents for the Indians the degree of faithfulness of all Englishmen.

Considered within the context of the chapter, the anecdote interrupts, as it were, Williams' narration of his attempt to explain the truth of Christianity to the Indians. The positioning of the anecdote thus suggests that the Indians will interrupt explanations of important spiritual matters in order to question the honesty and fairness of the Massachusetts colonists. The reader is left to ask the implied question: how will the Indians believe the English about God if the English are faithless in their other dealings with the Indians? In this way, Williams subtly implies that the Puritans are doing damage to the cause of converting the Indians, and such an insinuation would have troubled a reading audience that saw the mission of the Puritan colonists as that of converting the Indians. Moreover, the chapter seems to establish a link between the truth of everyday life and the cosmic truth of Christian revelation. A chapter that at first seems critical of the contentious and godless ways the Indians use to determine truth finally seems to endorse their faithfulness, or *Wunnaumwauonck*. And although they do possess the one truth of Christianity, the

Puritans appear singularly treacherous and faithless in their dealings with the Indians.

It is important to emphasize that Williams seems to go to great pains to represent the natural love of the natives as essentially a social force. Accordingly, while the severity of the Puritans has led to the disruption of community – especially Williams's community – the love of the Indians allows them to build a society based on mutual cooperation and trust. In Chapter XVI, "*Of the Earth, and the Fruits thereof, &c.*," Williams describes the love that enables the planting of crops.

> When a field is to be broken up, they have a very loving sociable speedy way to dispatch it: All the neighbours men and Women forty, fifty, a hundred & c, joyne, and come in to help freely.
> With friendly joyning they breake up their fields, build their Forts, hunt the Woods, stop and kill fish in the Rivers, it being true with them as in all the World in the Affaires of Earth or Heaven: By concord little things grow great, by discord the greatest come to nothing *Concordia parvae res crescunt, Discordia magnae dilabuntur.*[52]

The borrowed nugget from Sallust speaks directly to Williams's own views of the goals and functions of English society. In an atmosphere of love and concord, the individual is free to strive for his own spiritual perfection. Ironically, the Indians have been able to provide such harmony, while the Puritans have not, a conviction that Williams makes even plainer in chapter 12, "*Of their Government* and *Justice*," where he admires the sachims because "their agreement in the Government is remarkable."[53]

Elsewhere in the *Key*, Williams reiterates the Indian sensitivity to English behavior and thereby suggests that English foibles do not go unnoticed. In the chapter on religion, to which we have already referred, Williams elaborates on just how acutely the Indians are able to perceive details about their colonial neighbors.

> They apprehending a vast difference of Knowledge betweene the *English* and themselves, are very observant of the *English* lives: I have heard them say to an Englishman (who being hindred, broke a promise to them) You know God, Will you lie Englishman?[54]

Constructing the Indians as children, who possess an uncanny knack for perceiving the inconsistencies in their parents and other adults, Williams reminds his readers that the behavior of the English colonists will *signify* something to the Indians. Although the particular Englishman in question seems not to have committed an egregious offense – he was simply "hindred" – Williams effectively portrays the subjectivity of the Indians by rendering them "very observant."

We should here recall Thomas Harriot's text and Theodor DeBry's images from chapter 2. I suggested there that the effect of their work was to represent the native inhabitants as potentially dutiful children, who would look upon the English with a mixture of fear and love. Although Williams does not contradict such a construction of the native inhabitants, he does strongly imply that the fear and love of the native populations will not be static. Possessing critical intelligence, the native people will not respond to the English with fear and love unless English behavior merits that response. In the poem that concludes chapter 15, "*Of buying and selling*," Williams delivers an especially incisive attack on the English treatment of the Indians:

More particular:

Oft have I heard these Indians *say,*
These English *will deceive us.*
Of all that's ours, our lands and lives,
In th'end they will bereave us.

So say they, whatsoever they buy,
(Though small) which shewes they're shie
Of strangers, fearefull to be catcht
By fraud, deceipt, or lie.

Indians *and* English *feare deceits,*
Yet willing both to be
Deceiv'd and couzen'd of precious soule,
Of heaven, Eternitie.[55]

The context of this poem is significant. Located at the end of a chapter that discusses their trade with each other and with the English, the poem suggests that the Indians know when they are being had. As I asserted in the last chapter, there emerged in English colonial disourse the notion that the English would be trading their spiritual commodities for the temporal ones of the Indians. In this poem, Williams accuses the English colonists of violating the terms of that implicit contract by suggesting in the last stanza that they don't have any spiritual commodities to deliver to the Indians. And therefore, the Indians are left with nothing but fear.

Even in their conflict, which Williams discusses in chapter 29 "Of their Warre, &c.," the Indians display a remarkable civility. The vocabulary for the chapter begins with the Indian word for "peace" and ends with the Indian phrase: "Let us make friends." Between these words, Williams explores the range of the Indians' emotions and reactions to war and conflict. The significance of Williams's choice to begin the chapter's vocabulary with peace and end it with friendship bespeaks his conviction that Indian conflict is much less bloody than European conflict and, moreover, that the Indians are capable of resolving their differences harmoniously, a capacity he very much doubts exists in the Puritans.

The initial "peace" in the vocabulary list is soon interrupted with the simple declarative statement, "I am angry." After several phrases qualifying that anger, two phrases offer justifications for it: "He strucke mee," and "I am robbed." Perhaps what is most interesting about these initial vocabulary offerings is their defensive nature. Williams does not offer his readers a vocabulary of aggression, but rather one of defense. The implicit conflict in the chapter seems to have originated in an act of aggression – an act performed by someone outside the immediate group of natives with whom Williams converses. It remains ambiguous whether that aggression emanates from other Indians, or from the English, but in a sense it doesn't really matter. Williams seems to portray Indian warfare as defensive in nature, a portrayal that implicitly places the English in the position of aggressor in any conflict that might arise between the Indians and the English.

One of the most curious emotions the Indians feel during their battles is fear. In an exchange that begins simply with the word, "afraid," the reader can observe that fear quickly transforms itself into "churlishness" and "scorn". In other words, it would seem that attempts to intimidate this group of Indians have merely encouraged them to resist whatever aggression has been perpetrated on them. Fear, therefore, leads not to reconciliation but to an intensified conflict. This is of course significant, as many English people believed fear to be an effective means of bringing the native populations under control. Through his exploration of this rhetoric, Williams subtly dismantles such an assumption.

What seems to resolve the conflict in the chapter is not fear but love. The phrase, "I love you," occurs twice in Williams's phrase-book – once here in the chapter on war, and at the very beginning of the book in the first chapter (on salutation). The exchange containing the profession of love is worth examining.

Kunnanaumpasummish.	*Mercy, Mercy.*
Kekuttokaunta.	*Let us parley.*
Aquetuck.	*Let us cease Armes.*
Wunnishaunta.	*Let us agree.*
Cowammaunsh.	*I love you.*
Wunnetu nta.	*My heart is true.*
Tuppauntash.	*Consider what I say.*
Tuppauntamoke.	*Do you all consider.*
Cummequaunum cummittamussussuck ka	*Remember your Wives, and Children.*
Eatch keen anawayean	*Let all bee as you say.*
Cowawwunnauwem.	*You speak truly.*
Cowauontam.	*You are a wise man.*
Wetompatitea.	*Let us make friends.*

Love, it would seem, has provoked an affirmation of the value of families, truth, wisdom, and friendship. The conflict has not ended acrimoniously, but rather harmoniously with the articulation of a commitment to some of the most fundamental concepts on which English society is based. Williams, just prior to the resolution, tells us, "Their warres are farre less bloudy and devouring than the cruell Warres of Europe." Although Williams seems here to be speaking of the nature of the actual combat, it would also seem to be his intention to portray these struggles as occurring in a context of mutual respect and cooperation – facts which then enable the resolution of the conflicts.

Williams ends his chapter on war with a poem that is typically critical of the Puritans. Ivy Schweitzer has observed that these concluding poems almost always function to portray the Massachusetts Puritans as deficient. In addition, she suggests, the poems frequently offer a much more critical view of the Indians, whom he has just implicitly praised in the portions leading up to the poem. The effect of this operation, according to Schweitzer, is to present Williams as standing above both the natives and the Puritans. This poem would seem to fit Schweitzer's pattern. Williams does not praise but rather laments the constant warfare of the Indians. But he singles out for much sharper treatment the warlike tendencies of the "English Men, That boast themselves Gods Children, and Members of Christ to be."

In his re-appropriation of the Protestant rhetoric of fear and love, Williams couches his critique of the Massachusetts Puritans in terms that would be readily embraced by an audience eager to entertain the notion of a humane English colonialism. In other words, it was precisely this desire within his readership that not only rendered his critique so compelling but also managed to neutralize the more unsettling aspects of his text. We should not, however, lose sight of the fact that Roger Williams's *Key* presents us with our most radical critique of the idea that Englishness would, through colonialism, be rendered synonomous with Protestantness. And this critique is all the more remarkable when one considers that Williams achieved it by deploying the rhetoric that had been a staple of Protestant colonial discourse from its earliest instantiation. But what is perhaps most extraordinary about Williams's *Key* is the fact that his English readers seem not to have grasped its most radical implications – although his Massachusetts neighbors almost certainly did. In addition to revealing the necessarily tenuous connections that tied English national identity to a stringently articulated Protestantism, Williams's *Key* casts doubt on the possibility that colonial discourse could be used to unite the members of a nation hopelessly divided along numerous doctrinal, ideological and political lines. And yet Williams's success in obtaining a patent for his colony would seem to indicate the ongoing desire on the part of the English to imagine their colonies as places where English Protestant identity could be articulated in some pure or ideal form.

A letter from the Lord Protector's Council to the Governor of the Massachusetts Bay Colony, written in 1654, some eleven years after the publication of the Key, conveys the enduring nature of this English desire. Carried by Williams himself as he returned to America from one of his trips to London, the letter was intended to provide protection for Williams's own colony of Providence Plantations and to guarantee him safe passage through Massachusetts from whence he had been banished:

Taking notice, some of us, of long-time, of Mr. Roger Williams, his good affections and conscience, and of his sufferings by our common enemy and oppressor of God's people, the prelates; as also of his great industry and travels in his printed Indian labours in your parts (the like whereof we have not seen extant from any part of America), and in which respect it hath pleased both Houses of Parliament to grant unto him and friends with him, a free and absolute charter of civil government for those parts of his abode.[56]

Significantly, the Council cites Williams's "printed Indian labours," by which they presumably meant his *Key*, as a reason for granting him a charter. In their comment on the unusual nature of this volume, they echo Williams's own estimation of his work when it was published: "I present you with a *Key*: I have not heard of the like, yet framed, since it pleased God to bring that mighty *Continent of America* to light."[57] Moreover, the council's choice to refer parenthetically to the uniqueness of Williams's work could easily be interpreted as a not-so-subtle reminder to the Massachusetts Puritans that they should be less quick to criticize that which they themselves have failed to produce. Williams's *Key*, therefore, is recognized, not for the threat it might pose to English colonial desires, but rather for its cagey promise to fulfill those desires.

The skill with which Williams deployed the tropes of English Protestant colonial rhetoric to convince his readers that his colony embodied their own national aspirations would not be matched until John Eliot wrote his *Indian Dialogues*. As I shall argue, however, in the next chapter, Eliot's goals differed significantly from those of Williams. Rather than trying to construct his own colony, Eliot tries to argue for the importance of supporting his missionary work within the Massachusetts colony. And rather than attempting to persuade the *English* of the value of his project, Eliot will use the language of Protestant colonialism to convince his fellow *American* colonists of the importance of re-instilling their colonial work with a sense of purpose and urgency.

CHAPTER SIX

Fear and self-loathing:
John Eliot's Indian Dialogues

Attempting to articulate the differences between John Eliot and Roger Williams, one scholar suggests that, "Eliot has correctly been described as the apostle *to* the Indians while Williams was rather the apostle *among* them."[1] He was of course acknowledging, on the one hand, Williams's refusal to participate personally in the work of proselytizing the Indians and, on the other, Eliot's lifelong commitment to such a project. On the face of it, Eliot's work as the so-called "Apostle to the Indians" would seem to lend itself easily to the discourses of Protestantism and nationalism that we have been examining in this study. Eliot's relationship, however, to the discourse of nation was, as we shall see, a complicated one. While he zealously solicited support from people who remained in England, he also had to confront the disappointing reality that his work among the Indians was less valued among his fellow colonists than it was in England.

Published in 1671 in the Massachusetts Bay Colony, Eliot's *Indian Dialogues* represents his attempt to transform his labor among the Indians into a commodity that would be valued, not simply in England, but in the colony as well. He therefore puts forth his missionary enterprise as the most reliable way for the colonists to embody the ideals of Protestantism and Englishness. Implicitly suggesting that the real future of English Protestant identity lay not in England but in the colonies, Eliot frames his dialogues as an allegory of the ongoing struggle for survival of English Protestantism. Ultimately, Eliot sees in the conversion experiences of the Indians themselves a model for the spiritual renewal of a colony struggling to cope with both the internal strife of ecclesiastical conflict and the anxiety over England's uncertain future in the wake of the restoration.

Each of the four *Dialogues* rehearses a particular difficulty con-

155

fronting praying Indians as they tried to convert their unconverted brethren. In the first dialogue, Piumbukhou journeys home to his tribe to convince them to join him in converting to Christianity. At first, they are hostile and resist, but eventually they come around, presumably as a result of the rhetorical skills Piumbukhou has learned at the hands of Eliot. The second dialogue involves one of Eliot's earliest Indian converts, Waban, who is on a mission to convert his uncle Nishohkou, a powerful sachem. Nishohkou is willing to allow missionaries to preach to his people, but he is unwilling to convert himself.[2] Finally, in his explosive third dialogue, Eliot invents a fanciful conversation between Metacom (also known as King Philip) and two praying Indians. But these *Dialogues* are more than a handbook for native missionaries, as Eliot himself claims – if indeed they are that at all.

While Eliot's *Dialogues* are certainly concerned with the conversion of the Indians, they are also clearly preoccupied with the English context of those conversions. Eliot shrewdly frames each dialogue against the backdrop of a twofold English history that he invokes at strategic moments. These *Dialogues* display an acute – at times almost prescient – awareness of the precariousness of Protestantism on both sides of the Atlantic. At one moment, Eliot seems to address the plight of the oppressed nonconformists in England; at the next, he speaks to his fellow settlers' fears of declension. In 1671, radical Protestantism both in England and America found itself in crisis, and these crises formed the context for the *Dialogues*. For those nonconformists who remained in England at the Restoration, there was the troubling prospect of a king who appeared to incline increasingly toward Roman Catholicism. The publication of the *Dialogues* falls neatly between Charles's secret Treaty of Dover (1670) and his second *Declaration of Indulgence* (1672). In the former, he promised to convert to Roman Catholicism, while in the latter he suspended the penal laws against nonconformists and Catholics alike. If the Puritans in New England could take consolation in the fact that they had only to observe the restoration from a distance, Eliot is quick to remind his readers of problems that lie closer to home. Not only had the Massachusetts Bay Colony performed poorly in carrying out the conversion of the Indians, but in 1662, it confronted its own internal ecclesiastical crisis as the church elders grappled with the painful question of whether or not to baptize the children of adults who were not themselves full church members. The resulting Half-Way Covenant sparked a divisive debate that would last well into the 1670s. Thus it was that Eliot, like Williams, wrote to a culture divided. But, in the case of Eliot, whose audience was more likely a colonial one, the task at hand was not to offer a nation a way of imagining itself as whole again. It was instead that of presenting his fellow colonists with a means of healing and overcoming their divisions.

A REVOLTING NATION

Most English readers would have first encountered John Eliot's name during the 1640s and 1650s, in the so-called "Indian Tracts" published by various individuals interested in promoting the conversion of the Indians. Comprised of letters, testamonials, eye-witness accounts, verbatim reports, and solicitations, these tracts gave English readers a detailed sense of the workings of their missionary operations in America. Although Eliot himself was not responsible for the final compilations, his letters and accounts are prominently featured in the tracts. In at least one sense, these tracts functioned almost identically to the sermons we examined in chapter 4: they constructed the colonial work of prosyletizing the Indians as a national undertaking that would distinguish England from other nations. Like the Virginia sermons, the Indian tracts offered an explicit comparison between England's missionary achievements (or lack thereof) and those of other colonizing nations. These comparisons, which always figured England as lacking, were intended to encourage English readers to make material and spiritual investments in missionary work as a means of preventing England from being outdone by other nations in its attempts to "wynn and incite the Natives [to] the onlie true God and savior of mankinde."[3]

There is another sense, however, in which the Indian tracts functioned similarly to the Virginia sermons: they offered colonial work as an antidote to seemingly insurmountable domestic problems. Where the Virginia ministers offered colonial endeavor as a means of solving the most pressing national problems of their day – idleness, overpopulation, economic displacement – the compilers of the Indian tracts offered the American missionary undertaking as a way of avoiding the divisive religious and political conflicts that would plague England from the 1640s onwards. Missionary work, in other words, offered the English an opportunity to re-imagine itself as a nation. To be a Protestant in England in the mid-seventeenth century was to be a partisan in a struggle for the soul of the nation. The Indian tracts, therefore, were nothing short of allegories of an idealized Protestant national identity that was characterized, not by division and strife, but by holiness and harmony. The Indian tracts gave the English a chance to imagine their nation, not as it was, but as they would like it to be.

Two letters published in 1649 give an idea of the extent to which promoters of missionary activity attempted to frame it as a national cause that all Protestants could wholeheartedly support. In October of that year, Parliament had passed the bill that created the Society for the Propagation of the Gospel. This act of Parliament gave the Society (also known as "the Corporation") the authority to solicit funds in parishes throughout England.[4] The universities at Cambridge and Oxford responded by publishing their own appeals for support for the missionary work. These letters too were sent to ministers throughout England and Wales. Part of the appeal from Cambridge went as follows:

wee are earnestly sollicited to put our helping hands to a work so purely Christian (as their letter to us stiles it) and not at all engaged in the unhappy differences of these times.

The second appeal, emanating from Oxford, was similar:

This work is represented to us, and we doe in the like manner recommend it to you as a worke purely Christian, not at all relating to, or engaged in the unhappy differences of these sad and discomposed times.[5]

To the English people recovering from the trauma of a civil war, the American missionary enterprise offered itself as a "purely Christian" undertaking that Protestants of all sects could support. By donating their time and money to the missions, the English could participate in the writing of a narrative that was not marred by the "unhappy differences" that seemed inevitably to be attached to all political and religious discourse in the middle of the seventeenth century. In the words of George P. Winship, the conversion of the native populations "was a subject that took their minds away from the more immediate mundane concerns and into the realm of spiritual welfare in this world and the next, both their own future and that of the unconverted for whose redemption they were prepared to accept responsibility."[6]

By at least one measure the appeals to the English were wildly successful: according to Winship, they "created a pool of invested capital that refreshed the New England metropolis for a century and a third." These appeals not only took advantage of a "widespread longing" on the part of the English to "seek relief in pious deeds from the anxieties engendered by the uneasy political situations," but they also played on traditional fears that Catholic Spain was "threatening to create a vast body of adherents to Romanism who would overwhelm the Protestant settlers whenever the two came into contact."[7] In other words, missionary work not only seemed to exempt itself from the bitter debates within English Protestantism. It also offered the English a way of imagining themselves as a Protestant nation united against Roman Catholicism. And it did not seem to matter whether the missionary work was being performed by Puritans or by Presbyterians, so long as the missionaries were English and called themselves Protestant. As Michael Walzer has astutely observed, "During the 1640s, personal and national regeneration were constantly linked together: the individual's covenant with the covenant of a nation reborn, the saint's private warfare against satanic lust with the collective warfare against Satan's cohorts." Describing the ultimate effects of this linkage between the individual and the national covenant, Walzer asserts, "The practical culmination of covenant theology can be seen in the collective commitments undertaken in the 1630s and '40s by both the Scottish and English nations."[8]

Although Walzer does not discuss England's missionary enterprises in America, I would suggest that we treat them as just such a "collective commitment." Indeed, the Indian tracts as a whole attempt to construct the missionary undertaking as one that will offer England a means of differentiating its collective will from that of its Catholic rivals as well as affording unity and a stronger sense of purpose to those left at home. Of the six tracts published between 1647 and 1653, two were the products of the collective editorship of what was to become the board of the Society for the Propagation of the Gospel. The 1648 tract, *The Cleare Sun-shine of the Gospel Breaking forth upon the Indians in New England* was published one year before the formal incorporation of the Society, but seven of the sixteen men who signed its prefaces would also go on to sign the prefaces of the 1652 tract, *Strength out of Weaknesse; Or a Glorious Manifestation of the Further Progress of the Gospel among the Indians in New England.*

Before turning to the prefaces themselves, however, we should take a moment to acquaint ourselves with some of the men who signed them. Most were prominent Independent divines, some of whom had direct contact with the Puritans in New England.[9] John Owen, for instance, was perhaps the leading Independent minister in London during the 1640s. Philip Nye and Owen's colleague Thomas Goodwin were the editors of Thomas Hooker's posthumously published American sermons.[10] Simeon Ashe, William Bridge, Lazarus Seaman, and the former Smectymnuan Edmund Calamy were all parliamentary preachers during the 1640s.[11] William Gouge, whose preaching career began in the 1620s, and William Greenhill, who wrote the preface to Jeremiah Burroughes's, *The Excellency of a Gracious Spirit* (London, 1638) were also well known Independent divines by the 1640s.[12] Henry Whitefield, who edited one of the Indian tracts had served as a missionary in America. And William Spurstow would achieve prominence during the Restoration as one of the divines who consulted with Charles on his first *Declaration of Indulgence.*[13]

The point is not simply that the people sponsoring the missionary work were prominent, although that is in itself significant. Rather, it is important to understand that there was neither ideological conformity within the group, nor complete agreement between the group and the divines in New England. In fact, as Perry Miller asserted, Goodwin, Nye, and Owen were "men who might easily have come to New England and helped extirpate heretics," but who chose instead to declare that the Massachusetts "colony's law banishing Anabaptists was an embarrassment to the Independent cause in England."[14] Differences and divisions notwithstanding, the authors of the dedicatory epistle to *The Cleare Sun-shine of the Gospel Breaking forth upon the Indians in New England* set forth in no uncertain terms the importance of missionary work to the nation. Addressing their letter to the members of Parliament, these men hope that their report will serve as the occasion of the spiritual renewal of the nation.

The *report* of this mercy is *first* made to you, who are *Representatives* of this Nation, That in you *England* might bee stirred up, to be Rejoycers in, and Advancers of these promising beginnings.

They continue their appeal to the members of Parliament by stressing just how much the missionary work will contribute to a glorified national self-image.

In *order* to this what doth God *require* of us, but that we should *strengthen* the hands, *incourage* the hearts of those who are at *work* for him, *conflicting* with difficulties, *wrestling* with discouragements, to *spread* the Gospel, and in that, the *fame* and honor of this Nation, to the *utmost* ends of the earth?[15]

Sounding a familiar theme, these promoters assert that the missionary labor performed in the colony will increase "the fame and honour of this Nation." Although the letter mentions the "dif-ficulties" and "discouragements" of those who have chosen "to spread the Gospel," it seems at least equally concerned with allevi-ating the difficulties and discouragements of those left at home.

Following their letter to the Parliament, the assemblers of the pamphlet offer in their letter to the "Christian Reader" a strident challenge to support their missionary endeavors.

The Ordinances *are as much* contemned *here, as embraced there;* Religion *as much derided, the* ways *of godliness as much* scorned *here, as they can be* wished *and desired there;* generally *wee are* sick *of plenty, wee surfet of our abundance, the worst of Surfets, and with our* loathed Manna *and* disdained *food, God is* preparing *them a* Table *in the wildernes; where our* satieties, *wil be their* sufficiencies; *our* complaints, *their* contents; *our* burthens, *their* comforts; *if he cannot have an* England *here, he can have an* England *there;* and baptize *and adopt them into those* priviledges, *which wee have* looked *upon as our bur-thens. We have* sad decayes *upon us, we are a* revolting Nation, *a people* guilty *of great* defection *from God* (32).

Echoing the Virginia ministers from Chapter Four, these mission-ary promoters decry the current state of spiritual affairs in Eng-land and look to the colonies for a remedy to the problem. In language that recalls Benedict Anderson's characterization of a nation as "a sociological organism moving calendrically through homogenous, empty time," the epistle explicitly offers the colonial enterprise, and specifically its missionary arm, as a way of trans-porting England to the new world. But the England that is trans-ported will be superior to the England that is left behind – at least at first. What is dismissed in England will be valued in the colonies; what is a complaint in England will be a source of contentment in the colony; what is a burden in England will be a comfort in the colony. But as the epistle concludes, the spiritual vigor of the colonies is intended to serve as an "incentive" to England. In the meantime, as the promoters remind their readers, England is a "revolting nation." In 1648, in the middle of its revolution, England was indeed a "revolting nation." The darkly humored pun, though, cleverly plays on the fears of readers who worried that the revolution might turn out to be a "great defection from God." The promoters therefore present missionary work as a convenient way for their readers to rise above present difficulties and take part in a work that would be pleasing both to God and the Nation.

In the preface to the the 1652 tract, *Strength out of Weaknesse*, the promoters offer their readers similar inducements to help in the missionary work.

That when other Nations who have planted in those furthest parts of the Earth, have onely sought their owne advantage to possesse their Land, Transport their gold, and that with so much covetousnesse and cruelty, that they have made the name of Christianitie and of Christ an abomination, that the Lord should be pleased to make use of our Brethren that went forth from us to make manifest *the savour of Christ* among the people, and to winne their soules to him; How should wee rejoyce that the Lord hath so farre prosper'd such an undertaking.

. . .Such considerations as these, have filled and affected our hearts, in the reading and meditation of this great worke of the Lord, and wee hope being communicated may be a good means to awaken the godly and faithful of this Nation, to observe the Presence and appearances of God amongst his people there. . . (158)

By recalling (without naming) the cruel and covetous colonial exploits of the Spanish, the authors of the preface attempt to situate England's missionary enterprises in the context of the ongoing international rivalry between England and Spain – a rivalry that was no less fiercely contested during the 1650s than it had been earlier in the century.[16] But the prefators here do more than suggest that missionary work will advance England's interests in its geopolitical struggle with its Catholic rivals. Indeed, they assert that the effects of the publication of the Indian tracts will be felt at home. The missionary work of the English colonists, once "communicated may be a good means to awaken the godly and faithful *of this Nation*." In so asserting, the authors of the preface embrace the strategy of the Virginia ministers, who wrote almost fifty years before them: the successful prosecution of affairs in the colony will enable England to enhance its status as a nation.

It is important remember that it was not only English divines who suggested that the American missions might serve a vital function for the nation. New England divine Richard Mather, in his preface to the 1653 tract, *Tears of Repentance: Or, a Further Narrative of the Progress of the Gospel amongst the Indians in New England* also presented the missions in New England in explicitly national terms.

And Oh, let the English take heed, both in our dear Native Country, and here, lest for our unthankfulness, and many other sins, the Lord should take the Gospel from us, and bestow our mercy therein upon them as upon a Nation that would yeeld the fruits thereof in better sort than many of us have done. (225)

Mather darkly portends in this passage that God may punish the English by taking the Gospel from them and giving it to one of England's Catholic rivals. Such a threat played upon the English fears that the Spanish would be more successful than them in the conversion of the native populations. But it also suggests that the attempts to link the fate of the Gospel in America with the fate of the English nation were not simply the work of those living in England. Indeed, as David Cressy has suggested, even Richard Mather's son Increase frequently thought of his work in the colony as contributing to the well-being of the nation.[17]

So firmly was the missionary cause attached to England's sense of itself as a nation, that not even the Restoration in 1660 and its Act of Oblivion and Indemnity could do away with the Society for the Propagation of the Gospel. This act, which wiped clear all of the acts and ordinances of the *interregnum*, did leave the Society, which was chartered by the *interregnum* Parliament, temporarily without a charter. But by February of 1661–2, the new charter was sealed. True, the name and governing board had to be changed, but by and large the enterprise survived intact. In language similar to the above appeals from Oxford and Cambridge, we are told that no less a person than the King's Lord Chancellor, Edward Hyde, author of the infamous Clarendon Code, looked favorably upon the organization that was now known as The Corporation: he "approved of the worke, as that which could not be for any faction, or Evil end, but honourable to the King and Land."[18] The newly chartered Corporation even achieved the rather remarkable feat of retaining sequestered lands which it had purchased during the *interregnum*. Almost without exception, lands which were sequestered during the *interregnum* were returned to their royalist owners at the restoration. Evidently, not even the King wanted to risk stripping the assets from an enterprise that had such widespread public support.[19]

It seemed not to matter that Richard Baxter, a noted (some would say notorious) Nonconformist, had almost singlehandedly brokered the agreement for the new charter and chosen the board. In *Reliquiae Baxterianae*, Baxter himself describes how he met with the board of the old Society after the Restoration to discuss possible ways of reviving the Society. Although the board that Baxter helped to appoint was by no means made up entirely of Nonconformists, his political sagacity in selecting members whose credibility could not be questioned by the new regime was extraordinary. Baxter shrewdly tried to cleanse the board of any men that might offend the King: "we all agreed that such as had incurred the King's Displeasure by being Members of any Courts of Justice in Cromwells days, should quietly recede."[20] It also seemed not to matter that John Eliot, arguably the best known English missionary in North America, was a staunch Puritan, one of whose books was burned at the Restoration. In short, it seemed not to matter to the King and his government that the majority of the people who were engaged in missionary work were Nonconformists. Or, if it did matter, the King was unable to do anything about it. Apparently what was important was the idea that the English nation needed its missions.

SPIRITUALL FACTORIES/HOLY MERCHANDIZE

At the end of *Tears of Repentance,* the tract published in 1653 by Richard Mather, Joseph Caryl attaches an afterword, in which he describes the relationship between England and its colonial missions in explicitly mercantile terms:

O let old *England* rejoyce in this, that our brethren who with extream difficulties and expences have Planted themselves in the *Indian Wildernesses,* have also laboured night and day with prayers and tears and Exhortations to Plant the *Indians as a spirituall Garden,* into which Christ might come and eat his pleasant fruits. Let the gaining of any of their souls to Christ, and their turning to god from Idols to serve the living and true God, be more pretious in our eyes then the greatest gaine or return of Gold or Silver. This gaine of soules is a *Merchandize* worth the glorying in upon all the *Exchanges,* or rather in all the *Churches* throughout the world. *This merchandize is Holiness to the Lord:* and of this the ensuing Discourse presents you with a Bill of many particulars, from your spirituall *Factory in New England*, as the improvement of your former adventures thither, for the promoting of that heavenly Trade: as also for an encouragement not only to all those who have freely done it already, to adventure yet more, but also for the quickening of those who hitherto have not done it, now to underwrite themselves Adventurers for the advancement of so holy and hopefull a designe.[21]

In his characterization of the missionary enterprise as a mercantile adventure, Caryl accentuates the fact that the Indian discourse functioned as a commodity for England. He is, of course, not the first person to describe spiritual endeavors in economic terms. William Crashawe, for one, whose work we examined in chapter 4, argued that the Indians would exchange their material commodities with the English for spiritual ones. Although his move is not original, Caryl draws attention to the fact that the purpose and function of England's colonies was more than that of simply providing raw materials and other tangible commodites for consumption in England. Indeed, as Caryl says, the "gaine of soules is a Merchandize." As I have argued in the preceding pages, the attempts by New England's clergy to convert the Indians could and did function within a symbolic economy, in which people in England donated money and materials in return for being able to lay claim to the harvest of souls for their nation.

John Eliot's *Indian Dialogues* is an attempt to reinvent the economics of Indian disourse. Rather than constructing the *Dialogues* for English readers, who desired to reimagine themselves and their nation through the representations of native people, Eliot attempts to demonstrate to his fellow colonists that the work of converting the native people can produce "merchandize" for domestic consumption. For the Massachusetts Bay colonists struggling to heal the wounds of the divisive Half-Way crisis, Eliot's praying Indians offer a remarkable instance of the allegorical power of Indian discourse. For those who looked with despair toward England and the Restoration, Eliot offers the *Dialogues* as a retreat from the horrors of the Restoration. And for those who worried about the mounting tensions between the Massachusetts Puritans and the neighboring Indians, the *Dialogues* offer readers the hopes of peaceful cohabitation. The *Dialogues,* in other words, function as an allegory for the two most profound desires the Puritan colonists would have felt in the second half of the seventeenth century.

A fable deployed by Anthony, one of the praying Indians, in the third dialogue, serves to remind readers of the evocative power of missionary work. Although the immediate point of the fable is to lay out the logic for Eliot's desire to isolate his converted "praying Indians" in separate "praying towns," the fable suggestively links the missionary project with Protestant history.

ANTHONY. All that my brother hath said I second, and can bear witness unto. Only I will add one thing more of which I know more than he doth, because it was acted in the town where I live. There was some subtle endeavor to have mingled the praying and non-praying Indians under the power of non-praying Indians, contrary to public and evident condition. Against this did some of the wiser sort (who saw the trap) firmly stand, giving this reason: the fox came to the lamb's door, and would fain come in, but the lambs refused, saying, if he get in but one claw, he will not rest till he have wriggled in his whole body. Stop waters while they are small and superable.[22]

As he has constructed it, Eliot's fable posits an overwhelmed Christianity on the inside trying to stave off wily paganism on the outside. Eliot, however, seems unaware of the ways in which his fable is peculiarly inappropriate for the use he apparently intends it. For instance, the historical situation would seem to present a competing narrative. Paganism was, after all, on this continent first, and Christianity "wriggled" itself in. The fable, therefore, by positing Christianity on the inside, offers an implicit rewriting of colonial history. More than that, however, the fable offers Eliot's readers his own rendition of an old theme, namely that of Protestantism under siege.

It seems reasonable to assume that Eliot invented the fable of *The Fox and the Lambs* since it does not appear in any of the standard collections of the period.[23] It does, however, bear an uncanny resemblance to the two fables in the May Eclogue of Edmund Spenser's *Shepheardes Calender.* In fact, Eliot's fable is precisely what I imagine a composite of the two Spenserian fables would look like. The first one, the story of *The Wolf and the Sheep*, as told by the shepherd Piers, sets up the predatory relationship between

Catholic pastors and an unsuspecting Protestant flock. Next, Piers offers the story of the *The Fox and the Kid*, in which "Spenser produced a version of the ancient fable of *The Wolf and the Kid*, and by substituting a fox for the adversary achieved a greater emphasis on cunning."[24] As E. K. tells us in the "Argument" to the May Eclogue, "under the persons of two shepheards Piers and Palinodie, be represented two formes of pastoures or Ministers, or the protestant and the Catholique."[25] Thus the constituent dynamic of Spenser's May narrative is that of a sleepy, guileless Protestantism constantly under siege from a considerably more calculating and cunning Catholicism.

The May Eclogue's allegory of besieged Protestantism speaks directly to Eliot's fable of the *The Fox and the Lambs*. Sharing the agenda of the Leicester–Walsingham–Sidney faction in Queen Elizabeth's court, Spenser attempts to convince the Queen to adopt a more militantly Protestant (i.e., staunchly anti-Catholic) foreign policy.[26] Hence in his fable of *The Fox and the Kid* he attempts to paint an especially dire picture of the situation – a picture whose message is simply that the Catholic threat will not be apparent until it is too late to do anything about it. Spenser calls his fellow Protestants to shake off their complacency and join him in his recognition that Protestantism is in fact under siege.

Insofar as it is a retelling of the old Spenserian narrative of besieged Protestantism, Eliot's fable of the *Fox and the Lambs* is an attempt to suggest that the struggle to convert the Indians is merely the most recent chapter in Protestantism's struggle against Roman Catholicism. Eliot is trying in this dialogue to urge his fellow colonists not to look back to England, but to look at their own colony as the site of the struggle that must be won. Eliot suggests that his Indian missions will advance the interests of a global Protestantism and they are offered as an antidote to the disappointing and painful history of the restoration, but Eliot seems to be reminding his readers that the work that needs to be done needs to be done, not in England, but in New England.

As Eliot reminds us in his preface, his *Dialogues* are a blend of fact and fiction. But of the three dialogues, none is more fanciful than the third, whose principal character is Philip, also known as Metacom, the great sachem of the Wampanoags. In this dialogue, contrary to any known historical account, Philip has all but accepted Christianity. He tells his interlocutors, William and

Anthony, of the appeals of John Eliot and his son: "And I have had some serious thoughts of accepting the offer, and turning to God, to become a praying Indian, I myself and all my people." He goes on to tell them, however, that he does "have some great objections, which I cannot tell how to get over."[27] By the conclusion of the dialogue, the only obstacle standing in the way of Philip's conversion is instruction: "I am now in a great strait. My heart is bent within me to keep the sabbaths. But alas, neither I nor any of my people know how to do it, unless we have somebody to teach us."[28] What takes place between the two above quotes is not a catechism lesson – which was, incidentally, Eliot's preferred method of instruction. Rather, what transpires between Philip and the two praying Indians is an extraordinary political dialogue, the intent of which, it would seem, is not to convince Philip to convert but to convince Eliot's English colonial readers of the necessity and political importance of Philip's putative conversion.

Eliot is quick to illustrate the immediate, strategic value of Philip's conversion when he elaborates on Philip's "great objections." Philip worries less about the consequences of his own individual conversion than he does about the political repercussions that would result if his whole tribe were to convert to Christianity: "And hence it will come to pass, that if I should pray to God, and all my people with me, I must become as a common man among them, and so lose all my power and authority over them."[29] This statement may well reflect the fears of sachems like Philip, but more importantly, it reveals the colonial perception of Indian political structures. What is here articulated as a grave concern by Philip can be read by Eliot's readers as an implicit promise that Indian tribes will automatically follow their sachems to the baptismal font. The dialogue thus presents an easy and efficient way of bringing large segments of the native population under the yoke of Christianity. Presumably, such a turn of events would alleviate the constant friction that was to culminate in the genocidal frenzy of King Philip's War in 1675.

Whatever strategic value Philip's conversion might have represented to the English colonists, Eliot seems to be offering his readers an additional benefit. As promising as Philip's words might be to a colonial audience, they do take the form of a distinctly undemocratic pronouncement. The words "common," "power," and "authority" seem to jump off the page. Therefore, by joining Eliot in his missionary efforts, the colonists can help liberate the Indians from a tyrannical form of government. Later in the dialogue, Philip continues to employ the rhetoric of repression, when he notes that the praying towns are based on the principle of equality – a notion which causes him some anxiety: "This bringing all to an equality will bring all to a confusion."[30] By painting Philip as a politically repressive monarch, who refuses to accept Christianity, Eliot provides yet another reason for English settlers to support his missionary program. By so doing, they will be contributing to the establishment of a democratic commonwealth among the Indians.[31]

As we read on, we see that Eliot is quick to link repressive political structures to certain religious and ideological formations. Philip, William, and Anthony are interrupted in their conversation by the arrival of another sachem, who, Philip tells us, "hateth praying to God, and hath been a means of delaying my entrance into this way."[32] Like Philip, this unnamed sachem displays his undemocratic tendencies when he tells the other three present that he is willing to listen to their talk, but that he is very wary of it. As for the reading of the Bible, he fears what it will do to his control over his people:

And it will fill them with new light and notions, which withdraws them from our obedience, and leadeth them to make trouble and disturbance unto us in those old ways in which we and our forefathers have walked. And my counsel is to suppress the reading of that book.[33]

With his last sentence, Eliot has unambiguously moved the unnamed sachem into Roman Catholic territory. And in case Eliot's readers fail to notice this move, he underlines it with William's response. Referring to "a certain people who are called Papists," William explains that the sachem's "counsel" bears an uncanny resemblance to the draconian policies of Roman Catholic governments. The Catholics, after all, "suppress the reading of that book."

As with the rest of his *Dialogues*, Eliot tailors this one for his English colonial readers and not the Indians. It is unclear to what extent anti-Catholic rhetoric would have been included in Protestant missionary literature directed at native populations. But it is clear in the conversation that follows that the anti-Catholic references are intended to do more than make Indians want to be good Protestants. For an Indian in Massachusetts who had never encountered a Catholic, the significance of William's reference would have been lost. The settlers, however, would have associated Eliot's very pointed mention of Catholic suppression with a variety of related phenomena. Most obviously, William's words point to one of the fundamental tenets of the reformation, namely access to and interpretation of the scriptures. In breaking with Rome, Luther, for instance, had rejected the Catholic Church's profession that it was the only legitimate interpreter of scripture.[34] According to the Protestants, the Catholics had suppressed the scriptures in order to exercise a tyrannical authority over their flock, a charge, not coincidentally, reminiscent of Spenser's dire warnings in *The Shepheardes Calender*.

The debate between the Catholics and the Protestants on the issue of interpretive authority constitutes only the most general context for William's intervention in the above conversation. For Eliot, the issue of suppression of texts would have struck much closer to home. His own book, *The Christian Commonwealth*, which contained the provocative assertion that "Christ is the only right Heir of the Crown of England," was burned at the Restoration. Eliot himself was required to retract his statements in *The Christian Commonwealth* in March of 1661, and as James Holstun puts it, he did so "with a masterful display of truculent equivocation and ambiguous pronoun usage."[35] Even if they weren't aware of Eliot's own status as a victim of political censorship, his readers would almost certainly have known of the harsh political conditions under which their Nonconformist brethren lived back in England. They would also have heard with some discomfort and displeasure of the king's apparent leanings toward Roman Catholicism.

As the encounter between the two praying Indians and Philip continues, the Restoration subtext of a veiled Catholic threat suggests itself even more strongly. According to William, in most countries, the kings allow the priests to have an unreasonable authority over the people. Philip wonders why the kings do not put a stop to censorship by the priests, but his solution is to fight suppression of the book with suppression of the clergy:

And I wonder at the sachems, that they will suffer such vile ministers to abuse their people in that manner, why do they not suppress them? And why do they not command their people to print the Bible, and let it be free for any man that will buy them, and read them? I wonder at these things. Can you satisfy me in the reason thereof?

William responds by arguing that indeed "some sachems are as bad as the ministers," while there are "other sachems that are wiser and better minded, yet they cannot help it, because their ministers are so rich."[36] In effect, William argues that the personal character of the king matters very little. In one case, the priests work their evil with the king's blessing, while in the other, the sachem is simply overpowered by the priests. The Puritans in Massachusetts and the Nonconformists in England would have readily recognized William's argument against monarchy for what it was. Such arguments formed part of the standard rhetorical apparatus of radical Protestantism. John Milton, for instance, in his *Ready and Easy Way* predicted quite accurately in 1660 the situation that William describes to Philip, namely that of a king constantly beleaguered by family and counsellors with Catholic leanings. More specifically, Milton feared (correctly as it turns out) that Charles's putative bride would be "in most likelihood outlandish and a papist." And there was "besides a queen mother such already."[37]

Charles himself consistently gave substance to Protestant fears of Catholic infiltration. His mother's outrageous attempts to convert her children to Roman Catholicism were well known, and his marriage to Catherine of Braganza simply fulfilled Milton's prediction.[38] But as if that wasn't enough to make Protestants uneasy, Charles's own political maneuvering often aroused suspicion. In 1663, in response to the king's first Declaration of Indulgence, Clarendon had warned Parliament that "royal dispensations could be used to give Anglican bishoprics to papist priests."[39] Then in 1670, Charles actually promised to convert to Catholicism in his secret Treaty of Dover. Even his second Declaration of Indulgence in 1672, which would have legalized religious dissent, was criticized by many Protestants because it promised leniency to Catholics as well as Nonconformists.[40]

There is no way that John Eliot could have known in 1671 of either the secret 1670 Dover Treaty or of the 1672 Declaration. The date of the publication of the *Indian Dialogues* must thus remain a happy coincidence, but the persistent Protestant fears of Catholic conspiracy have, as I have suggested, a long history. And that history, with the restoration as its most recent chapter, forcefully suggests itself as one of the subtexts of Eliot's *Dialogues*. If the only purpose of these *Dialogues* was to instruct would-be Indian converts, the digression into Catholicism would be completely gratuitous. If, however, the *Dialogues* have some ulterior purpose, then the apparent digression on the Papists might have some significance. Eliot is doing several things here with this diatribe against Catholicism. First, he is linking the political structures of Indian culture with those of Catholicism. Thus, by converting Indians, the Puritans can, by analogy, be participating in the destruction of Romanism. Secondly, if establishing a commonwealth is indeed still a Protestant hope, Eliot provides his readers with an intermediate goal that is far less dangerous and extreme than trying to overthrow the English throne. In a sense, Eliot says to his readers that the fight against monarchy can begin in their own back yards. In addition, the passage on Catholicism works suggestively: By mentioning Catholics and Indians in the same breath, Eliot is playing on the Puritan fears I mentioned earlier of being overrun by Catholic missionaries. But finally, and most importantly, Eliot invokes Catholicism as an emblem of everything that Protestantism is not. By working to convert the Indians, Eliot argues, the Puritans will be doing nothing new. They will merely be participating in the two principal activities that have defined their English Protestant colonial identity from the start, namely converting heathens and keeping Roman Catholicism at bay.

SO DIM A WORK

By the time he published his *Indian Dialogues* in 1671, John Eliot was in an odd position. Financially, he was still well-supported by the Society for the Propagation of the Gospel, but politically within the colony he was isolated. The publication of the *Dialogues* marks a departure for Eliot in his work. Rather than asking for material support from his English brethren, as he did so successfully in the Indian tracts, Eliot tries in the *Dialogues* to appeal to his fellow settlers for *their* support of his work among the Indians. Eliot attempts to convince his readers to support him by suggesting that their long-sought goal of a true Christian Commonwealth is almost a reality among his praying Indians. James Holstun argues that it was precisely this aspect of the praying towns that appealed to Eliot's English supporters: "Amid the rising millenarian speculation, the imaginative appeal of the praying towns lay not in their missionary or political unity, but in the purity of their experiment in utopian discipline."[41] With his *Dialogues*, Eliot tries to instill among his colonial colleagues the same enthusiasm for his work that his English supporters have long shown through their unswerving generosity.

Ostensibly the *Dialogues* were part of Eliot's efforts to form a native troop of missionaries who would attempt the conversion of their fellow Indians. At least that is what he tells us in his introductory letter to the Commissioners of the United Colonies in New England:

I find it necessary for me to instruct them (as in principles of art, so) in the way of communicating the good knowledge of God, which I conceive is most familiarly done by way of dialogues.[42]

Again in his brief preface, Eliot explains his choice of form:

It is like to be one work incumbent upon our Indian churches and teachers, for some ages, to send forth instruments to call in others from paganry to pray unto God. Instructions therefore of that nature are required, and what way more familiar than by way of dialogues?[43]

The most obviously puzzling aspect of Eliot's claim is that of the language of the *Dialogues*. Written in English, they seem an unlikely tool to convert Indians, most of whom could not speak, let alone read any English. Moreover, one of the centerpieces of Eliot's ministry was precisely the notion of preaching to the Indians in their native tongue. That was why he had translated and published the *Bay Psalm Book* and the Algonquin *Bible*, as well as a host of other books and tracts including Richard Baxter's *A Call to the Unconverted*. There is more at work in the *Dialogues* than the attempt to provide his "Indian" teachers with yet another tool with which to ply their trade.

Eliot's repetition of the word "familiar" is also important. A fair question to ask at this point is: Familiar to whom? These *Dialogues* might be many things to an Indian who did not speak English, but familiar would not be one of them. Furthermore, even if the *Dialogues* were in Algonquin – a project Eliot says he plans to undertake – how familiar would they be to the Indians? The dialogue is a distinctly Western form, and it would hardly have been familiar to Indians whose own language was not a written one. The *only* people for whom these dialogues would have been familiar were the English settlers. These dialogues were not written for the Indians, as Eliot pretends, but for the English colonists whom Eliot hoped to convince to support his work.

If the dialogue was a cultural form that would have been "familiar" to educated English settlers, we should not assume that Eliot's *Dialogues* would have fully assumed that quality for his colonial readers. While I am insisting that this text was written for the settlers and not the Indians, I would also argue that familiarity was not one of Eliot's goals. In fact the contrary is true. One of the points of the *Dialogues* was precisely to produce a document that would be jarring to the colonists. Eliot achieves an effect of estrangement in part by constructing his *Dialogues* as exclusively Indian interchanges. In contrast to Spenser's dialogue on the Irish colonial efforts and Roger Williams's "implicit dialogue" in his *A Key into the Language of America* – texts in which the colonial voice is easily located – Eliot's innovation is to do away with the English presence altogether. In Spenser's case, we have two Englishmen, one of whom has been to Ireland, discussing the fate of that colony. And in Williams's *Key*, we have an implicit cultural exchange between nameless Indians and nameless settlers. In the *Indian Dialogues*, however, the only speakers are Indians. While the settlers are absent from the *Dialogues*, their ideas are not. As I will argue in a moment, Eliot intended his *Dialogues* to be a rehearsal not of Indian conversions *per se*, but of the reasons the English colonists should support his work.

While Eliot's pamphlets and letters to England provided him with a seemingly endless stream of contributions of both cash and supplies, they could not guarantee him the political support of his fellow English settlers. In fact, Eliot had a strained relationship with the Commissioners of the New England Company, to whom he addresses his introductory letter. Eliot, it seems, continued to solicit contributions directly from supporters in England while also collecting money and supplies from the Commissioners. And when questioned on this practice, he consistently failed to provide the Commissioners with a complete accounting of all of his sources of income.[44] Thus Eliot's letter to the Commissioners is itself significant, as it represents his recognition of the power of the colonial authorities, whom he has hitherto ignored. But if Eliot's letter is a solicitation, it does not signal that he will shy away from controversial issues. And one such issue was that of native lands:

My earnest request unto yourselves, is, that in all your respective colonies you would take care that due accommodation of lands and waters may be allowed them, whereupon to townships and churches may be (in after ages) able to subsist; and suffer not the English to strip them of all their lands, in places fit for the sustenance of the life of man.[45]

I would suggest that what appears to be an innocent promotion of Eliot's project, the establishment of "praying towns," is in fact a reference calculated to touch upon the sensitive question of native lands. As I argued in the last chapter, Roger Williams brought the issue of Indian land rights to the attention of English readers in several of his writings. In fact, the alleged dispossession of the Indians proved to be one of the more effective weapons in Williams's polemical arsenal.[46]

In the above passage, we can begin to see the polemical edge of Eliot's *Dialogues*, but we should note a crucial difference between him and Williams. Whereas Williams's goal was to hinder Massachusetts's efforts to derail his Rhode Island charter, Eliot always offers a face-saving route of escape to the targets of his polemic. Here, as a means of deflecting the troublesome charge of stripping the Indians "of all their lands," Eliot suggests to his readers the convenient solution of supporting his "praying towns." In response to every criticism and dilemma they adduce, the *Dialogues* offer Eliot's missionary work as the answer. The *Dialogues* are, in a sense, a cleverly framed job-description – Eliot's relentless attempt to create a demand for his services.

As he consistently does throughout the *Dialogues*, Eliot here attempts to show how his work will accomplish important tasks for the colony. Eliot's discussion of the issue of native lands forms part of a larger attempt to produce a new, sanitized history of Anglo-Indian contact. In the *Dialogues*, we find Eliot attempting such a project by recontextualizing the story of the Indians' first contact with the English. In the first dialogue the converted Indian Piumbukhou challenges his unconverted kinsman's assertion that the stories of the Bible are fiction. The kinsman asks Piumbukhou:

May not we rather think that *English* men have invented these stories to amaze us and fear us out of our old customs, and bring us to stand in awe of them, that they might wipe us of our lands, and drive us into corners, to seek new ways of living, and new places too? And be beholding to them for that which is our own, and was ours, before we knew them.[47]

This quote presents the reader with several possible interpret-ations. First of all, Eliot's preface to the *Dialogues* gives credence to this Indian's charge. If the *Dialogues* are what Eliot says they are, then at least one Englishman, Eliot, is not above inventing stories. After all, according to Eliot, these *Dialogues* are really nothing more than a blend of fact and fiction whose aim it is to get the Indians to behave in a certain way. He is able to evade the charge of untruthfulness by claiming that he is presenting an ideal version of what the truth would be.

The kinsman's charge, however, does not stop at claiming that the stories are invented. Their purpose, he argues, is to deprive the Indians of their land. If we read the charge of the Indian and consider Eliot's plan for setting up "praying towns," then we see that what this Indian charges and what Eliot intends are not that far apart. Eliot's goal was to separate the Indians from the English settlers, and in most cases the land for the "praying towns" was literally in a corner, in a part of the land that the white settlers didn't want for their own. Since we cannot dismiss the kinsman's charge altogether, we must assume that Eliot is here offering the English settlers a way of "rewriting" Anglo-Indian relations in a way that leaves the English less open to the charge of stealing the Indian lands. Once again, Eliot softens the polemical edge of his writing by presenting his readers with a ready defense. And as usual, the primary component of that defense is Eliot's missionary work itself.

Piumbukhou immediately counters his kinsman with a flat denial: "The Book of God is no invention of Englishmen." This denial, of course, also has at least two implications. Piumbukhou is referring to the Bible, but quite literally, the Indian-language Bible is the invention of an Englishman, namely Eliot himself. Piumbukhou's defense of English culture, however, goes beyond the Bible.

Yet this is also true, that we have great cause to be thankful to the English, and to thank God for them. For they had a good country of their own, but by ships sailing into these parts of the world, they heard of us, and of our country, and of our nakedness, ignorance of God, and wild condition. God put it into their hearts to desire to come hither, and teach us the good knowledge of God; and their King gave them liberty to serve God according to the word of God. And being come hither, we gave them leave freely to live among us. They have purchased of us a great part of those lands which they possess. They love us, they do us right, and no wrong willingly. If any do us wrong, it is without the consent of their rulers, and upon our complaints our wrongs are righted.[48]

By portraying his praying Indians as eloquent defenders of the English, Eliot reminds his readers just how useful Indians can be. We should also note that the above quotation is especially tailored to the Restoration: in terms that will soon seem ironic, Piumbu-khou dutifully mentions the king in flattering terms. What Eliot is offering here to his fellow colonists is Indian support. Thus the kinsman who debates Piumbukhou is not a straw man. He is presenting the anti-Puritan case in its strongest form, a case that circulated in London, and was one of the most significant obstacles to marshalling home support for colonial efforts.

In his introductory letter to the *Indian Dialogues*, Eliot reminds the commissioners of the embarrassingly slow progress on one of the Bay Colony's primary directives: "I find few English students willing to engage into so dim a work as this is. God hath in his mercy raised up sundry among themselves [i.e., the Indians] to a competent ability to teach their countrymen."[49] We should not fail to notice the implicit edge in this apparently straightforward assessment of his work: by claiming to do the "dim" work, Eliot leaves his readers to suppose that the other colonists are engaged in work that is perhaps more immediately rewarding or lucrative. We should also remember that Eliot's *Dialogues* appear in the wake of the divisive Half-Way Covenant, which was the product of the 1662 Synod, and which set off a debate that would preoccupy the colony through the 1670s.

While the "Half-Way Covenant" might at first seem only distantly linked, if at all, to the conversion of the Indians, I want to argue that both were symptoms of a larger identity crisis. The crisis that produced the "Half-Way Covenant" was sparked by the increasingly urgent question of what to do with the children of colonists who were not full church members. Should they be baptized and granted some sort of Half-Way status as intermediate church members? Or should they be treated just like any other non-believer who would only receive baptism after demonstrating convincing evidence of conversion and election? The question of church membership for children would have been moot, had there not been the fairly widespread perception that the younger generations had lost some of the seriousness and sense of purpose and mission of the earlier generations.[50] Thus, it is important that Eliot tells his superiors that "students" are unwilling to take on the missionary work. By so doing, he alludes to the painful perception that the younger generation is less spiritually inclined. Rather than pursuing the "dim work" of religion, the younger people, comfortable because of their parents' labors, can afford to forget God and seek their own personal gain.

In contrast to the backsliding Puritan youth, Eliot presents the Indians whom he has trained to convert their own brethren to Christianity. To the elders of Massachusetts Bay yearning for the "good old days" when God and church were supposedly everyone's primary concern, Eliot presents his missionary program as the key to a renewed emphasis on spirituality. In his *Dialogues*, Eliot attempts to seize an opportunity to garner colonial support for his work. In spite of the generous support Eliot found for his work back in England, the New England colonists seemed to treat the conversion of the native populations more as a necessary evil than as a project to be enthusiastically embraced. To be sure, the colony leaders were grateful that Eliot tended to the business of converting the Indians. He did, after all, give them credibility in England. But they seemed uninterested in doing anything more than the bare minimum necessary to support his work.[51]

Eliot had discovered that while the colonial government was only too happy to sanction his efforts to organize the Indians into some form of civil government, they were much less willing to let the Indians form their own churches.[52] Theologically, Eliot's work among the Indians was also questionable to some more stringent Puritans. As James Holstun has pointed out,

The Eliot Indian tracts are almost Arminian in their implicit assumption that the Indians as a whole can choose grace without ever worrying about the election or non-election of the individual Indians. Both converts and missionaries seem to see the very fact of the Great English Migration as a sufficient sign of God's special grace to the Indians.[53]

A stricter Puritanism, say of the sort that Roger Williams practiced, required that those who would convert do so completely because of the grace of God acting on their individual souls. But even Puritans who were considerably less strict than Williams, would have had trouble with Eliot's apparent Arminianism.[54] While I would agree with Holstun's assessment of the Indian tracts, it is not a simple matter to dismiss Eliot's approach to missionary work or conversion as unmitigated Arminianism. As Edmund Morgan points out, Eliot was not exactly consistent on this point. In some letters to Richard Baxter, Eliot "advocated admitting everyone to the privileges of the church." His practice, however, in New England showed no evidence of such a sentiment.[55] Moreover, in other places in the Eliot–Baxter correspondence, we find that Eliot is far more stringent on the issue of baptism than Baxter. In response to Eliot's separation of the Covenant of Grace from the Baptismal Covenant, Baxter's response is dismay: "While I highly honour yr person, I confesse I read yr words with admiration [i.e., amazement] as speaking very strange doctrine to me (wch. I must gladly tell you ye congregationall men here, of chiefe name, are utterly against and are wholly of my mind)."[56]

To be sure, Eliot's positions on doctrinal questions are relevant here. But I would suggest that even more to the point is the role that the Indian conversions played in the Bay Colony's culture at large. Few people offered vocal opposition to the project of converting the Indians.[57] But the status of Indians spoke directly to the issue of the Half-Way Covenant and infant baptism. Increase Mather, for example, after he had transformed himself into a supporter of the Half-Way Covenant, used the status of the Indians to buttress his arguments.

Have we for our poor Childrens sake in special, left a dear and pleasant Land, and ventured our Lives upon the great waters, and encountred with the difficulties and miseries of a wilderness, and doth it at last come to this, that they have no more Advantage as to any *Church care* about them, then the *Indians* and *Infidels* amongst whom we live?[58]

Thus the Half-Way Covenant became, in a sense, another way of demonstrating God's favor. After all, if the Puritans of the Bay Colony were not specially chosen by God, then there would be no reason for them to expect special treatment for their children. Conversely, however, if they were chosen, then it would be wrong for them to give their children "no more Advantage" than the Indians. The Indians' role in such an argument is not insignificant: their existence provides the Puritans with a ready justification for treating their own children differently.

Using the Indians once again as an example, Mather lights upon what he views as the ultimate absurdity of those opposed to the infant baptism of church members who merely owned the covenant.[59] Taken to its logical extreme, this position would yield the bizarre phenomenon of churches without any baptized members.

Finally, if membership in the particular (strictly taken) or Instituted Church be necessarily required before Baptisme, it will then follow, that an Instituted Church may (and in some Cases ought to) Consist of none but unbaptized persons. Suppose a Company of Indians should be Converted to the Faith of Christ; according to this notion, they must first of all be formed into an Instituted Church and then baptized, so there is an Instituted Church, and not one baptized member in all the Church. A thing never known in Apostolical dayes.[60]

Apparently, Mather is here ignoring what was the accepted practice in Indian conversions, not to mention the position of his father.[61] Eliot's own adherence to the notion that Mather ridicules in this passage is well known. In his Indian tracts, Eliot documents the various steps that the Indians must take before they are baptized.[62] And given Eliot's explicit intention of forming his praying Indians into congregations separate from the English, the situation that Mather describes above is all but unavoidable.

If, as Edmund Morgan has argued, the "Half-Way" crisis in part resulted from a "tangle of problems created in time by human reproduction," we must not overlook that tangle of problems created by the Indian conversions.[63] Eliot's praying Indians, in addition to requesting land for their praying towns, threatened to outdo the Puritans in their godliness. But just as importantly, the Indian conversions, as Increase Mather (perhaps inadvertently) pointed out in the above passage, posed a serious challenge to the logic of Puritan covenant theology. The work of converting the Indians forced the Puritans to reconsider their positions on a range of issues pertaining to apparently unrelated internal church polity. Thus Eliot's *Indian Dialogues* participate directly in the debates that raged over such questions as infant baptism and church membership. By aggressively confronting the most sensitive issues of his day, Eliot tries to argue for the urgency and importance of his own project.

SLEEPING IN FEAR; SWIMMING IN LOVE

If the *Indian Dialogues* represent a dramatic shift away from Eliot's earlier preoccupation with his supporters in England, they resolutely reaffirm the power of fear and love in the making of English colonial identity. In fact, in each of the four dialogues, the climax occurs in language that suggests that, through the conversion process, the Indians will learn the proper display of the emotions of fear and love. Moreover, in addition to depicting the conversion as inevitably involving fear, the dialogues also suggest that self-loathing forms a crucial component in an Indian conversion. As Neal Salisbury comments, the Puritan mission program "was directed against the individual and collective identity provided by tribal culture."[64] The point of the conversions was to isolate the Indians both individually and tribally – or at least that was the effect. James P. Ronda puts Salisbury's point in much bolder language: "The Indian who embraced Christianity was compelled in effect, to commit cultural suicide. He was required to renounce not only his own personal past, but that of his forefathers as well, forsaking – and despising – all traditional beliefs and practices."[65] Indeed each of the dialogues presents readers with a recognition that the Indians are aware of the fact that conversion means the complete renunciation of their pasts.

For the Massachusetts colonists contemplating the threat posed by increasingly hostile Indians, the prospect of those Indians expressing fear and love would have offered comfort. In addition, however, to demonstrating that the natives would not trouble the settlers, Eliot also showed that they were ready to be accepted into the church. In short, Eliot offers his readers proof that the former selves of these natives were indeed completely eradicated. I would suggest that Eliot's representations function in two ways. First, by representing the Indians as terrorized – as living in constant fear – Eliot is trying to minimize the threat that they posed to the English settlers. Moreover, he shows that the Indians are afraid not of the English, but rather of life without the English and their message of Christian hope. But perhaps even more startling in these representations is the fact that the Indians offer the Puritans a sincere portrayal of the proper attitude of a Puritan: self-loathing. In this sense, the dialogues offer readers, many of whom have never had a conversion experience, a powerful representation of penitent converts coming at Christianity afresh. While there is certainly a racial edge to Eliot's depictions of self-loathing, the self-loathing was in fact an important part of the conversion process. That is, Eliot's newly converted Indians subtly remind his readers that they are in fact supposed to loathe the pre-conversion self. Hence Eliot's depictions of fear and self-loathing are intended as allegorical representations both of the proper Puritan conversion process and, more generally, of his vision of how Puritan congregations should function.

Departing from previous representations of Indians fearing and loving English settlers, Eliot instead offers his readers Indians who fear God and loathe themselves. In other words, Eliot shows us the Indians as inhabiting precisely the structure of belief that the Puritans were supposed to inhabit. In this sense, Eliot's *Dialogues* share a good deal with the Jeremiad literature that achieved a particularly shrill tone after the restoration. Eliot attempts, therefore, to focus his readers' attention on this side of the Atlantic by suggesting that his praying Indians are behaving precisely as the Puritans were supposed to behave. Insofar as it is the Indians who model the appropriate self-loathing attitude that the Jeremiads attempted to encourage, Eliot's *Dialogues* function, not as a conversion manual for the Indians, but as a powerful corrective for his own fellow colonists who have lost their way. Accordingly, in the first dialogue, the converted Indian Piumbukhou describes to his unconverted kinsman the considerable benefits of converting to Christianity.

And by faith in God's protection we sleep quietly without fear, whereas you that do not pray, nor believe, nor commit your selves to God, you do always sleep in fear and terror.[66]

As is consistent in Eliot's *Dialogues*, the condition of living in fear is the lot of the unconverted. The world that Eliot imagines, therefore, is a world where there is no more need for fear. The Indians themselves will no longer sleep in fear because they will know they are protected by God. And the English will no longer fear the Indians, because the Indians will be united with them.

The kinsman's response to Piumbukhou's description of a life without fear follows the pattern that Eliot will use throughout the *Dialogues*. The kinsman comes to the realization that he will have to renounce everything in his life if he is to realize the life without fear that Piumbukhou describes.

KINSMAN. I feel my heart broken and divided. I know not what to do. To part with our former lusts and pleasures is an hard point and I feel my heart very loth and backward to it. Many objections against it. I cannot but confess, that I do not in my inward heart approve of them. I know they are vile and filthy, and I desire to forsake them. They are like burning coals in my bosom. I will shake them out if I can. I am ashamed of my old ways, and loth I am to keep that which I am ashamed to be seen in... But the greatest difficulty that I yet find, is this. I am loth to divide myself from my friends and kindred. If I should change my course and not they, then I must leave and forsake their company, which I am very loth to do. I love my sachem, and all the rest of you my good friends. If I should change my life and way, I greatly desire that we might agree to do it together.[67]

After accepting Piumbukhou's teaching, the kinsman, whose feelings of shame and self-loathing literally divide his heart, begins to revile himself. Significantly, in strategically offering his readers the possibility that Indians such as this one might convert with others, Eliot reminds us that the process of conversion is properly conducted within the context of a social transformation. In suggesting that this kinsman will convert with his fellow Indians, Eliot offers his readers a model for a similar kind of communal reaffirmation of faith among his fellow colonists.

The second dialogue offers us a similar series of moments. Waban, who encounters a penitent Indian on the way to visit his uncle, manages to convince the Penitent to convert and live by God's commandments.

PEN. This little sight and experience I have hath so filled my heart with a sense of my own vileness, that I see matter of endless confession. And I see so much nothingness in my self that I see endless matter of petition and supplication. And I see my self infinitely obliged to God for the riches of his free grace to me a rebellious work, that I see infinite matter of praise, thanksgiving and admiration.[68]

Like the unnamed kinsman in the first dialogue, the Penitent is overcome with a sense of his own vileness. In fact, he is overcome to such a degree that he can only see nothingness in himself – the perception of which is of course already a sign that he has begun to embrace the ways of Christ. After he has made his own self-loathing pronouncements, the Penitent describes the fear that he feels, and Waban responds:

PEN. Your words do put a fear into my heart. I know that old customs of sin are very hardly left, and I have been so long accustomed to sin, that I am afraid of my self.
WABAN. Fear is a good watchman: *happy is the man that feareth always*.[69]

The Penitent has become so thoroughly self-loathing that he cannot escape the fear of the self. In other words, the Penitent has embraced the ways of the English to such an extent that he cannot any longer live without fearing what he once was. Insofar as being English is constituted by a fear of the Indians, the Penitent has turned English. The Indians who convert will therefore always live in fear, and as Waban says, "Fear is a good watchman." Eliot seems to suggest here that the process of conversion, because it will leave the Indians fearing themselves, will also leave them in a permanently submissive posture.

Near the end of his dialogue with the two praying Indians, Philip signals a similar readiness to submit both to the English and to the Lord. Like the other Indians in the *Dialogues* who have preceded him, Philip describes his own conversion process in terms of self-loathing.

> KEIT. Who can oppose or gainsay the mountainous weight of these arguments? I am more than satisfied. I am ashamed of my ignorance, and I abhor myself that I ever doubted of this point. And I desire wholly to give myself to the knowledge of, and obedience to the Word of God, and to abandon and forsake these sins which the Word of God reproveth and condemneth.[70]

Like the other Indians, Philip abhors himself, but that self-abhorrence turns out to be a function of the love shown to him by the Christian Indians.

> KEIT. Words that come swimming in love, with the full sails of wisdom, have great power to calm heart storms of grief and trouble. I now find it true. My soul is wounded for my sin in profaning the sabbath day. Now I desire to look deeper into the matter. I desire you would open unto me the sabbath, that I may know my former sins, and further duty.[71]

In a sense, Eliot offers here another version of the formula of colonialism we discussed in chapter 4. Here, however, instead of suggesting that the English settlers will exchange spiritual commodities for material ones, Eliot suggests that the spiritual discourses of the Puritans will offer the Indians psychological comfort.

In the fourth and final dialogue, the praying Indian John confronts another penitent Indian who by now follows the familiar pattern of fear followed by self-loathing. As the Penitent contemplates his past, his "outward condition is full of affliction." He feels an overwhelming fear. John responds by reassuring him that the fear is to be expected and desired.

JOHN. This is a wholesome fear, and you shall find it will end well. My counsel is, mingle hope with your fear, viz. that God doth outwardly afflict you, that he might drive your distressed soul into the bosom of Jesus Christ, who will graciously pardon all your sins, and save your soul from those eternal flames, which you so much dread.[72]

Echoing Waban's pronouncement of the utility of fear, John suggests that the fear is really desirable for it is this fear that will keep the Penitent mindful both of what he has done with his past and of God's commandments. A couple of pages later, following the pattern of the other Indians, the Penitent has moved from fear to self-loathing.

PENIT. . . .It is sometimes a quieting argument to my heart, to be patient under my outward crosses, because they be mustard on the world's nipples, to keep me from surfeiting upon the creature. If I look into the glass of God's law, and behold the face of my life, and of my soul, as they are there represented, I am afraid of myself. I abhor my self. I am confounded. God's sabbaths have I profaned; God's work I have neglected; God's grace I have despised and resisted. I have broken the whole law of God. Every command have I violated.[73]

Like Waban's penitent Indian, this penitent finds that his conversion experience has left him fearing himself. And beyond that, he abhors the self that he once was.

Perhaps the most startling expression of self-loathing in the *Dialogues* comes at the very end of the discussion between John and the penitent Indian. As he re-iterates his rejection of his former self, the penitent gives readers a sense of what the ultimate purpose of the dialogues might have been.

PENIT. My dearest friend, God hath made you an instrument in his hand to lay before me unspeakable consolation. And I cannot deny but I feel it in my heart. I am another man than I was. I looked upon my self the most miserable of men. I now am happy being united with Christ. O blessed change! I am in admiration at this. I admire the Grace of God to a dead, lost, damned sinner. I am come into a new world. I have other desire than I had, and other purposes. I see things in another frame than I was want to see them. I must live a new life and steer a new course.[74]

One cannot help but read this passage and wonder whether, by offering his readers Indians who have "come into a new world" and now "have other desire," Eliot wasn't suggesting that his project of converting the Indians would function similarly to the Great Migration earlier in the century. In describing the conversion of the Indians, Eliot hopes to give the Puritans a new way of re-imagining their own declining culture. The allegory of the *Indian Dialogues,* therefore, consists in its explicit linking of the narratives of Indian conversion and Puritan reform. Through the peaceful process of converting the Indians to Christianity, Eliot hopes to be able to do the more important work of re-converting his colonial brethren. The narrative of the conversion of the Indians, in other words, functions for Eliot as an allegorical one that will reinvigorate Protestantism and give it a new sense of purpose.

Coda

And as the moon rose higher the inessential houses began
to melt away until gradually I became aware of the old island
here that flowered once for Dutch sailors' eyes – a fresh,
green breast of the new world. Its vanished trees, the trees
that had made way for Gatsby's house, had once pandered in
whispers to the last and greatest of all human dreams; for a
transitory enchanted moment man must have held his breath
in the presence of this continent, compelled into an aesthetic
contemplation he neither understood nor desired, face to face
for the last time in history with something commensurate to
his capacity for wonder.

And as I sat there, brooding on the old unknown world, I
thought of Gatsby's wonder when he first picked out the green
light at the end of Daisy's dock. He had come a long way to
this blue lawn and his dream must have seemed so close that
he could hardly fail to grasp it. He did not know that it was
already behind him, somewhere back in that vast obscurity
beyond the city, where the dark fields of the republic rolled
on under the night.

Gatsby believed in the green light, the orgiastic future that
year by year recedes before us. It eluded us then, but that's
no matter – tomorrow we will run faster, stretch our arms
farther. . . And one fine morning –

So we beat on, boats against the current, borne back cease-
lessly into the past.

F. Scott Fitzgerald, *The Great Gatsby*

I have chosen to end this book about colonial writing with the
concluding reveries of Nick Carraway, the narrator of *The Great
Gatsby*, because they provide us with something in the way of a
cautionary tale about the uses and abuses of the colonial moment.
In other words, I end with *Gatsby*, not to suggest that all colonial
writing, and in turn all colonial studies, lead inevitably to an

American national identity. In fact, I cite *Gatsby* as an eloquent example of the dangers of assuming as Nick does, that the colonial period was characterized by the sort of sureness that his poetic conclusion seems to assume. In a sense this book has been nothing more than an extended plea for a re-examination of some of the fundamental assumptions that govern our studies of the colonial period. If the texts we have examined lead inevitably to Gatsby, they do so only by offering readers an earlier version of the uncertainties and self-doubt that surround the construction of an identity. That is to say, these texts show that the colonial moment is much more accurately characterized by that experience of a "future that year by year recedes" before those who are trying desperately to grasp it, than it is by some fanciful notion, albeit "transitory" and "enchanted," of "aesthetic contemplation" and "wonder."

If, in its particulars, the structure that Nick delineates is a modern one, we must also understand that it is similar to the one occupied by European colonizers attempting to grasp their own dreams. Therefore, we must also recognize that Nick is mistaken to assume that the men and women who ventured to the New World were any more successful in achieving that moment of "aesthetic contemplation" than he or his contemporaries have been. That moment, filled with transcendence and emptied of uncertainty, eluded the colonizers just as it would later elude Nick. And like Nick, the colonizers found themselves attempting to describe experiences that always seemed to promise more than they could deliver.

For Nick, whose own world is shaped by a devastating sense of loss – most poignantly illustrated by the death of Gatsby himself – the temptation to look to the past for coherence and meaning is almost overwhelming. Nick therefore constructs a fiction. And, insofar as it offers him a representation of a parallel world marked by the fulfillment of some ultimate – almost inarticulable – desire, that fiction could be said to be an allegory. In other words, embodied in the relationship between Nick and the Dutch sailors, whom he believes held "their breath in the presence of this continent," is another version of that allegorical structure we have been examining here. To recognize this, it seems to me, is to acknowledge the perils inherent in any exploration of the past that seeks to find what the present lacks or demands.

Implicit in the preceding chapters has been my insistence that we resist the temptation to construct fictions of the colonial period that are driven, in one way or another, by our present needs. Indeed, my critique of earlier American Studies narratives was precisely that they were driven by the need to discover in the colonial period something resembling the seeds of the later incarnation of the "American Self". The authors of these narratives, because they did not scrutinize the status of *English* identity during the period of colonization, were unable to recognize the fragility of the very identity against which they supposed the colonists were able to define and construct their *American* identity. In other words, they committed an error not unlike that committed by Nick Carroway at the end of *The Great Gatsby*.

To caution against the writing of history that too readily conforms to the demands of the present does not, it seems to me, prevent me from looking beyond 1671, the declared endpoint of this study. The writings we have examined in this study do indeed show a steady progression away from concerns with specifically English national identity and toward an independent colonial identity. This progression would only accelerate in the waning years of the seventeenth century and early years of the eighteenth. I would suspect that this increasingly independent strain was as much a function of the growth of the printing industry in the colonies, as it was the result of any single political or ideological development. We might get at this fact by asking two simple questions: Would Roger Williams have written his *A Key to the Language of America* in the same way if he were writing for a colonial audience rather than a metropolitan one? I think not. Would John Eliot have written his *Indian Dialogues* in the same way if he knew that the majority of his readers would be Londoners rather than Bostonians? Again, I think not. To ask these questions is not to say that a writer's audience determines everything. But when one is dealing with allegories, as I have argued these texts to be, the question of an assumed readership is extremely important.

Although my study suggests a trend, I would be hesitant to posit a date or to suggest a particular text that marks the moment when we can begin to talk about a specifically American identity. In fact, the usefulness of such pronouncements has always escaped me. What I would prefer to do instead is to suggest that the subsequent colonial experience would always be inflected by its

English antecedents, even long after the point when an American identity can be said to have materialized. Moreover, I would suggest that the ways in which early English colonizers struggled with notions of identity were not significantly different from the ways later American colonists would grapple with the same questions, albeit in different terms. If this study has anything to say about later periods of colonial history or of American history, therefore, it has as much to do with the process of identity formation itself as it does with the specific features of that formation during the colonial period. To be sure, one can discern in the self-contradictory determination, on the part of the English, to encourage the native inhabitants to fear and love them, the origins of a subsequent American ambivalence toward native others. The specific historical outlines of such an ambivalence, however, would need to be carefully traced out, lest we commit another anachronism. But that is a story, the telling of which, I will leave to another time.

Notes

INTRODUCTION

1 See Tom Conley, "DeBry's Las Casas," *Amerindian Images and the Legacy of Columbus*, ed. Rene Jara and Nicholas Spadaccini, Hispanic Issues (Minneapolis: University of Minnesota Press, 1992), 103–31. Also see Bernadette Bucher, *Icon and Conquest: A Structural Analysis of the Illustrations of de Bry's Great Voyages*, trans. Basia Miller Gulati (Chicago: University of Chicago Press, 1981), 10.

2 The most prominent instance of this tendency is to be found in Stephen Greenblatt's *Marvelous Possessions: The Wonder of the New World* (Chicago: University of Chicago Press, 1991). According to Greenblatt, wonder is "the central figure in the initial European response to the New World, the decisive emotional and intellectual experience in the presence of radical difference" (14). While I would not dispute his contention that wonder is present in many of the European narratives of New World experiences, I would suggest that Greenblatt's argument is significantly weakened by his persistent refusal to acknowledge (among others) the fundamental differences between Catholic and Protestant encounters with the New World. In other words, Greenblatt seems unwilling to historicize "wonder," and transform it into a term with historical and cultural depth. In a provocative argument that presents a different set of problems for scholars of the colonial period, Roland Greene argues that the outlines of the structure of colonial desire can be discerned within Petrarchanism itself. According to Greene, "If early modern Petrarchanism was widely understood as an internationally sanctioned medium for the deliberation of both kinds of issues – if, in fact, its usages were taken to indicate that sixteenth-century poets, explorers, and readers knew these as in effect the same issues of desire, conquest, and exploitation – then imperialist discourse would seem to emerge through many more openings than recent work on colonial history, law, and politics has found for it (242). See "The Colonial Wyatt: Contexts and Openings," *Rethinking the Henrician Era: Essays on Early Tudor Texts and Contexts*, ed. Peter C. Herman (Urbana: University of Illinois

Press, 1994), 240–66. While Greene's essay presents readers with a refreshingly new way to read Wyatt and other renaissance writers, I would be reluctant to subsume the notion of colonial desire under the heading of Petrarchanism.

3 See Stephen Slemon, "Post-Colonial Allegory and the Transformation of History," *Journal of Commonwealth Literature*, 23, no. 1 (1988): 162.

THE ALLEGORICAL STRUCTURE OF COLONIAL DESIRE

1 For useful introductory and biographical material on Las Casas, as well as the original Spanish version of the *Brevíssima relación*, see the modern Spanish edition of his works, *Tratados de Fray Bartolomé de Las Casas* (Mexico City: Biblioteca Americana, 1965).

2 See Perry Miller, *The New England Mind: The Seventeenth Century* (Cambridge, MA: Harvard University Press, 1939). Miller traces the "intellectual content of Puritanism. . .to four principal sources. One was European Protestantism, the reinterpretation of the whole Christian tradition effected by the reformers. Secondly, because at the time of the settlement of New England Protestantism was already undergoing transformations, we must consider certain peculiarly seventeenth-century preoccupations and interests. Thirdly, there was humanism, the stimulus and the challenge of the revived learning and the still fresh discovery of classical culture. Fourthly, there was the all-pervading influence of medieval scholasticism, as yet unchallenged within Puritan hearing by the new physics and the mathematical method. There were other sources of lesser importance, as will appear in the course of our narrative, but these were the four quarries from which the Puritan scholars carved out their principal ideas and doctrines" (92).

3 See Perry Miller, *Errand into the Wilderness,* Cambridge, MA: Harvard University Press, 1956, 6.

4 On this point see Miller, *The New England Mind: From Colony to Province* (Cambridge: Harvard University Press, 1953), 20–3.

5 Roy Harvey Pearce, *The Savages of America, a Study of the Indian and the Idea of Civilization* (Baltimore: Johns Hopkins University Press, 1953), 25.

6 Francis Jennings suggested that the European voyages to America were nothing short of an invasion, an outgrowth of a "crusader ideology" that had evolved in Europe during the Middle Ages and Renaissance. In the specific instance of the English settlement of New England, Jennings characterized the Puritan efforts to control the Indians as "conquests" that ended ultimately in the decimation of the native population. Although very little of Jennings's evidence was new, what was new was his assumption that Puritan behavior could

be the subject of an almost derisive critique. According to Jennings, "Traditional histories tell a different tale that need not be repeated here. The novelty of my findings derives, I believe, from unorthodox assumptions about persons and a critical attitude toward the evidence of familiar sources. In contrast with traditional assumptions that Puritans possessed the humanity implied by civilization while Indians lacked it, I have assumed that both Indians and Puritans were neither more nor less than human" (180). Jennings was also characteristically contentious in admitting his biases: "it seems fair to say, I have recognized in myself a strong aversion toward the Puritan gentry and have tried to compensate for it by documenting heavily from their own writings whenever possible. It may be well to notice that I have tried to practice restraint but not concealment of my distaste, and to say further that it was acquired in the course of the research. I started the study with pervasive skepticism and busy curiosity, and my present biases are largely the result of wrestling with the Puritan gentry's own writings to extract bits of reliable data from excruciating cant and masterful guile. Those who can swallow the cant, of course, will find it neither painful nor guileful, but they have an obligation to take into account the bits of data" (185). See Francis Jennings, *The Invasion of America: Indians, Colonialism, and the Cant of Conquest* (Chapel Hill: University of North Carolina Press, 1975).

7 In a departure from Jennings's polemical style, several historians have attempted to argue for the complexity of the colonial encounter and, as a result, have produced accounts that focus on events other than wars and battles. James Axtell, for instance, encourages students of the period to think of the encounter between Indians and white settlers in terms other than those of explicit invasion. He says, "Despite a few famous outbreaks of armed aggression, especially during the intercolonial wars of the eighteenth century, the conquest of North America was fought largely in times of declared peace, with weapons other than flintlocks and tomahawks." See his *The Invasion Within: The Contest of Cultures in Colonial North America* (New York: Oxford University Press, 1985), 4. Karen Ordahl Kuperman also took exception to those historical accounts that characterized the English attitude toward the Indians as one of "contemptuous dismissal," and instead argued "that neither savagery nor race was the important category for Englishmen looking at Indians" (2). In Kuperman's analysis, the English attitude toward the Indians differed very little from their attitude toward other cultures. And after a detailed examination of the way that the English represented their encounters with the Indians, Kupperman was able to assert that, "The really important category was status" (86). After carefully examining the ethnographic record, Kupperman was able to conclude

that the English "were consciously describing another society, one which was strikingly different from their own, but which was understandable and recognizable as a society by their own definition" (105). And instead of discovering widespread revilement of Indian culture and customs, Kupperman found that the English often expressed their admiration for Indian ways and recognized "that the Indians were better adapted to life in America than the English were" (104). Ultimately, Kupperman determined that the study of Anglo-Indian relations would also have to include consideration of the English perceptions of themselves and of other European cultures as well: "If we are really to understand how the English viewed the Indians, then we must not only analyze the way they described the Indians, but also how they saw their own culture and their fellow Europeans" (114). In the end, Kupperman rejects the notion that racism drove the early English colonial efforts, but does not rule it out for the subsequent colonial engagement: "It was the effect of unrestricted power, not preconceived racism, which caused the English to treat the American Indians as they did. If, in the period after 1640, the American Indians were the subjects of racism by English people, the conclusion must be that this racism was a product of, not the cause of, the treatment of Indians by colonists" (188). See her *Settling with the Indians: The Meeting of English and Indian Cultures in America, 1580–1640* (Totowa, NJ: Rowman and Littlefield, 1980). Implicitly extending the conclusions of Kupperman's study, Neal Salisbury suggested that we consider Europe's colonial expansion in the context of the social and economic forces that were producing dramatic changes in the Old World and rendering the colonial project so urgent in the first place. "In the final analysis," Salisbury argued, "it was not simply the manifest differences between Indians and Europeans that explain the conquest but rather the unprecedented economic and social revolution that had begun to transform parts of Western Europe, particularly England, and was now spreading to North America" (12). It would be a mistake, in Salisbury's view, to characterize the encounter between the English and the native populations exclusively as a clash of cultures that was almost inevitably bound to result in the destruction of one of them. Therefore, instead of constructing the encounter in explicitly ideological or racial terms, Salisbury devotes most of his study to an exploration of the subtle economic and social changes that the arrival of the English set in motion. For instance, Salisbury describes the Indians as a "reciprocating" society, meaning that they viewed the exchange of goods as a means of keeping the world in balance. The English, on the other hand, were "non-reciprocating." That is, they viewed the exchange of goods as a means of accumulating wealth. According to Salisbury, the Indian acceptance of the English attitudes led to a specialization that ultimately created an economic structure in which they were dependant on the English. See pp. 49–58. In a similar sort of analysis, Salisbury suggests that the Great Migration of the 1630's exported to New England many of the same forces that were transforming English agriculture, namely industrialization and consolidation. Just as the English arrival led to the dissolution of the Indian system of "reciprocity" so too did the English attitudes toward the land change the ways that the Indians farmed and lived off the land. See pp. 166 ff. See his *Manitou and Providence: Indians, Europeans, and the Making of New England, 1500–1643* (New York: Oxford University Press, 1982).

8 I am not forgetting here either Douglas Leach's *Flintlock and Tomahawk: New England in King Philip's War* (New York: Macmillan, 1958) or Alden Vaughan's *New England Frontier, Puritans and Indians 1620–1675* (Boston: Little Brown, 1965), both of which were written before the 1970s. I would simply assert that both of these studies construct the confrontation between the Puritans and the Indians as a struggle between an advanced society and a primitive one. I would therefore endorse Neal Salisbury's claim that these studies "tended to perpetuate earlier assumptions that cultural differences explained the rapidity and relative ease of the English conquest." See *Manitou and Providence*, 5–6. One study that did attempt to tell a different story was Nancy Ostreich Lurie, "Indian Cultural Adjustment to European Civilization," *Sixteenth-Century America: Essays in Colonial History*, ed. James Morton (Chapel Hill: University of North Carolina Press, 1959), 33–60. Lurie presciently argued that there was a process of mutual accommodation between the Indians of Virginia and the English settlers: "Scientific knowledge of generally predictable group reactions thus suggests that the degree of ethnocentrism was probably equal on both sides of the contact between Indians and Europeans in Virginia. Recognition of the Indians's self-appraisal is necessary for a clear understanding of their basis of motivation and consequent behavior in relation to Europeans" (39).

9 Some scholars have even gone so far as to suggest that the history of contact between the English settlers and the natives actually determined the nature and shape of American culture. This would be Richard Slotkin's claim when he argued that, "Puritans came to define their relationship to the New World in terms of violence and warfare. Narratives of the Indian wars of New England became the first significant genre of New World writing and formed the literary basis of the first American mythology." See his *Regeneration Through Violence: The Mythology of the American Frontier 1600–1860* (Middletown, CT: Wesleyan University Press, 1973), 56. Slotkin's is just one of several studies that has used the colonial treatment of the Indians as a starting point for a discussion of racism and violence in subsequent American history. Richard Drinnon, for instance,

discovers in the colonial period what he calls a "functional racism" that would evolve and operate in American history until the present day. See his *Facing West, the Metaphysics of Indian-Hating and Empire-Building*, 1990 edn. (New York: Schocken, 1980), *passim* but especially chapters 4 and 5. Dana Nelson takes a slightly different approach. Arguing for a "sociological criticism of literature," Nelson examines colonial American literary representations of Native Americans and argues that, although they do not reveal a "concretized idea" of race, "the *situation* named by these various texts deals with what we now categorize as 'race': the arbitrary enforcement and institutionaliz-ation of Anglo superiority in United States history" (21). See *The Word in Black and White: Reading "Race" in American Literature, 1638–1867* (New York: Oxford University Press, 1992).

10 See Sacvan Bercovitch, *The Puritan Origins of the American Self* (New Haven: Yale University Press, 1975), 36–7.

11 In an earlier article, Bercovitch suggests that there are in fact two kinds of typological writing extant in the colonial period. His purpose was to revise Perry Miller's earlier claim that Roger Williams dis-tinguished himself from the Puritan orthodoxy in New England by indulging in typological thinking and writing. According to Miller, "typology had for centuries been a special subdivision of the allegori-cal." Typology, though, was rejected by Protestant reformers, includ-ing Luther and Calvin because, the "typological method along with every other variant of the allegorical," led to too capricious a reading of the scriptures. See Perry Miller, *Roger Williams: His Contribution to America* (New York: Atheneum, 1962), 34–5. Against Miller, Bercov-itch argues as follows: "In sum, the conflict stood between two views of typology, which might be called the allegorical and the historical modes. William stresses the spiritual progress of the Church, arguing that the meaning of the whole *Church* of *Israel, Roote* and *Branch*, from first to last. . . . [is] *figurative* and *allegorical.*" See Sacvan Bercovitch, "Typology in Puritan New England: The Williams-Cotton Contro-versy Reassessed," *American Quarterly*, 19 (1967) 175–6.

12 Thomas H. Luxon, *Literal Figures: Puritan Allegory and the Reformation Crisis in Representation* (Chicago: University of Chicago Press, 1995), 26. Luxon later concludes that the distinction between allegory and typology is at best problematic, and at worst untenable: "If the his-tory of ancient Israel was intended by God as an allegory, then of course reading it allegorically produces the literal sense God intended. Is this, then, what is meant by typology – a method that authorizes as literal and claims to make perfectly perspicuous to even 'the most ignorant person' meanings that might appear to many to be quite flagrant perversions, even inversions, of the text?" (96).

13 Angus Fletcher, *Allegory: The Theory of a Symbolic Mode* (Ithaca: Cornell University Press, 1964), 2.

14 In the most articulate recent argument for allegory as a genre, Maureen Quilligan stresses the importance of recognizing the generic aspects of allegory: "the class of works to which *The House of Fame, The Romance of the Rose,* and *The Crying of Lot 49* belong is a class of literature very much 'hung up with words' [quote is from Oedipa Maas]. This class is 'allegory,' and the argument of this book is that allegory is, in fact, a genre – a legitimate critical category of a prescriptive status similar to that of the generic term 'epic.'" Although I do not quarrel with Quilligan's readings of these texts, I would argue that the generic definition of allegory is unnecessarily limiting. See *The Language of Allegory: Defining the Genre* (Ithaca: Cornell University Press, 1992) 14.

15 Fletcher makes precisely this distinction in distinguishing his project from the earlier work of Edwin Honig: "Honig's book seems to me to be concerned chiefly with accounting for the *creative* aspects of allegory. Honig wants to show how allegory comes into being, what are the cultural determinants *from without.* My own approach, despite the chapter I devote to the psychoanalytic theory of allegory, is less genetic, and more formal. I am not so much concerned with individual authors or individual periods as with the form that any given allegory will be likely to present to a sophisticated reader, regardless of the ways by which it came into being." See Fletcher, *Allegory*, 12–13. For the relevant material in Honig, see his *Dark Conceit: The Making of Allegory* (Evanston: Northwestern University Press, 1959), 39–50.

16 In describing the difference between symbol and allegory Lewis says, "Symbolism is a mode of thought, but allegory is a mode of expression. It belongs to the form of poetry more than to its content" See C. S. Lewis, *The Allegory of Love* (New York: Oxford University Press, 1936), 48.

17 A compelling, if at times reluctant, case for the importance of allegory in all interpretive endeavors is to be found in E. D. Hirsch, Jr., "Transhistorical Intentions and the Persistence of Allegory," *New Literary History*, 25 (1994): 549–67. Basically Hirsch argues that allegory is indispensable in getting at intention, which is ultimately the foundation on which interpretation must rest. In this sense his article is an updated reiteration of his argument in his book *Validity and Interpretation.* Hirsch sets up two extremes. On the one hand, there are unbridled allegorists, for whom all interpretation is an allegorical operation severed from any notion of authorial intention. On the other, there are the strict originalists, who argue that only the author's original intention (as defined extremely literally) can regulate interpretation. Hirsch lays the problem out as follows: "Originalists need to realize that allegory is a *necessary* tool for interpreting all transoccasional writings, and that pure originalism risks turning

our written inheritance into a dead letter. But the risks go in both directions. While rejection of allegory leads to pure backward-pointing anachronism that deprives interpretation of present applicability, unconstrained allegory, or its fraternal twin anti-intentionalism, leads to pure forward-pointing anachronism that risks turning a literary work or the Constitution into a 'blank piece of paper"' (562).

18 According to Jameson, "The usefulness of Benjamin's analysis lies however in his insistence on a temporal distinction as well: the symbol is the instantaneous, the lyrical, the single moment in time; and this temporal limitation perhaps expresses the historical impossibility in the modern world for genuine reconciliation to endure in time, for it to be anything more than a lyrical, accidental present. Allegory is, on the contrary, the privileged mode of our own life in time, a clumsy deciphering of meaning from moment to moment, the painful attempt to restore a continuity to heterogeneous, disconnected instants." Allegory therefore becomes a mode that expresses the will toward reconciliation between object and spirit. In Marxist terms, symbol would seem to correspond to false-consciousness, insofar as the reconciliation it offers takes place outside of history. Allegory, on the other hand, expresses the desire for reconciliation in explicitly historical or temporal terms, and it simultaneously concludes by recognizing that such a desire is unattainable. See *Marxism and Form* (Princeton University Press, 1971), 71–2. It is important to note that the attribution of temporality to allegory is not exclusively a Marxist move. Paul deMan, in the context of a very different project from that of Jameson, arrives at essentially the same conclusion: "In the world of the symbol it would be possible for the image to coincide with the substance, since the substance and its representation do not differ in their being but only in their extension: they are part and whole of the same set of categories. Their relationship is one of simultaneity, which, in truth, is spatial in kind, and in which the intervention of time is merely a matter of contingency, whereas in the world of allegory, time is the originary constitutive category. . .it remains necessary, if there is to be allegory, that the allegorical sign refer to another sign that precedes it." See *Blindness and Insight* (Minneapolis: University of Minnesota Press, 1971; 1983), p. 206–7.

19 See Walter Benjamin, *The Origin of German Tragic Drama*, trans. John Osborne (London: Verso, 1977), 164–5.

20 *Ibid.*, p. 178.

21 As J. Hillis Miller has remarked, the preceding passage from Benjamin implies two different theories of the workings of time. The phrase "process of an eternal life" connotes what he calls the "Hegelian" theory of the workings of time, in which "nature, history, and

art are the process of an eternal life (*Prozess eines ewegen Lebens*). They move dialectically and harmoniously through better and better toward a goal which will be their absolute spiritualization, their vanishing or disembodiment in the fulfillment of a total meaning." In contrast to the Hegelian notion, Benjamin posits his own theory of how time functions on things. Miller continues, "In the other theory nature, history, and the work of art are inhabited by no such teleological spiritual drive. Their tendency is rather toward an irresistible decay. This decay has the effect of bringing into the open detached fragmentary bits of matter not transfigured by any totalizing idea. Nature, history, the artwork become body merely body, without soul, a dead body so to speak, as a ruined building is moving toward becoming a heap of rubble, without informing shape or wholeness, as if its ruination through time were to reveal what it has secretly been all along." The effects of such a process, Miller asserts, are "devastating." Allegory, therefore becomes a mode which operates as a repository of a process of decay. See "The Two Allegories," *Allegory, Myth, and Symbol*, ed. Morton W. Bloomfield (Cambridge, MA Harvard University Press, 1981), 363.

22 The term "manichean allegory" comes from Abdul Jan Mohamed's analysis of a later epoch of colonial writing in "The Economy of Manichean Allegory: The Function of Racial Difference in Colonialist Literature," *Critical Inquiry*, 12 (1985): 59–87. According to Jan Mohamed, colonialist discourse can best be understood through an examination of "its ideological function in relation to actual imperialist practices. Such an examination reveals that any evident 'ambivalence' is in fact a product of deliberate, if at times subconscious, imperialist duplicity, operating very efficiently through the economy of its central trope, the manichean allegory. This economy, in turn, is based on a transformation of racial difference into moral and even metaphysical difference. Though the phenomenological origins of this metonymic transformation may lie in the 'neutral' perception of physical difference (skin color, physical features, and such), its allegorical extensions come to dominate every facet of imperialist mentality" (61). It is not my purpose to offer a specific critique of Jan Mohamed's analysis here, but I feel it is important to emphasize the inappropriate fit between his notion of "manichean allegory" and the writings of early English colonization. In an argument that presents similar difficulties, Eric Cheyfitz sees in the colonial period the emergence of a dynamic that would characterize American attitudes toward the "other" into the twentieth century. According to Cheyfitz, eloquence, linguistically speaking, is the equivalent of technology. Therefore, since native populations will always lack that eloquence, they will lack the technology to master the world. The colonial enterprise, therefore, always begins with the colonizers depriving

another group of its language. Hence, "translation was, and still is, the central act of European colonization and imperialism in the Americas" (104). See *The Poetics of Imperialism: Translation and Coloniz-ation from "The Tempest" to "Tarzan"* (New York: Oxford University Press, 1991).

23 See Joel Fineman, "The Structure of Allegorical Desire," *Allegory and Representation*, ed. Stephen J. Greenblatt (Baltimore: Johns Hopkins University Press, 1981), 26–60. In suggesting that allegory could be described in psychoanalytic terms, Fineman follows Angus Fletcher, who had suggested something similar. Here's Fletcher: " Let us sup-pose then that the proper analogue to allegory is the *compulsive syn-drome*, which Freud himself had made parallel to religious behavior. One condition must be laid down: that we are not talking about the compulsive behavior of authors as men; we are talking about literary products which have this form, a form we can discern regardless of its causes, a form which for our purposes exists as a thing in itself. In each of the five areas we have mapped out – agency, imagery, action, causality, and theme – there should be some psychoanalytic clarification of the true nature of allegory" (286). Fletcher then goes on to connect the five areas to specific psychoanalytic terms as fol-lows: Agency (obsessional anxiety); Image (the *idée fixe*); Action (compulsive rituals); causality (magical practices); Theme (ambivalence in "antithetical primal words"). Fineman extends Flet-cher's observations as follows: "I therefore psychoanalytically assume that the movement of allegory, like the dreamwork, enacts a wish that determines its progress – and, of course, the dream-vision is a characteristic framing and opening device of allegory, a way of situat-ing allegory in the *mise en abyme* opened up by the cognate accusatives that dream a dream, or see a sight, or tell a tale. On the other hand, with this reference to psychoanalysis, I mean also to suggest that analysis itself, the critical response to allegory, rehearses the same wish and therefore embarks on the same pilgrimage, so that psycho-analysis, especially structural psychoanalysis, by which today we are obliged to mean Lacan, is not simply the analysis of, but the exten-sion and conclusion of, the classical allegorical tradition from which it derives – which is why psychoanalysis so readily assimilates the great archetypes of allegorical imagery into its discourse: the labyr-inths, the depths, the navels, the psychomachian hydraulics" (26–7).

24 Lacan lays out this particular feature in his essay, "The agency of the letter in the unconscious, or reason since Freud" in his *Ecrits: A Selection*, trans. Alan Sheridan (New York: Norton, 1977). According to Lacan, "One cannot go further along this line of thought than to demonstrate that no signification can be sustained other than by reference to another signification: in its extreme form this amounts to the proposition that there is no language (*langue*) in existence for

which there is any question of its inability to cover the whole field of the signified, it being an effort of its existence as a language (*langue*) that it necessarily answers all needs. . .it is in the chain of the signifier that the meaning 'insists' but that none of its elements 'consists' in the signification of which it is at the moment capable. . .We are forced, then, to accept the notion of an incessant sliding of the signified under the signifier. . ..What this structure of the signifying chain discloses is the possibility I have, precisely in so far as I have this language in common with other subjects, that is to say, in so far as it exists as a language, to use it in order to signify *something quite other than* what it says. This function of speech is more worth pointing out than that of "disguising the thought" (more often than not undefinable) of the subject; it is no less than the function of indicating the place of this subject in the search for the true" (150–5).

25 See Jacques Lacan, *The Four Fundamental Concepts of Psycho-analysis*, trans. Alan Sheridan (New York: Norton, 1978) 235.

26 According to Rose, "When the child asks something of its mother, that loss will persist over and above anything which she can possibly give, or say, in reply. Demand always 'bears on something other than the satisfaction which it calls for,' and each time the demand of the child is answered by the satisfaction of its needs, so this 'something other' is relegated to the place of its original impossibility. Lacan terms this 'desire'. It can be defined as the 'remainder' of the subject, something which is always left over, but which has no content as such. Desire functions much as the zero unit in the numerical chain – its place is both constitutive *and* empty. . . At the same time, 'identity' and 'wholeness' remain precisely at the level of fantasy. Subjects in language persist in their belief that somewhere there is a point of certainty, of knowledge and of truth. When the subject addresses its demand outside itself to another, this other becomes the fantasied place of just such a knowledge or certainty. Lacan calls this the Other – the site of language to which the speaking subject necessarily refers." See Juliet Mitchell and Jacqueline Rose, eds., *Feminine Sexuality: Jacques Lacan and the École Freudienne* (New York: Norton, 1982), 32.

27 See Homi Bhabha, *Location of Culture* (London: Routledge, 1994), 44–5.

28 Bhabha has in fact been criticized, unfairly I would suggest, for precisely this aspect of his work. See, for instance, Abdul Jan Mohamed's critique in "The Economy of Manichean Allegory." Here's Jan Mohamed: "While otherwise provocative and illuminating, his [Bhabha's] work rests on two assumptions – the unity of the 'colonial subject' and the 'ambivalence' of colonial discourse – that are inadequately problematized and, I feel, finally unwarranted and unacceptable. . . Bhabha's unexamined conflation allows him to

circumvent entirely the dense history of the material conflict between Europeans and natives and to focus on colonial discourse as if it existed in a vacuum. This move in turn permits him to fetishize what he calls 'colonial' discourse (that is, the discourse of the dominators *and* the dominated) and map its contradictions as the problematics of an 'ambivalence,' as 'indeterminacy,' that is somehow intrinisic to the authority of that discourse. By dismissing 'intentionalist' readings of such discourse as 'idealist' quests, Bhabha is able to privilege its 'ambivalence' and, thereby, to imply that its 'authority' is genuinely and innocently *confused*, unable to choose between two equally valid meanings and representations. To impute in this way, at this late date, and through the back door, an innocent or naive 'intention' to colonialist discourse is itself a naive act at best. Wittingly or otherwise, Bhabha's strategy serves the same ideological function as older, humanistic analyses: like Mahood, he represses the political history of colonialism, which is inevitably sedimented in its discourse" (59–60).

29 For the most complete discussion of the Aristotlean dimensions of this debate, see Anthony Pagden, *The Fall of Natural Man: The American Indian and the Origins of Comparative Ethnology* (Cambridge University Press, 1982), esp. ch. 3.

30 See Bartolomé de Las Casas, *The Spanish Colonie, Or Briefe Chronicle of the Acts and Gestes of the Spaniards in the West Indies, Called the Newe World* (London, 1583). The translator is identified on the title page only by the initials M. M. S. and then later in the text as James Aliggrodo. No explanation is given for this apparent discrepancy.

31 *Ibid.*

32 *Ibid.*

33 The full title of Phillips's translation is *The Tears of the Indians, Being an Historical and True Account of the Cruel Massacres and Slaughters of above Twenty Millions of innocent People; Committed by the Spaniards in the Islands of Hispaniola, Cuba, Jamaica, & c.* (London, 1656).

34 The engravings included in the 1656 translation of Las Casas are based on engravings from the third volume of Theodor DeBry's *America*, about which I will say more in the next chapter.

35 The quote is from *The Cleare Sun-shine of the Gospel Breaking forth upon the Indians in New England* (London, 1648); *Collections of the Massachusetts Historical Society*, 3rd series, 4 (1834): 60. See also *Tears of Repentance: Or, a Further Narrative of the Progress of the Gospel amongst the Indians in New England* (London, 1653); *Collections of the Massachusetts Historical Society*, 3rd series, 4 (1834).

36 See Ola Elizabeth Winslow, *John Eliot "Apostle to the Indians"* (Boston: Houghton Mifflin, 1968) 79 ff.

37 Las Casas, *The Tears of the Indians*.

38 *Ibid.*

39 See, for instance, John Underhill, *Newes From America. . . Containing a True Relation of Their War-like Proceedings These Two Years Last Past* (London, 1638); see also Edward Johnson, *Wonder-working Providence* (London, 1653) 111. For a contemporary account of the Pequot war, see Richard Drinnon, *Facing West,* 35–45. As an interesting sidenote to my discussion here, Drinnon observes that the two English protagonists in the Pequot War, John Mason and John Endicott, had served in the Dutch Netherlands.

40 Las Casas, *The Tears of the Indians.*

41 See Arthur Percival Newton, *The Colonising Activities of the English Puritans* (New Haven: Yale University Press, 1914) 3–20 ff. See also J. Leitch Wright, Jr. *Anglo-Spanish Rivalry in North America* (Athens: University of Georgia Press, 1971) 44ff.

42 See Richard Hakluyt, "Discourse of Western Planting" in *The Original Writings of the Two Richard Hakluyts,* 2nd series (London: The Hakluyt Society, 1935), *passim* but especially 234–5.

43 See D. B. Quinn and A. M. Quinn, "A Hakluyt Chronology" in *The Hakluyt Handbook*, ed. D. B. Quinn, vol. 1 (London: The Hakluyt Society, 1974), 284.

44 Hakluyt argued as follows: "Besides this in our way as wee passe to and froe wee shall have in tempestes and other necessities the portes of Ireland to our aide and no nerer coaste of any enemye. Moreover by the ordinary entercourse wee may annoye the enemyes to Ireland and succour the Queenes Majesties faithfull subjects, and drawe the Irishe by little and little to more civilitie, and in shorte tyme wee may yelde them from the coastes of America whatsoever commodities they nowe receave at the handes of the Spaniardes." See "Discourse of Western Planting", 267.

45 Nicholas Canny, *The Elizabethan Conquest of Ireland: A Pattern Established, 1565–76* (London: Harvester Press, 1976), 60ff. Canny also suggests that Sidney may have gotten some of his ideas about supporting colonial projects while he served as Mary's emissary in Spain, although he insists that such links between Sidney and Spain are merely speculative.

46 See *ibid.,* 85ff. He notes that joint stock had been used in trading ventures, but never a colonization project.

47 For a complete account of the development of the joint-stock company, see W. R. Scott, *The Constitution and Finance of English, Scottish and Irish Joint-Stock Companies to 1720* (Cambridge University Press, 1912), 3 vols. See esp. vol. 1, 86 ff. and 440–1.

48 *Ibid.,* vol. 1, 48–9.

49 See Hakluyt, "Discourse of Western Planting", 217. The idea of exporting religious dissent would, of course, gain widespread acceptance in colonial operations of the next century. So too would the notion of combining colonial adventure with missionary work, an issue that I take up at some length in later chapters.

50 See *ibid.*, 234–5.
51 See *ibid.*, 257.
52 See Richard Helgerson, *Forms of Nationhood: The Elizabethan Writing of England* (University of Chicago Press, 1992), 4.
53 See Claire McEachern, *The Poetics of English Nationhood, 1590–1612* (Cambridge University Press, 1996), 6.
54 This was of course the view put forth by Perry Miller as he attempted to locate the origins of American identity in the colonial period. Miller argued as follows: "In England the party was never able to formulate the grounds for unanimity, because divergences within the ranks grew apace, and political triumph signalized the beginnings of intellectual disintegration... The writings of New England divines do not set forth its every aspect in full detail, but omissions may be supplied from the works they studied or endorsed. Puritanism in New England can be isolated for the purposes of study as Puritanism in England cannot be." For Miller, who was writing as American Studies was just beginning to take shape as a discipline, the task was to demontrate that the American self constituted a legitimate object of study. And the origins of that self were to be found in the hitherto neglected writings of the Puritans. Rather than finding in the Puritans all that had come to seem antithetical to what was generally considered American, Miller found in the Puritans precisely the consistency and "unanimity" that would support the claim that the American self could be traced back to the colonial period. See *The New England Mind: The Seventeenth Century*, 91. Arguing against Miller, Sacvan Bercovitch suggested that it was precisely the fundamental lack of unanimity among the colonists that, paradoxically, forced them to define themselves and their communal project in such unambiguous terms. Such a deliberate act of self-definition, according to Bercovitch, was never necessary for the English, as they always knew who they were. Bercovitch puts it this way: "One way or another, that is, country, saint, and church reflected one another, in the definition of the colony. Each of the three identities was fundamental to the whole, but what most clearly radiated the special nature of the undertaking, its *somma luce*, was its christianographical locale. Sainthood and church-membership implied one another, and both implied the New England Way; the idea of America implied all three in the proper apocalyptic context, justified the non-separating congregational theocracy, expressed the relationship of England to New England, and assured the settlers of success. Christic selfhood was a tremendous barrier against the terrors of self-discovery, but, as the English saints were about to discover, it left the individual prey to the mutability of providence. The American Puritan self was a garden enclosed from the threat even of secular failure. In part, it was precisely the enormity of the threat that prompted the emigrants' extra-

ordinary definition of themselves. The English Protestant may have trembled at the uncertainty of his sainthood, but he knew, proudly, that he was an Englishman." See, *Puritan Origins of the American Self*, 101–2. While Englishmen may well have known with some degree of certainty that they were Englishmen in 1702 when Cotton Mather published his *Magnalia,* this was certainly not the case in the early years of the seventeenth century. Indeed, this is one of the most serious flaws in Bercovitch's otherwise brilliant analysis of Mather, namely that he collapses the seventeenth and eighteenth centuries. Part of what I will show in the pages ahead is precisely the fact that Englishmen writing in the early years of colonization did not know who they were. And more importantly, the colonial project constituted a self-conscious attempt to tackle these fundamental questions of English identity. For an alternative account of American exceptionalism, I refer readers to Jack P. Greene, who suggests that the problem with the American exceptionalist line of thinking lies not in the belief in exceptionalism *per se*, but in the belief that exceptionalism is an American phenomenon. See Jack P. Greene, *The Intellectual Construction of America* (Chapel Hill: University of North Carolina Press, 1993), esp. chs. 2 and 3.

55 See Liah Greenfeld, *Nationalism: Five Roads to Modernity* (Cambridge, MA: Harvard University Press, 1992), 51–3. According to Greenfeld, "The radical shift in attitude which was expressed in the application of the word 'nation' to a people, and which in more than one way signified the beginning of the modern era, was already under way in the 1530s. In the course of the sixteenth century this shift had affected a substantial segment of the English population, and by 1600, the existence in England of a national consciousness and identity, and as a result, of a new geo-political entity, a nation, was a fact. . . The evolution of the national consciousness was reflected in the changing vocabulary. In the period between 1500 and 1650 several crucial concepts altered their meaning and came into general use. These concepts were 'country,' 'commonwealth,' 'empire,' and 'nation.' The changes in meaning were concentrated in the sixteenth century. The four words became understood as synonyms, acquiring the sense which, with slight alterations, they retained later, but which differed from their separate meanings before" (30–1).

56 See *ibid.*, 63.

57 See Linda Colley, *Britons: Forging the Nation 1707–1837* (New Haven: Yale University Press, 1992), 54. As her usage of the term "Great Britain" suggests, Colley is dealing with the development of national identity during the eighteenth century. Nonetheless, I would contend that many of her claims hold true for the earlier period as well. In particular, her chapter on Protestantism seems to provide a very useful framework for anyone interested in exploring the relationship

between England's struggles with its Roman Catholic neighbors and its ongoing attempt to declare itself unequivocally Protestant.

58 See Robert Berkhofer, Jr., *The White Man's Indian: Images of the American Indian from Columbus to the Present* (New York: Knopf, 1978), 23.

59 See Robert A. Williams, *The American Indian in Western Legal Thought: The Discourses of Conquest* (New York: Oxford University Press, 1990), 185. Williams also suggests that the emergence of a coherent national and religious identity must be seen in the context of the economic aspects of colonialism: "In Discovery-era England particularly, the Reformation worked perhaps the most profound transformations throughout all discursive domains of society, redefining and crystallizing a vision of national identity and destiny. The West's most potent, aggressive will to empire emerged from the convergence of radical Protestantism's consuming rivalry with Rome and its papal agent in the New World, Spain, and a national economy freed from religious constraints and primed to create surplus national wealth in the world trading system" (119).

60 See Benedict Anderson, *Imagined Communities: Reflections on the Origin and Spread of Nationalism* (London: Verso, 1983), 12–19. Anderson describes the relationship between culture and poltical ideology as follows: "What I am proposing is that nationalism has to be understood, by aligning it not with self-consciously held political ideologies, but with the large cultural systems that preceded it, out of which – as well as against which – it came into being" (19).

61 Anderson is unusual to the extent that he constructs his argument in largely cultural terms, and it is these terms that make his study so useful to those of us trying to analyze the cultural aspects of the concept of nation. For a different kind of analysis, see E. Gellner, *Nations and Nationalism* (Ithaca: Cornell University Press, 1983). Gellner does suggest that, "Two men are of the same nation if and only if they share the same culture, where culture in turn means a system of ideas and signs and associations and ways of behaving and communicating" (7). But he goes on to treat culture as a stable category, rather than as a site of conflict and change.

62 See Anderson, *Imagined Communities*, 23–5. In quite a different context, Frank Kermode suggests that the notion of "the Classic" finds its origins in the dissolution of Latin as a universal language. Significantly, Kermode asserts, "The Empire is the paradigm of the classic: a perpetuity, a transcendent entity, however remote its provinces, however extraordinary its temporal vicissitudes." Although he doesn't make the direct connection between allegory and colonialism that I am making here, Kermode does suggest that "Allegory has always been one of the instruments by which old texts are accommodated to modern cultures." In other words, for Kermode, "the Classic" and Empire have always demanded similar hermeneutic stra-

tegies in order to render them coherent. See *The Classic* (Cambridge, MA: Harvard University Press, 1975), 28 and 39.

63 See Anderson, *Imagined Communities*, pp. 25 and 31. The notion of "time as either homogenous or empty," comes of course from Thesis XVIII in Benjamin's *Theses on the Philosophy of History*. See his *Illuminations*, trans. Harry Zohn (New York: Shocken Books, 1969), 264.

FEAR AND LOVE: TWO VERSIONS OF PROTESTANT AMBIVALENCE

1 See Mary B. Campbell, "The Illustrated Travel Book and the Birth of Ethnography: Part I of De Bry's America," *The Work of Dissimilitude: Essays from the Sixth Citadel Conference on Medieval and Renaissance Literature*, ed. David G. Allen and Robert A. White (Newark: University of Delaware Press, 1992). In an assessment with which I concur wholeheartedly, Campbell goes on to describe the importance of the Harriot-DeBry collaboration as follows: "As preserved in DeBry's edition of the *Briefe and True Report*, Harriot's text and White's pictures are not only new in the history of the travel book but, looked at from our own position in the ensuing history of ethnography, they stand (together) as an originating work in that genre" (178).

2 See Bernadette Bucher, *Icon and Conquest: A Structural Analysis of the Illustrations of DeBry's Great Voyages*, trans. Basia Miller Gulati (University of Chicago Press, 1981), 10. See also Benjamin Keen, *The Aztec Image in Western Thought* (New Brunswick: Rutgers University Press, 1971). He also argues that "no publisher did more to popularize the so-called Black Legend in Germany and throughout Europe than Théodore DeBry and his sons Jean Théodore and Jean Israel" (163). For an interesting reading of the DeBry edition of Las Casas, see also Tom Conley, "DeBry's Las Casas," *Amerindian Images and the Legacy of Columbus*, ed. Rene Jara and Nicholas Spadaccini, (Minneapolis: University of Minnesota Press, 1992), 103–31.

3 Volume 2 of the *Great Voyages* was Le Moyne de Morgues' *Brevis Narratio* of Laudonière's expedition to Florida in 1565. I would assert that Le Moyne's narrative also reveals many of the same features as the narratives of Harriot and Léry. LeMoyne's narrative and images offer in a sense a combination of the features I am suggesting are divided between Harriot and Léry.

4 Richard Helgerson makes a similar point with regard to Richard Hakluyt who also was a compiler of other peoples' work. But rather than think of Hakluyt as simply a compiler, Helgerson urges us to think of him in more visionary terms: "Hakluyt's task – the collective task of the various intersecting communities for which his name and his book stand as convenient markers – was thus not merely to record what the English had done and what the world was like, though these are the goals he explicitly set himself. He had also to reinvent both

England and the world to make them fit for one another" (153). See *Forms of Nationhood: The Elizabethan Writing of England* (University of Chicago Press, 1992).

5 See Paul H. Hulton, *America, 1585 : The Complete Drawings of John White* (Chapel Hill: University of North Carolina Press, 1984), 9ff.

6 See Bernadette Bucher, *Icon and Conquest*, 3. Bucher notes that copperplate engraving had been in existence since the late fifteenth century but had not become prevalent until the later sixteenth century.

7 Claude Levi-Strauss, *Tristes Tropiques*, trans. John and Doreen Weightman (New York: Atheneum, 1973), 83.

8 Villegagnon denied ever having invited Léry and his cohort to Brazil. On this piont see Jean de Léry, *History of a Voyage*, 232, note 3. Léry was himself a protégé of Admiral Gaspard de Coligny, the Protestant hero of the St. Bartholomew's Day massacres who was murdered by the duke of Guise. Thus when he arrived in Brazil to discover that the leader of the French colony was a closet-Catholic, and not the Reformer that he pretended to be, Léry was surprised.

9 Jean de Léry, *History of a Voyage to the Land of Brazil*, trans. Janet Whatley (Berkeley: University of California Press, 1990), 4.

10 See Claude Levi-Strauss, *Tristes tropiques*, 81. Villegagnon's final act of treachery did not reveal itself until Léry had arrived safely back in France. Recounting a story that is eerily reminiscent of Claudius's attempt to do away with Hamlet, Léry tells us that "Villegagnon, without our knowing anything about it, had given to the master of our ship (who knew nothing of it either) an indictment that he had formed against us, with the express order to the first judge in France to whom it would be presented, not only to arrest us, but also to put us to death, by having us burned as the heretics that he said we were." See Léry, *History of a Voyage*, 216–17.

11 For an account of the various misadventures of Léry's manuscript, see Whatley's excellent introduction to her translation of *History of a Voyage*, xvi–xvii.

12 See Frank Lestringant, *Cannibals: The Discovery and Representation of the Cannibal from Columbus to Jules Verne*, trans. Rosemary Morris (Cambridge: Polity Press, 1997), 74.

13 See Léry, *History of a Voyage*, 132.

14 See *ibid.*, 41.

15 See *Tristes tropiques*, Lévi-Strauss, 83.

16 See Lestringant, *Cannibals*, 76–7.

17 See *ibid.*, 71.

18 See Homi Bhabha, *Location of Culture* (London: Routledge, 1994), 86. Bhabha's emphasis.

19 See Léry, *History of a Voyage*, 163.

20 See Roger Schlesinger, ed., *Portraits from the Age of Exploration: Selections from André Thevet's* Les vrais pourtraits et vies des hommes illustrés (Urbana: University of Illinois Press, 1993), 2.

21 See Léry, *History of a Voyage*, 68.
22 Compare Léry's narrative with Andre Thevet, who offered a much less generous portrayal of the natives of Brazil.
23 See Léry, *History of a Voyage*, 102.
24 See *ibid.*, 198.
25 Michel de Certeau, *The Writing of History*, trans. Tom Conley (New York: Columbia University Press, 1988), 218. For another reading of Léry's text, see Stephen Greenblatt, *Marvelous Possessions: The Wonder of the New World* (University of Chicago Press, 1991), 14–22. Greenblatt's reading focuses on the episodes of wonder in Léry's text. While I do not dispute the specific claims of Greenblatt's reading of Léry, I would hesitate to suggest, as he does, that wonder constitutes the resting place of any reading of this text.
26 De Certeau, *The Writing of History*, 213.
27 I am here borrowing Steven Mullaney's vocabulary of "staging" and "rehearsing." Although his essay is not primarily concerned with Léry's work, he does see Léry as participating in the phenomenon that he calls "the rehearsal of cultures." Mullaney defines his use of the term as follows: "Knowledge of another culture in such an instance [i.e. Henri II's royal entry into Rouen in 1550] is directed toward ritual rather than ethnological ends, and the rite involved is ultimately organized around the elimination of its own pretext: the spectacle of the Other that is thus celebrated and observed, in passing. To speak of Renaissance curiosity or fascination with other cultures hardly begins to address what is odd in such an anthropology, geared not toward the interpretation of strange cultures but toward their consummate performance. What we glimpse in the field outside Rouen is not a version of the modern discipline of anthropology, but something preliminary to it; not the interpretation, but what I would call the *rehearsal* of cultures." See "Strange Things, Gross Terms, Curious Customs: The Rehearsal of Cultures in the Late Renaissance," *Representing the English Renaissance*, ed. Stephen Greenblatt (Berkeley: University of California Press, 1988), 73.
28 J. H. Elliott, *The Old World and the New 1492–1650* (Cambridge University Press, 1970), 95.
29 See Raphael Holinshed, *Chronicles*, vol. 2 (London, 1586), 107.
30 Las Casas, *The Spanish Colonie*, D2 v.
31 Thomas Harriot, *Briefe and true report of the New Found Land in Virginia* (London: 1588), E1 v.
32 See *The Portable Machiavelli*, ed. and Peter Bondanella and Mark Musa (New York: Viking Press, 1979).The above quote comes of course from *The Prince*, c. 17, "On Cruelty and Mercy and Whether It Is Better to Be Loved than to Be Feared or the Contrary." In this chapter, Machiavelli argues as follows: "And men are less hesitant about harming someone who makes himself loved than one who makes

himself feared because love is held together by a chain of obligation which, since men are a sorry lot, is broken on every occasion in which their own self-interest is concerned; but fear is held together by a dread of punishment which will never abandon you" (131). The question of Harriot's Machiavellian tendencies is one which I will take up shortly when I discuss Stephen Greenblatt's reading of Harriot's text. If one argues, as Stephen Greenblatt does, that Harriot is indeed testing "a Machiavellian hypothesis," then one would have to concede that the result of Harriot's test leads him to part company in some significant ways from Machiavelli. See Stephen Greenblatt, "Invisible Bullets: Renaissance Authority and its Subversion" in *Political Shakespeare: New Essays in Cultural Materialism*, ed. Jonathan Dollimore and Alan Sinfield (Ithaca: Cornell University Press, 1985), 31.

33 See Harriot, *Briefe and true report*, E2 v.

34 See Anthony Pagden, *Lords of All the World* (New Haven: Yale University Press, 1995). Pagden argues, "For most of the English settlers, however, evangelization – when they considered it at all – was only one part of an enterprise which blurred any real distinction between military glory, Gods work and profit" (35). We see such a blurring going on here in Harriot, for whom "true religion" simply represents the ultimate commodity in a series of transactions. I discuss this way of figuring religion in more detail in c. 4.

35 Harriot, *Briefe and true report*, E4 r.

36 *Ibid.*, E4 v.

37 In attempting to interpret this episode in Harriot, I have found it helpful to consider Tzvetan Todorov's distinction between "sacrifice" and "massacre." According to Todorov, "Sacrifice. . .is a religious murder: it is performed in the name of the official ideology and will be perpetrated in public places, in sight of all and to everyone's knowledge. . . The sacrifice is performed in public and testifies to the power of the social fabric, to its mastery over the individual. Massacre, on the other hand, reveals the weakness of this same social fabric, the desuetude of the moral principles that once assured the group's coherence; hence, it should be performed in some remote place where the law is only vaguely acknowledged: for the Spaniards, America or even Italy. Massacre is thus intimately linked to colonial wars waged far from the metropolitan country. The more remote and alien the victims, the better: they are exterminated without remorse, more or less identified with animals. The individual identity of the massacre victim is by definition irrelevant (otherwise his death would be a murder): one has neither time nor curiosity to know whom one is killing at that moment. Unlike sacrifices, massacres are generally not acknowledged or proclaimed, their very existence is kept secret and denied. This is because their social function is not recognized, and we have the impression that such action finds its justification in

itself: one wields the saber for the pleasure of wielding the saber, one cuts off the Indian's nose, tongue, and penis without this having any ritual meaning for the amputator." See *The Conquest of America: The Question of the Other*, trans. Richard Howard (New York: Harper & Row, 1984), 144.

38 I will be citing the version of Stephen Greenblatt's "Invisible Bullets" essay that is reprinted as ch. 2 in *Shakespearean Negotiations*. For the above quote see *Shakespearean Negotiations: The Circulation of Social Energy in Renaissance England* (Berkeley: University of California Press, 1988), 30.

39 See *Shakespearean Negotiations*, 30–2.

40 See *ibid.*, 37.

41 See Hugh Honour, *The New Golden Land: European Images of America from the Discoveries to the Present Time* (New York: Pantheon, 1975), 26. Honour adds, "And when they reappear more prominently in illustrations to a digest of John Smith's *General History of Virginia, New England and the Summer Isles*, they figure as little more than an inconvenient hindrance to the establishment of a Protestant colony." For a brief summary of the publication data and contents for all thirteen volumes of the *Great Voyages*, see Michele Duchet, ed., *L'Amerique de Theodore DeBry: une collection de voyages protestante du XVIe siécle : quatre études d'iconographie* (Paris: Editions du Centre Nationale de la Recherche Scientifique, 1987), 15–17. Unfortunately, Duchet's volume, which is one of the best introductions to DeBry's work has not (yet) been translated into English.

42 As Mary Campbell has argued, one of the effects of the DeBry engravings is to transform Harriot's text from a pamphlet whose primary intention is to acquaint readers with the economic advantages of colonialism into a work of ethnography. Campbell makes the point this way: "The book becomes what we now call ethnographic largely as a result of De Bry's choices for illustration and his unusually suggestive opening and closing illustrations (which do have to do only theoretically with the situation depicted by the rest of the book, and to which I will return later)" (182). See "The Illustrated Travel Book and the Birth of Ethnography: Part 1 of De Bry's *America*," *The Work of Dissimilitude: Essays from the Sixth Citadel Conference on Medieval and Renaissance Literature*, eds. David G. Allen and Robert A. White (Newark: University of Delaware Press, 1992), 177–95.

43 See Daniel Defert, "Collections et nations au XVIe siecle," 47–67. Defert argues, "Les gravures de DeBry n'illustrent pas le prospectus d'Hariot, elles le développent, le magnifient, en déploient toutes les implications" (67). [I translate Defert as follows: "DeBry's engravings do not illustrate Harriot's prospectus, they develop it, they magnify it, they deploy all of its implications."] Defert goes on to argue that it would be a mistake to interpret DeBry's images as simply

forming part of an ethnographic discourse. Rather they must be read as participating in a political discourse as well.

44 See Elliott, *The Old World and the New 1492–1650*, 23.
45 See Mary C. Fuller, *Voyages in Print: English Travel to America, 1576–1624* (Cambridge University Press, 1995), 45.
46 See Greenblatt, "Invisible Bullets," 28.
47 See Léry, *History of a Voyage*, 26–7.
48 Pagden describes a similar phenomenon in his book. He suggests that part of what constitutes the "fall of natural man" is the process whereby the Indians were transformed in the Spanish perception from "nature's children" to "nature's slaves". Anthony Pagden, *The Fall of Natural Man* (Cambridge University Press, 1982), pp. 59–108.
49 See Campbell, "The Illustrated Travel Book and the Birth of Ethnography," 189.

FORGOING THE NATION: THE IRISH PROBLEM

1 Quoted in "Introduction" David B. Quinn, ed., *The Voyages and Colonising Enterprises of Sir Humphrey Gilbert*, 2 vols., vol. 1 (London: Hakluyt Society, 1940), 17. For a more detailed account of Gilbert's practices in Ireland, see Thomas Churchyard, *A Generall Rehearsall of Warres* (London, 1579). According to Churchyard, Gilbert's "maner was that the heddes of all those (of what sort soever they were) which were killed in the daie, should bee cutte of from their bodies, and brought to the place where he encamped at night and should there bee laied on the ground, by eche side of the waie leading into his owne Tente: so that none could come into his Tente for any cause, but commonly he muste passe through a lane of heddes, whiche he used *ad terrorem*, the hedde feelyng nothying the more paines thereby: and yet did it brynge great terrour to the people, when thei sawe the heddes of their dedde fathers, brothers, children, kinfolke, and freendes, lye on the grounde befroe their faces, as thei came to speake with the saied Collonell" (d3, v).

2 One of the most forceful (and better known) attempts to lay the burden of English atrocities at Spenser's feet comes of course from Stephen Greenblatt in his influential *Renaissance Self-Fashioning: From More to Shakespeare* (Chicago: University of Chicago Press, 1980). According to Greenblatt, "Spenser's own account presses in upon us the fact that he was involved intimately, on an almost daily basis, throughout the island, in the destruction of Hiberno-Norman civilization, the exercise of a brutal force that had few if any of the romantic trappings with which Elizabeth contrived to soften it at home. Here, on the periphery, Spenser was an agent of and an apologist for massacre, the burning of mean hovels and of crops with the deliberate intention of starving the inhabitants, forced relocation of peoples,

the manipulation of treason charges so as to facilitate the seizure of lands, the endless repetition of acts of military 'justice' calculated to intimidate and break the spirit. We may wish to tell ourselves that a man of Spenser's sensitivity and gifts may have mitigated the extreme policies of ruthless men, but it appears that he did not recoil in the slightest from this horror, did not even feel himself, like his colleague Geoffrey Fenton, in mild opposition to it" (186). For a similar claim, see David Norbrook, *Poetry and Politics in the English Renaissance* (London: Routledge, 1984), 141.

3 The tradition of reading *A View* as a text that speaks unambiguously for itself has deep roots. Elizabeth Merrill, for instance, compares *A View* with the *Faerie Queene* as follows: "The reader who loses himself – happily to be sure – in the mazes of the *Faerie Queene* finds here [in *A View*] a discourse so clear and coherent in its thought and arrangement that it might seem almost mechanical." See *Dialogue in English Literature* (New York: Henry Holt, 1911), 64. Stephen Greenblatt also seems to treat *A view* as a more transparent text than the *Faerie Queene*, arguing that, in the *Faerie Queene,* Spenser effects "the allegorical separation of rhetoric and violence." In *A View*, however, he would have us believe, there is no such separation. See "Murdering Peasants: Status, Genre, and the Representation of Rebellion," *Representing the English Renaissance*, ed. Stephen Greenblatt (Berkeley: University of California Press, 1988), 23. A welcome corrective comes from Patricia Coughlan who takes previous critics to task for failing to emphasize what she calls the "fictive mode of existence of *A View*." Whereas she moves from *A View* out into Spenser's poetry, I try to treat *A View* on its own terms. See " 'Some Secret Scourge Which Shall by Her Come unto England': Ireland and Incivility in Spenser," *Spenser and Ireland: An Interdisciplinary Perspective*, ed. Patricia Coughlan (Cork University Press, 1989), 46–74. Another essay that gestures at the dialogical frame of *A View* is David J. Baker, " 'Some Quirk, Some Subtle Evasion': Legal Subversion in Spenser's *A View of the Present State of Ireland,*" *Spenser Studies* 6 (1986): 147–63. In a response to Ciaran Brady, Nicholas Canny urges us to take seriously a proposition he had advanced in an earlier article, namely that we try to read Spenser's *A View* as a relatively sophisticated articulation of English political theory. Only then will we be able to understand the precise nature of the text's originality. While ultimately I would want to qualify Canny's assertion that "Spenser pursues his line of argument to its chilling denouement," I see my argument here as one which attempts to situate Spenser in a particular sub-genre of political theory, namely colonial theory. And I would also want to insist on a more rhetorically complicated reading of *A View* than Canny seems willing to entertain. See his "Edmund Spenser and the Development of an Anglo-Irish Identity," *Yearbook of English Studies*

13 (1983): 1–19; and, with Ciaran Brady, "Spenser's Irish Crisis: Humanism and Experience in the 1590s," *Past and Present*, 120 (1988): 201–15.

4 Jonathan Goldberg argues that *A View* was suppressed because it articulated explicitly the terms of "a case that cannot be stated." See *James I and the Politics of Literature* (Baltimore: Johns Hopkins University Press, 1983), 8–9. In an interesting extension of Goldberg's argument that *A View* demystified power relations, Bruce Avery suggests that *A View* was threatening because it showed how easily strategies for dealing with the Irish could be applied to the English at home. In other words, following Goldberg, he argues that *A View* was too honest. See "Mapping the Irish Other: Spenser's *A View of the Present State of Ireland*," *English Literary History* 57 (1990): 263–79. Clarke Hulse puts forth a different argument: "[Spenser] sees the Anglo-Irish as the major obstacles to victory: offspring of both cultures, they threaten to mediate his polarity, to reconcile England and Ireland. Herein probably lies the reason for the suppression of *A View*, for Elizabeth counted on the Anglo-Irish to reconcile the two cultures. She persisted in seeing Ireland as a domestic and feudal matter. The large-scale military campaigns involved in Spenser's proposals would only mean vast expenditures and the likelihood of foreign intervention, such as precipitated the Smerwick massacre... The humanist-colonial analysis of *A View* challenged and disturbed Elizabeth's position in a way that the humanist-mythological analysis of the *Faerie Queene* did not". See "Spenser, Bacon, and the Myth of Power," *The Historical Renaissance: New Essays on Tudor and Stuart Literature and Culture*, ed. Heather Dubrow and Richard Strier (University of Chicago Press, 1988), 330. Andrew Hadfield suggests, "A much more likely explanation is that *A View* failed to appear because of a serious dispute between members of the Stationers' Company as to who had rights to publish Spenser's works" (461). Nonetheless, he notes, "What is clear from this list is that Spenser's tract was the only analytic, exhortationary work on Ireland entered into *The Stationers' Registers* during Elizabeth's reign" (462). See "Was Spenser's *View of the Present State of Ireland* Censored? A Review of the Evidence," *Notes and Queries*, 41, no. 239 (1994). In a sobering article, Jean Brink reminds us of how much we *do not* know about the composition and publication history of *A View*: "Recent studies of *A View* have been predicated upon the assumption that this dialogue circulated in manuscript because the English government prevented its publication. No documentary evidence, however, has been cited to demonstrate that either the Privy Council or the bishop of London suppressed it." See Jean R. Brink, "Constructing *A View of the Present State of Ireland*," *Spenser Studies*, 11 (1994): 204. It seems to me that Brink's point is very well taken, but I don't think that we need to

bring the study of *A View* to a grinding halt simply because there are unresolved textual questions. We need instead to sort out the sorts of claims we are making about the text. She is absolutely right to look skeptically on claims that rest on the assumption that the text was censored. But not everything that one can say about *A View* rests on that assumption.

5 The two most persuasive accounts of Spenser's attempts to construct an English national identity through the *Faerie Queene* are Richard Helgerson, *Forms of Nationhood: The Elizabethan Writing of England* (University of Chicago Press, 1992), and Claire McEachern, *The Poetics of English Nationhood, 1590–1612* (Cambridge University Press, 1996). Willy Maley, in an examination of Spenser's use of language that builds on the work of Richard Helgerson, argues that "Spenser's language was dialectical as well as archaic, synchronic as well as diachronic. He was not simply 'affecting the ancients,' but imitating Irish English. This sheds light on the 'imaginative refeudalization. . . of Elizabethan culture,' the appropriation of antiquity in the interests of a patriotic yearning for a lost nationhood. It also reminds us that Ireland was not simply an arena of confrontation between ready-made English and Irish nations, but, paradoxically, a site of struggle between competing forms of Englishness. Metropolitan identity could be both questioned and constructed in the colonial margins." See "Spenser's Irish English: Language and Identity in Early Modern Ireland," *Studies in Philology* 91 (1994): 431. For Helgerson's argument, see "Barbarous Tongues: The Ideology of Poetic Form in Renaissance England," *The Historical Renaissance: New Essays on Tudor and Stuart Literature and Culture*, ed. Heather Dubrow and Richard Strier (University of Chicago Press, 1988), 273–92.

6 See C. S. Lewis, *The Allegory of Love* (New York: Oxford University Press, 1936): 349.

7 More recent readers of *A View* have questioned earlier assertions (by Greeenblatt and others) that Irenius functions in *A View* as "Spenser's spokesman." John M. Breen puts it this way: "It is naive and methodologically flawed to treat the opinions expressed by Irenius and Eudoxus as simply belonging to Edmund Spenser. I have argued for placing Spenser's *A View* in the context of Renaissance dialogue and historiography so as to demonstrate the generic complexity of *A View*." See "Imagining Voices in *A View of the Present State of Ireland*: A Discussion of Recent Studies," *Connotations: A Journal for Critical Debate*, 4 (1994): 129. See also Annabel Patterson, who performs a detailed analysis of the various moments where Eudoxius seems to contradict or challenge Irenius. Of these moments she says, "If one reads the dialogue without preconceptions of what Spenser's views *must* have been, the less clear it becomes that Irenius is the only conveyor of authorial opinion or that he conveys that opinion

transparently. Eudoxius (sometimes Eudoxus) is identified by his name as a man of good judgment and/or of good reputation, and he alternates between straight man, feeding Irenius the necessary questions, and independent thinker, who asserts the value of many aspects of Irish culture that Irenius means to suppress." See her "The Egalitarian Giant: Representations of Justice in History/Literature," *Journal of British History*, 31 (1992): 115–16.

8 I would therefore agree with Andrew Hadfield when he says, "*A View* is not a tract advocating 'genocide' as some would have it, but rather, cultural and linguistic destruction." See "Spenser's *View of the Present State of Ireland*: Some Notes Towards a 'Materialist' Analysis of Discourse," *Studia Anglistica Upsaliensia*, 65 (1988): 270.

9 See Benedict Anderson, *Imagined Communities: Reflections on the Origin and Spread of Nationalism*, (London: Verso, 1983), 15. Elaborating on the nature of this imagined community, Anderson asserts the following: "The idea of a sociological organism moving calendrically through homogenous, empty time is a precise analogue of the idea of the nation, which is also conceived as a solid community moving steadily down (or up) history" (31). I would suggest that this formulation is particularly useful to us as we attempt to explore the failure of English national identity to produce order in Elizabethan Ireland. As Anderson explains in the notes, the notion of "homogeneous, empty time" derives from Walter Benjamin's *Theses on the Philosophy of History*. In his book, Anderson shrewdly avoids placing the emergence of what he calls "nation-ness" within a specific chronology, instead choosing to connect it loosely with two phenomena: the exploration of the non-European world and the decline of Latin. For another, equally flexible definition of nationalism, see E. Gellner, *Nations and Nationalism* (Ithaca: Cornell University Press, 1983). Gellner defines the nation as follows: "What then is this contingent, but in our age seemingly universal and normative, idea of the nation? Discussion of two very makeshift temporary definitions will help to pinpoint this elusive concept. 1. Two men are of the same nation if and only if they share the same culture, where culture in turn means a system of ideas and signs and associations and ways of behaving and communicating. 2. Two men are of the same nation if and only if they *recognize* each other as belonging to the same nation. In other words, *nations maketh man*; nations are the artifacts of men's convictions and loyalties and solidarities. A mere category of persons (say, occupants of a given territory, or speakers of a given language, for example) becomes a nation if and when the members of the category firmly recognize certain mutual rights and duties to each other in virtue of their shared membership of it. It is their recognition of each other as fellows of this kind which turns them into a nation, and not the other shared attributes, whatever they may be, which separate that category from non-members" (7).

10 See Richard Helgerson, *Forms of Nationhood: The Elizabethan Writing of England* (University of Chicago Press, 1992), 4. I would also point readers to Liah Greenfeld's analysis of the evolution of the word "nation" in her book, *Nationalism: Five Roads to Modernity* (Cambridge, MA: Harvard University Press, 1992). According to Greenfeld, "The radical shift in attitude which was expressed in the application of the word 'nation' to a people, and which in more than one way signified the beginning of the modern era, was already under way in the 1530s. In the course of the sixteenth century this shift had affected a substantial segment of the English population, and by 1600, the existence in England of a national consciousness and identity, and as a result, of a new geo-political entity, a nation, was a fact... The evolution of the national consciousness was reflected in the changing vocabulary. In the period between 1500 and 1650 several crucial concepts altered their meaning and came into general use. These concepts were 'country,' 'commonwealth,' 'empire,' and 'nation.' The changes in meaning were concentrated in the sixteenth century. The four words became understood as synonyms, acquiring the sense which, with slight alterations, they retained later, but which differed from their separate meanings before" (30–1).

11 See Edmund Spenser, *A View of the Present State of Ireland* (Oxford University Press, 1970) 37.

12 I would want here to register my strenuous disagreement to Walter S. H. Lim's suggestion that Spenser reveals the Irish to lack an identity. According to Lim, "Spenser's Irish are not only barbaric and uncivilized, they do not possess an identifiable ethnic or national identity. The origins of the people who have come to be known as the Irish are lost as a result of different ethnic interactions... In order to reinforce this absence of identity, Spenser proceeds to argue that there is no such character as a real Spaniard... Ireland's uncivilized and anarchic, and nationally indistinct state is a thematic constant in both Spenser's *A View* and *The Faerie Queene*." See "Figuring Justice: Imperial Ideology and the Discourse of Colonialism in book 5 of *The Faerie Queene*," *Renaissance and Reformation Renaissance et Reforme*, 19 (1995): 58.

13 See Spenser, *View*, 45.

14 Emphasis is mine. See *ibid.*, 153.

15 Emphasis is mine. See *ibid.*, 155–6.

16 David J. Baker describes the problem differently: "The Queen's government had not been able to amalgamate her Irish colony into a coherent whole, either in practice or on paper. The result was a congeries of indeterminate territories assembled under a rubric – "Ireland" – which could name but, strictly speaking, could not refer to, the country so called. In one sense English power called Ireland into being, in another sense Ireland was not really there at all. Unlike

England, which, arguably at least, was a "nation", or was being constructed as one, Ireland was a terrain where the categories of English nationalism manifestly did not apply, a space that, in several ways, the colonizers could not map (82). See "Off the map: charting uncertainty in Renaissance Ireland," in *Representing Ireland: Literature and the Origins of Conflict, 1534–1660*, ed. Brendan Bradshaw, Andrew Hadfield, and Willy Maley (Cambridge University Press, 1993).

17 Emphasis is mine. See Spenser, *View*, 47–8.

18 Both Campion and Stanyhurst refer to this problem before Spenser. And after Spenser, Davies devotes some considerable time to the analysis of it.

19 See Linda Colley, *Britons: Forging the Nation 1707–1837* (New Haven: Yale University Press, 1992), 5.

20 Emphasis is mine. See *View*, 63, 64, and 65. Andrew Hadfield and Willy Maley also read the above passages as attempts to grapple with the intractable questions that identity poses to anyone who would colonize: "Like Spenser, Donne perceives in the colonial experience the risk of a loss of identity, an abandonment of self. Thus colonial adventure can be both an opportunity to fashion an identity – as the archetypal English gentleman – and an abyss into which one's identity may disappear. Through literature, the poet hopes to cultivate and refine the art of memory in order to preserve both name and nationhood. One thinks here of the closing lines of John of Gaunt's emotive speech in *Richard II*: "That England that has wont to conquer others/ Hath made a shameful conquest of itself" (II. I. 65–6). Thus, the determination of an English self depends upon the subjection of an Irish other." See "Introduction: Irish Representations and English Alternatives," in *Representing Ireland: Literature and the Origins of Conflict, 1534–1660*, ed. Bradshaw, Hadfield, and Maley, 9.

21 Emphasis is mine. See Spenser, *View*, 67. On the question of the degeneration of the English language in Ireland, see Andrew Hadfield's comparison of *A View* with contemporary political theory. Hadfield interestingly concludes his argument by linking *A View*, not to Book 5 of *The Faerie Queene*, but to the Mutabilitie Cantoes: " 'The 'Two Cantos of Mutabilitie' flirt with the possibility of a Protean victory and in allegorizing the fall taking place in Ireland say what *A View* can never consider: that Ireland is the place from where all chaos originates and which will suck in and consume all attempts to redeem it. It is the site where (the English) language turns against itself and ceases to be able to transform its 'other'; the master tropes of *A View* have no privileged status in this world. Conquest is shown to be an arbitrary act devoid of distinction and significance. Myth has become the nightmare of history; *The Faerie Queene* is the Irish 'other' of *A View*." See "Spenser, Ireland, and Sixteenth-Century Political Theory," *Modern Language Review* 89 (1994): 18.

22 See Raphael Holinshed, *Chronicles* (London, 1586) vol. 2, 4. According
to Stanyhurst, "So long as these impaled dwellers did sunder themselves as well in land as in language from the Irish," they were able
to avoid the problems that have since beset the English in their
attempt to reverse the "barbarous savageness" of Ireland. According
to Stanyhurst, however, the "posteritie" of these original settlers was
less vigilant, and as a result "the Irish language was free dennized
in the English pale." For Stanyhurst, linguistic backwardness was not
to be viewed as quaint archaism but rather as one of the steps in an
inevitable chain reaction, the result of which was nothing short of
total rebellion. He offers an ambitious inventory of various forms of
cultural and political degradation of which "this present ruine and
decaie" of the English language is only part. Stanyhurst describes
the interrelation this way: "They were invironed and compassed with
evill neighbours. Neighbourhood bred acquaintance, acquaintance
waffed in the Irish toong, the Irish hooked with it attire, attire haled
rudeness, rudeness ingendered ignorance, ignorance brought contempt of lawes, the contempt of lawes bred rebellion, rebellion raked
thereto warres, and so consequentlie the utter decaie and desolation
of that worthie countrie" (5). On the question of the relationship
between Spenser and Stanyhurst, see Willy Maley, "Spenser's Irish
English: Language and Identity in Early Modern Ireland," *Studies in
Philology* 91 (1994). Maley argues, "Stanyhurst argues, *contra*
Spenser – who favored integration and assimilation – for partition
and proscription as a solution to degeneration" (418). Later, Maley
elaborates as follows: "Spenser purified the dialect of the tribe,
whereas Stanyhurst stuck to his source, finally abandoning it in favor,
not of a modernised version, but for Latin, which he had referred to
in Holinshed as 'the language that is universallie spoken, throughout
the greater part of the world'" (428–9). See also Maley's shorter
piece comparing Spenser to Stanyhurst: "Spenser's *View* and Stanyhurst's *Description*," *Notes and Queries*, 43, no. 241 (1996): 140–2.

23 See Spenser, *View*, 151.

24 See *ibid.*, 152.

25 See *ibid.*, 3.

26 See *ibid.*, 3–4.

27 For an illuminating discussion of the proliferation of the trope of the
"prince as physician" in contemporary political discourse see A. D.
Hadfield, "The Course of Justice: Spenser, Ireland and Political Discourse," *Studia Neophilologica: A Journal of Germanic and Romance Languages and Literature*, 65 (1993). In comparing Spenser to Erasmus,
Hadfield observes, "Erasmus also works out a sliding scale, a classifi-
cation, of legal judgements, which includes the possiblity that force
must at some point replace the use of reason. At times there are
direct linguistic parallels between the two works, when each writer

resorts to identical tropes to justify and explain his respective argument. The stock image of the prince as doctor to the wounded body of the state (a commonplace of sixteenth-century political writing, but not always used in exactly the same way) appears in both texts" (189).

28 Emphasis mine. See Spenser, *A View*, 5.

29 Emphasis mine. See *ibid.*, 22–23. David J. Baker comments interestingly and extensively on the passage I quoted as well as on the larger legal questions raised by *A View*. See " 'Some Quirk, Some Subtle Evasion': Legal Subversion in Spenser's *A View of the Present State of Ireland*," *Spenser Studies*, 6 (1986): esp. 154.

30 See Brendan Bradshaw, "Robe and Sword in the Conquest of Ireland" in *Law and Government under the Tudors*, ed. Claire Cross, David Loades, and J. J. Scarisbrick (Cambridge University Press, 1988), 143. Bradshaw argues that we must read Spenser's *View* as a Machiavellian text that uses 'the needs of the state' to justify an extreme reaction to Ireland's ills. He also argues that we must look at the text as typically Protestant. And finally, he suggests that what distinguished Spenser from his contemporaries was his commitment to the use of ethnology to implement his program of destruction.

31 See Sheila T. Cavanagh, " 'That Fatal Destiny of that Land': Elizabethan Views of Ireland" in *Representing Ireland* ed. Bradshaw, Hadfield, and Maley, 128. While I applaud Cavanagh's attempt to read *A View* as an ambivalent text, I think that she goes too far when she claims that "Spenser never advocated the wholesale slaughter or famine which certain critics choose to credit him with." To be sure, *A View* presents readers with a muddled blueprint of a plan of action, in which a variety of options are available. One of these is the use of slaughter and famine, and I don't think it's as easy to rule it out as she suggests. For a more complete version of her argument on this point see her article, " 'Such was Irena's countenance': Ireland in Spenser's Prose and Poetry," *Texas Studies in Language and Literature*, 28 (1986): 24–50.

32 See Spenser, *View*, 37.

33 Emphasis mine. See *ibid.*, 49–50.

34 Julia Reinhard Lupton argues that "waste" is "the key word" in Spenser's *View*: "Spenser's tract defines Ireland as wasteland (desolate, depeopled, and unpossessed) in order to defend an active policy of further wasting followed by restorative 'plantation'" (93). See "Mapping mutability: or, Spenser's Irish Plot," *Representing Ireland*, ed. Bradshaw, Hadfield, and Maley.

35 See Spenser, *View*, 77.

36 Annabel Patterson suggests that Spenser's discussion of the folkmote is to be connected with an ongoing debate over "the value of places and occasions for self-government." In her reading of *A View*, neither

Irenius nor Eudoxius reliably functions as a spokesperson for Spenser. She rejects, therefore, the notion that "Irenius is the only conveyor of authorial opinion or that he conveys that opinion transparently." In the case of the folkmotes, it is Eudoxius, who articulates the position with which we might assume Spenser to have sympathy, namely "the democratic position." My own analysis does not contradict Patterson's, but it does push the discussion in a different direction. See her "The Egalitarian Giant: Representations of Justice in History/Literature," *Journal of British History* 31 (1992): 116–17.

37 In fact, many of the "personal" customs of the Irish were the subject of humorous portrayals by English writers. Edmund Campion, for instance, ironically described the wearing of glibs as follows: "Proud they are of long crisped glibbes, and doe nourish the same with all their cunning: to crop the front thereof they take it for a notable peece of villany" (18). See his *Historie of Ireland* which was first published with Spenser's *View* by Sir James Ware in Dublin in 1633 under the title, *Two Histories of Ireland*. Spenser's association with Campion, however, was not merely an accident of publication. Although Campion's text was composed some twenty-five years before Spenser wrote *A View*, Spenser would almost certainly have known about it through its mention in Holinshed's *Chronicles*. Moreover, his Catholicism notwithstanding, Campion shared another connection with Spenser, namely his ties to the militantly Protestant faction of Elizabeth's court – the same faction credited with obtaining for Spenser his first appointment in Ireland as secretary to Lord Grey. In other words, Campion's patrons were the very same men who, throughout the middle of Elizabeth's reign, urged her to adopt a more aggressive colonial policy, first in Ireland, and later in America. On this last point, see Nicholas Canny, *The Elizabethan Conquest of Ireland: A Pattern Established, 1565–76* (London: Harvester Press, 1976.), 60 ff. For another humorous description of mantles and glibs, see John Derricke, *The Image of Irelande with a Discoverie of Woodkarne* (London: 1581) D1, v. More a playful reprise of received prejudices than a serious attempt to describe or analyze Irish culture, Derricke's *Image* presents its readers with a series of predictable clichés about the Irish. Andrew Hadfield and Wiley Maley suggest that Derricke's text "belongs to the same tradition of complaint or satire [as *The Mirror for Magistrates*], yet could also be seen as an attempt to press the case for greater honours for his patron, Sir Henry Sidney, or as crude anti-Irish propaganda." See Hadfield and Maley, "Introduction: Irish Representations and English Alternatives" in *Representing Ireland, ed. Bradshaw, Hadfield, and Maley*, 7.

38 See Spenser, *View*, 51–2.

39 See *ibid.*, 53.

40 See Bradshaw, *Robe and Sword*, 159.

41 Emphasis mine. See Spenser, *View*, 11–12.

42 It was of course during a fateful trip to Ireland in 1399 to quell the
rebellion of Art MacMurrough, that Richard II was replaced by his
rival Henry Bolingbroke. See T. W. Moody and F. X. Martin, eds.,
The Course of Irish History (Cork: The Mercier Press, 1984). They
remind us that "no other monarch was to visit Ireland during the
middle ages" (158). I would suggest that Elizabeth, whose own title
to the crown derived from the conflict between the Yorkists and the
Lancastrians, would have been very mindful of the dangers presented
by Ireland.

43 Emphasis mine. See Spenser, *View*, 132–3.

44 See *ibid.*, 125.

45 See *ibid.*, 152.

46 See *ibid.*, 155.

47 As Andrew Hadfield concludes, "*A View* is therefore a contradictory
work, a fact of which Spenser was probably all too painfully
aware" (9). See "Spenser, Ireland, and Sixteenth-Century Political
Theory," *Modern Language Review* 89 (1994): 9.

48 See Spenser, *View*, 159–60.

49 See *ibid.*, 168.

50 See *ibid.*, 86.

51 See Nicholas Canny, "The Ideology of English Colonization: From
Ireland to America," *William and Mary Quarterly*, 3rd series, 30
(1973): 595.

52 Here is the complete passage from which the quote is extracted:
"The Elizabethans' colonial wars in Ireland are of critical importance
in any investigation of English Discovery-era colonizing discourses.
Until England could develop a practice of colonization, with the subsequent ruptures in a theory-bound discursive field that praxis inevitably reveals, its colonizing discourses would necessarily remain
underdeveloped and derivative. Ireland provided an unparalleled
opportunity to test the new practices of empire perfected by the successful Spanish New World enterprise and to articulate them in a
peculiarly English discursive style. This same style, blending together
medievally derived legal theories on the diminished status and rights
of a normatively divergent savage people, anti-Spanish religious and
mercantile nationalism, and English innovations of Spanish colonizing practice, would complete the thematic constructing of the
colonizing discourse later carried by Elizabeth's Protestant crusaders
to the New World." See Robert A. Williams, *The American Indian in
Western Legal Thought: The Discourses of Conquest* (New York: Oxford
University Press, 1990), 136. Williams's view in the above passage is
anticipated by Francis Jennings's analysis. See *The Invasion of America:
Indians, Colonialism, and the Cant of Conquest* (Chapel Hill: University of
North Carolina Press, 1975), 45–8. Edward Said attempts to connect

Spenser and the earlier English colonization of Ireland with the much broader concept of global imperialism – a notion, I would suggest, that needs to be (at the very least) saturated with a great deal more specificity. According to Said, "The idea of English racial superiority became ingrained; so humane a poet and gentleman as Edmund Spenser in his *View of the Present State of Ireland* (1596) was boldly proposing that since the Irish were barbarian Scythians, most of them should be exterminated." See his *Culture and Imperialism* (New York: Vintage, 1993), 222.

PREACHING THE NATION: THE SERMON AS PROMOTION

1 For an articulation of this position, see Wesley Frank Craven, *The Dissolution of the Virginia Company* (Gloucester, MA: Peter Smith, 1964). Craven says, "Whatever else may have entered into the activities of the [Virginia] company, it was primarily a business organization with large sums of capital invested by adventurers whose chief interests lay in the returns expected from their investments" (24). For a more recent discussion of the question of the composition and motives of the Virginia colony, see chs. 1 and 2 in Jack P. Greene, *Pursuits of Happiness: The Social Development of Early Modern British Colonies and the Formation of American Culture* (Chapel Hill: University of North Carolina Press, 1988).

2 See Perry Miller, *Errand into the Wilderness* (Cambridge, MA: Harvard University Press, 1956), 106.

3 John Parker, *Books to Build an Empire: A Bibliographical History of English Overseas Interests to 1620* (Amsterdam: N. Israel, 1965), 201. Parker here refers specifically to Robert Gray, but he elsewhere makes the same claim for William Symonds and William Crashaw.

4 Mary Fuller argues, "The disavowal of profit [by Humphrey Gilbert] was deeply and problematically rooted in the attitudes of Englishmen who sought to stage cultural superiority by needing nothing from America. The benefit of travel to America was to be not gain but loss – the purging of intemperate humors or excess population, or the self-sacrificing effort to give away the riches of English religion and culture." See *Voyages in Print: English Travel to America, 1576–1624* (Cambridge University Press, 1995), 12.

5 See Robert Gray, *A Good Speed to Virginia* (London, 1609) fol. B1 r–v. Very little is known about Gray except that he was the rector of St. Benet Sherehog in Cheapward. For another discussion of Gray and his sermon, see John Parker, "Religion and the Virginia Colony, 1609–10," *The Westward Enterprise: English Activities in Ireland, the Atlantic, and America, 1480–1650*, ed. K. R. Andrews, N. P. Canny, and P. E. H. Hair (Detroit: Wayne State University Press, 1979), 255 ff.

 6 See Karen Ordahl Kupperman, "The Beehive as a Model for Colonial Design," *America in European Consciousness, 1493–1750*, ed. Karen Ordahl Kupperman (Chapel Hill: University of North Carolina Press, 1995), 287. I might add to Kupperman's claim, that the same social vision that displaced onto the laborers the desire for productive activity also displaced onto the native populations the desire for civility and Christianity.

 7 See William Shakespeare, *The Life of King Henry the Fifth* (I. II. 183–9).

 8 See Gray, *A Good Speed*, fol. B1 v.

 9 As I suggested in the first chapter, Benedict Anderson's formulation of the concept of "nation-ness" is helpful in understanding and describing the European desire for colonies in the early seventeenth century. Anderson's analysis might also be usefully recalled here as we attempt to comprehend the function both of Gray's images of the hive and the body as well as his account of the English rejection of Columbus. To borrow more explicitly from Anderson, I would argue that Gray implicitly constructs England as "a sociological organism moving calendrically through homogenous, empty time." Such an "organism," Anderson suggests, "is a precise analogue of the idea of the nation, which is also conceived as a solid community moving steadily down (or up) history." See *Imagined Communities: Reflections on the Origin and Spread of Nationalism* (London: Verso, 1983), 31.

10 See Gray, *A Good Speed*, fo. B4 r.

11 See *ibid.*, fol. C2 r.

12 See *ibid.*, fol. C2 v.

13 See *ibid.*, fol C2 v-3 r.

14 See *ibid.*, fol. C3 r.

15 See *ibid.*, fol. C4 r.

16 See *ibid.*, fol D2 r.

17 See *ibid.*, fol D2 v-3 r.

18 See William Symonds, *A Sermon Preached at White-Chappel, In the Presence of Many, Honourable and Worshipfull, the Adventurers and Planters for Virginia* (London, 1609).

19 See *ibid.*, 19–22.

20 See *ibid.*, 32–4.

21 According to Mary Fuller, "The anxiety which these documents manifest concerning unauthorized reports suggests that individual colonists and sailors also wrote, and said, a good deal; yet surviving reports showing the early colonial enterprise in a harsh (read: objective?) light are rare. The varied tales of the disaffected exist primarily as moments embedded in the authorized texts of men like Harriot and Crashaw, where they are stigmatized or (as in William Symond's *Virginia: A Sermon*) made into the passive part of a dialogue which the author is bound to win" (90).

22 See Symonds, *A Sermon Preached at White-Chappel*, 13.

23 It is interesting to note that Symonds's argument echoes James's famous pronouncement at the Hampton Court conference in 1604 (which Milton quotes in his tract, *Of Reformation*): "No Bishop, no King." It is not clear whether Symonds knew James's line, but it does seem clear that he rather shrewdly ties the propriety of the colonial project to the propriety of the monarchy. One could paraphrase this component of Symonds's argument as follows: "No colonies, no King."

24 See Symonds, *A Sermon Preached at White-Chappel*, 14.

25 The revelations of Las Casas quickly found their way into other tracts which trumpeted Spain's moral bankruptcy and, by comparison, England's unassailable moral superiority. Among other disseminations of Las Casas there were the works of Hakluyt and Purchas as well as Theodor de Bry's *America*, which contained graphic pictoral representations of Las Casas's descriptions of the various methods of torture used by the Spanish conquerors, including the feeding of natives to the dogs. For a discussion of these texts, see chs. 1 and 2 above.

26 See William Crashaw, *A Sermon Preached in London before the right honorable the Lord Lawarre, Lord Governor and Captaine Generall of Virginea, and others of his Maiesties Counsell for that Kingdome, and the rest of the Adventurers in that Plantation* (London, 1610), fol. K3 r. Crashaw, a puritan divine, was the father of Richard Crashaw, the poet.

27 See *ibid.*, fol. C3 v.

28 See *ibid.*, fol. D3 r.

29 See *ibid.*, fol. D3 v.

30 See *ibid.*, fol. D3 v.

31 See *ibid.*, fol. D4. r.

32 See *ibid.*, fol. F4 r.

33 See *ibid.*, fol. H3 r.

34 See Alexander Whitaker, *Good Newes from Virginia* (London, 1613), 33.

35 See *ibid.*, 18–19.

36 See *ibid.*, 20.

37 George R. Potter and Evelyn Simpson, eds., *The Sermons of John Donne*, 10 vols. (Berkeley: University of California Press, 1959), vol. 4, 280.

38 *Ibid.*, 272.

39 *Ibid.*, 272–3.

LOVE AND SHAME

1 On this point, see Larzer Ziff, *Puritanism in America: New Culture in a New World* (New York: Viking, 1973), 171–5. See also David S. Lovejoy, "Roger Williams and George Fox: The Arrogance of Self-Righteousness," *New England Quarterly* 66, no. 2 (1993): 199–225. Lovejoy says, "Since the founding of Rhode Island in 1636, Roger Williams had immersed himself in the ways of New England Indians,

had written a brilliant book about their language, and certainly had a closer everyday relationship with the New World aborigines than any English settler in the seventeenth century, John Eliot included" (219). In describing Williams's ability to "treat Indian culture with respect," Perry Miller claims, "He was the only Englishman in his generation who could do so." See *Roger Williams: His Contribution to America* (New York: Atheneum, 1962), 52.

2 I will defer my discussion of the critical work pertaining to Eliot until the next chapter. With respect to Williams, however, the only recent extensive study of his *Key* has been Ivy Schweitzer's chapter in her book *The Work of Self-Representation: Lyric Poetry in Colonial New England* (Chapel Hill: University of North Carolina Press, 1991). I am indebted to Schweitzer's work on Williams in more ways than the notes to this chapter may indicate, for it was Schweitzer who first gave a coherent and rigorous account of the workings of Williams's polemic within the *Key*. My work, no doubt, goes in a different direction, but it is safe to say that I couldn't have made my argument without recourse to her work. Besides Schweitzer's chapter, there have been only a handful of articles concerning the *Key* in the past decade or so.

3 I am thinking in particular here of the work of Ola Elizabeth Winslow, who wrote biographies of both Williams and Eliot. Although her work tends to be more reverential than critical, her two books still remain valuable sources of biographical information see *Master Roger Williams* (New York: Macmillan, 1957) and *John Eliot: "Apostle to the Indians"* (Boston: Houghton Mifflin, 1968). In the hagiographical mode there is also Cyclone Covey, *The Gentle Radical: A Biography of Roger Williams* (New York, 1966). I should add here that the case of Roger Williams is complicated. His writings on toleration and liberty of conscience have received extensive critical attention. But even in this area, Williams has sometimes been ill-served by scholars who have seen him as the founding father of religious liberty as it was articulated in the Constitution. See, for instance, James E. Ernst, *The Political Thought of Roger Williams* (Seattle: University of Washington Press, 1929). As Perry Miller lamented, "A serious disservice has been done to the liberal, the Protestant, the patriotic traditions of this country by well-meaning panegyrists who, in making Williams over into their own terms, have made him unavailable to a day which has need of him." See Miller, *Roger Williams,* 27. Thanks, in large part, to the work of Miller, there has since emerged a vigorous scholarly debate about the political and theological aspects of Williams's thought. See for instance Edmund S. Morgan, *Roger Williams, the Church and the State* (New York: Norton, 1967). Frequently in discussions of Williams's views on religion and politics, scholars have acknowledged his contribution to the discourse on native Americans. But so far, that aspect of Williams's corpus remains understudied.

4 Of Roger Williams's role in the Pequot War, Richard Drinnon says, "In fact, Williams acted as a one-man Office of Strategic Services, watching out for 'any perfidious dealing,' warning Winthrop that the Pequots had heard of his preparations for war, proposing a Narragansett hit-and-run raid that would 'much enrage the Pequots for even against them, a thing much desirable,' and sending a sketch of the Pequot forts and a Narragansett battle plan against them, including night-assault n'– a plan that was later followed in all its essentials save one: 'That it would be pleasing to all natives, that women and children be spared, etc.'" See *Facing West, the Metaphysics of Indian-Hating and Empire-Building*, 1990 edn. (New York: Schocken, 1980), 41. About John Eliot, Francis Jennings has suggested that he undertook his missionary work only after embarrassing revelations that Massachusetts was not doing its part to live up to that part of its charter that required them to make an effort "to wynn and incite the Natives. . .to the knowledge and obedience of the onlie true God and Savior of Mankinde, and the Christian Fayth." See "Goals and Functions of Puritan Missions to the Indians," *Ethnohistory*, 18 (1971): 197–8.

5 Typical of the assessment of the literary merit of Williams's *Key*, before Ivy Schweitzer argued that we take the poetry in it seriously, is John Garrett's dismissal of it as "sententious doggerel verse." See *Roger Williams, Witness Beyond Christendom, 1603–1683* (New York: Macmillan, 1970), 127.

6 See John Winthrop, *The History of New England*, ed. James Savage (Boston, 1825), vol. 1, 162–3.

7 *Ibid.*, 175.

8 See Henry Chupack, *Roger Williams* (New York: Twayne, 1969), 69. Here, he lays out the standard argument for the effect of the *Key* in getting Williams's name into circulation among influential people in the government. Among these, was Sir Henry Vane, a friend of Milton's.

9 William Wood's *New England's Prospect* (London, 1634) is frequently suggested as a model for Williams's *Key*, I would argue that the two books are really quite different. At first, the similarities between *New England's Prospect* and the *Key* are striking. Not only does *New England's Prospect* contain twenty chapters devoted to a description of Indian life, but Wood also includes "A Small Nomenclator" of the Indian language at the end of his volume. Wood's eight-page glossary of Indian words and phrases, arranged alphabetically according to the Indian spelling, pales in comparison to Williams' much more extensive treatment of the Indian language in the *Key*. But more to the point, Wood's "nomenclator" appears almost as an afterthought, and the author himself admits that it will probably be of little practical value. Wood himself describes it as follows: "Because many have

desired to hear some of the natives' language, I have here inserted a
small nomenclator, with the names of their chief kings, rivers,
months and days, whereby such as have insight into the tongues may
know to what language it is most inclining; and such as desire it as
an unknown language only, may reap delight, if they can get no profit" (117). Wood thus offers the Indian language to his readers as a
commodity, the linguistic equivalent of a momento or souvenir.

10 Williams, *Key*, 90.
11 See Schweitzer, *The Work of Self-Representation*, 194.
12 See Edwin S. Gaustad, *Liberty of Conscience: Roger Williams in America*
(Grand Rapids: William B. Eerdmans Publishing Co., 1991), 137.
13 *Ibid.*, 62.
14 See Schweitzer, *The Work of Self-Representation*, 184. Perry Miller cor-
roborates this assertion by arguing that Williams rejected the Puritan attempts to find in the Old Testament proof of New England's
divine election: " He belonged to that rare and furtive brotherhood
who, here and there throughout the centuries, have taken the New
Testament to mean not a continuation but a repudiation of the Old.
He would be a Christian but not a Christianized Jew." Later Miller
elaborated as follows: "he [Williams] believed that in all human history there had been only one nation in covenant with Jehova, only
one chosen people, and that this unique federation had vanished
from earth on the morning of Christ's resurrection." See his *Roger
Williams: His Contribution to America* (New York: Atheneum, 1962), 32
and 54. See also Edmund S. Morgan, *Roger Williams, the Church and
the State* (New York: Norton, 1967). Morgan says, "Williams had the
confidence of every Protestant that Christ would come again, subdue
Satan, and destroy Antichrist, but he was not sanguine about the
imminence of the date, nor did he find reason to suppose that the
millennial headquarters would be located in England. Williams had
an unusual capacity for looking squarely at facts, and neither the
facts of English history nor the evidence of Scripture seemed to him
to support the popular view of England's appointed role in the struggle with Antichrist" (10). Morgan takes up this point in greater
detail later: "For England to be an elect nation it would have to be
composed entirely of John Lamberts – that is, of true Christians –
and this was precisely what could not happen to any nation" (101).
Lambert, as Morgan tells us, was burned at the stake in 1538 for
expressing religious views contrary to those of Henry VIII.
15 The quotation is from Jean de Léry, *History of a Voyage to the Land of
Brazil*, trans. Janet Whatley (Berkeley: University of California Press,
1990), 132. For a more complete discussion of Léry, see ch. 2 above.
16 Williams, *Complete Writings*, vol. 7, 36.
17 *Ibid.*, 37.
18 *Ibid.*, 37.

19 See Christopher Hill, *The World Turned Upside Down: Radical Ideas During the English Revolution* (London: Penguin, 1972), *passim*. Hill documents in some detail the various conflicts among the radical sects. See especially ch. 9, which discusses the ways in which Ranters and Seekers were villified.

20 See Thomas Morton, *New English Canaan* (Amsterdam, 1637), 111 and 114.

21 *Ibid.*, 125.

22 There were other differences as well. As harsh and direct as his attack on the Massachusetts and Plymouth Puritans was, Morton was a much easier figure for the Puritans and Pilgrims to dismiss. In the opening pages, Morton identified himself as both a royalist and a member of the Church of England, moves which enabled the Puritans to distance themselves from his critique. Not only was he *not* a Puritan, but he engaged in activities that rendered him vulnerable to the charge of having "turned Indian." Those activities included apparently selling arms and liquor to the Indians, as well as the unforgivable sin of sleeping with them. See Bradford, *History of Plymouth Plantation*, ed. William T. Davis (New York: Charles Scribner's Sons, 1908), 236–43. Winthrop says that he was punished for "many injuries offered to the Indians"; see Winthrop, *The History of New England*, vol. 1 (Boston, 1825), 34–6. Readers will also remember that the story of Thomas Morton and his settlement at Mt. Wollaston offered Nathaniel Hawthorne the material for his story "The Maypole of Merrymount." In that story, Hawthorne tries to "recast" Morton as a hero of sorts. See also Drinnon, *Facing West*, 3–20. He gives a provocative analysis of both Morton and Hawthorne's depiction of him.

23 I should add here that it would of course have been far more difficult for the Puritans to distance themselves from Williams who, upon his arrival in Massachusetts, was immediately recognized as a godly person and offered the prestigious post of minister at the church in Boston, a post that John Cotton would later hold. Although (and perhaps even because) he turned down the post, Williams presented his co-religionists with an unprecedented threat. See Winthrop, who records the arrival of Williams: "The ship Lyon, Mr. William Pierce master, arrived at Nantasket. She brought Mr. Williams, (a godly minister) with his wife. . ." (41). Later on, Winthrop recounts the story of Williams's refusal to join with the congregation at Boston. See 52ff. Bradford treats Williams ambivalently, calling him "a man godly and zealous, having many precious parts, but very unsettled in judgmente" (299). That Bradford felt obliged to concede his godliness at all is an indication of the grudging respect that the other Puritans felt they owed Williams.

24 For a fascinating (and brief) history of Gregory Dexter, Williams's printer for the *Key*, see Bradford F. Swan, *Gregory Dexter of London*

and New England, 1610–1700 (Rochester: Leo Hart Co., 1949). Swan makes the case that Dexter was just the man to go to if one had an especially polemical printing job. For instance, William Prynne, after he was imprisoned in the wake of the publication of *Histrio-Mastix*, published *Instructions to Church Wardens* illegally while he was still in jail in 1637. Gregory Dexter was his printer. Some other of Dexter's credits include John Milton's *Of Prelatical Episcopacy*, his *Of Reformation*, and the second edition of John Cotton's *The Doctrine of the Church, To which are committed the Keys of the Kingdome of Heaven*. Ivy Schweitzer suggests that this last pamphlet may well have given Williams the idea for the name of his *Key*. While I believe that my argument for the polemical nature of the *Key* finally rests on an examination of the text, this information about the printing business also suggests that Williams's engagement of Dexter was not simply an accident. Rather, I believe that Williams and Dexter connected because Williams had written the kind of book Dexter liked to print.

25 Williams, *Key*, 130.

26 The court of Charles was notoriously and unapologetically foppish. Indeed the trademark of the Cavaliers was their long hair, and that of the Puritans was their "round heads." The term "roundhead" of course became a derisive way of referring to Quakers in the 1650s. See Christopher Hill, *The World Turned Upside Down: Radical Ideas During the English Revolution* (London: Penguin, 1972), 233–5. Williams was not the only one to comment on the undesirabilty of long hair. Thomas Hall, for instance, about a decade later, would inveigh against the tendency of his countrymen to wear their hair long. See *The loathsomnesse of long haire, or, A treatise wherein you have the question stated, many arguments against it produc'd, and the most materiall arguguments [sic] for it refell'd and answer'd : with the concurrent judgement of divines both old and new against it : with an appendix against painting, spots, naked breasts, &c.* (London, 1654).

27 Reproductions of this seal appear in various places including John Canup, *Out of the Wilderness* (Middletown: Wesleyan University Press, 1990) 59.

28 Williams, *Key*, 185.

29 Peter Hulme offers an insightful analysis of nakedness in his "Tales of Distinction: European Ethnography and the Caribbean," in *Implicit Understandings: Observing, Reporting, and Reflecting on the Encounters between the Europeans and Other Peoples in the Early Modern Era*, ed. Stuart B. Schwartz (Cambridge University Press, 1994), 157–97. According to Hulme, "In the classical tradition 'naked' often implied an unalloyed truth contrasted with the deceit made possible by the cunning garments of rhetoric. . . This was seen as an advantage: That lack of contamination by other faiths or idols left them as pure as the supposedly unused soil – purer, so Las Casas and others could argue,

than the nominally Christian Europeans who killed and enslaved them. But of course purity of heart could only be built on total denial of existing culture: the fundamental trope of colonial discourse" (184–5). With specific reference to the *Key*, John J. Teunissen and Evelyn J. Hinz make a similar point: "If clothing is truly the mark of the civilized man and symbolic of his regenerate spiritual condition, then the nakedness of the Indian has to be a cause of sadness since, conversely, first it must be symbolic of his fallen condition, and second, his preference for nakedness must reveal his stubborn unregeneracy. If nakedness symbolizes openness and honesty, however, then the European's superabundance of clothing becomes a matter for suspicion and condemnation." See their "Anti-Colonial Satire in Roger Williams's *A Key into the Language of America*," *Ariel* 7, no. 3 (1976): 16.

30 Williams, *Key*, 188.
31 *Ibid.*, 175.
32 Roderick Nash, *Wilderness and the American Mind* (New Haven: Yale University Press, 1967), 24. See also Peter N. Carroll, *Puritanism and the Wilderness. The Intellectual Significance of the New England Frontier* (New York: Colombia University Press, 1969), 55, and Perry Miller *Errand into the Wilderness* (Cambridge, MA: Harvard University Press, 1956), Ch. 1 *passim*.
33 Williams, *Key* , 175.
34 *Ibid.*, 225. The Latin is from Martial, *Epigrams*, 13, 94. Williams repeats it in his *Bloody Tenent Yet More Bloody*. See Williams, *Complete Writings of Roger Williams* (New York: Russell and Russell, 1963), vol. 4, 34–5, where it is translated as follows: "We naked Does, prey undefended, fall."
35 Williams, *Key*, 226.
36 *Ibid.*, 227.
37 *Ibid.*, 227.
38 Williams, *Complete Writings*, vol. 2, 46–7. Neal Salisbury remarks that similar arguments were used on the Indians and wealthy landowners during the civil war: those who did not work the land had no right to withhold it from those who did. See *Manitou and Providence: Indians, Europeans, and the Making of New England, 1500–1643* (New York: Oxford University Press, 1982) 177. Williams may not have disagreed with that position, but his argument is that the Indians do indeed have a sense of property, and that they do work the land. See also Francis Jennings, *The Invasion of America: Indians, Colonialism, and the Cant of Conquest*, (Chapel Hill: University of North Carolina Press, 1975), 128ff.
39 See William Cronon, *Changes in the Land* (New York: Hill and Wang, 1983), 57.
40 See William Richard Fisher, *The Forest of Essex* (London, 1887), 37.

41 *Ibid.*, 48.
42 See Oliver Rackham, *The Last Forest* (London: J. M. Dent & Sons, 1989) 102.
43 Williams *Key*, 228.
44 In a fascinating article on the importance of affect in Roger Williams's *Bloudy Tenent of Persecution*, Anne G. Myles makes a convincing case for the absolute centrality of the emotions in a proper understanding of Williams's work. Myles argues, "The text [Bloudy Tenent] works profoundly on the reader in a logic of images that addresses the emotions with the same argument that literal language directs toward the understanding." Borrowing the word "sentient" from Elaine Scarry, she demonstrates the way that Williams is shifting from the Old Testament model to a New Testament model of how truth is validated. In this transition, Myles explains (paraphrasing Scarry), she sees "a process by which embodiment and suffering replace wounding as the medium of God's truthful relationship to humankind" (154–56). See "Arguments in Milk, Arguments in Blood: Roger Williams, Persecution, and the Discourse of the Witness," *Modern Philology* 91 (1993): 133–60. I would suggest that there is still much work to be done in this regard with respect to Williams's *Key*, which seems to rely, for its persuasive power, on effect as much is it does on logic.
45 Williams, *Key*, 97–8.
46 *Ibid.*, 99.
47 *Ibid.*, 116.
48 *Ibid.*, 128.
49 *Ibid.*, 134.
50 *Ibid.*, 135.
51 *Ibid.*, 136–37.
52 *Ibid.*, 170.
53 *Ibid.*, 201.
54 *Ibid.*, 197.
55 *Ibid.*, 220.
56 John Russell Bartlett, ed., *Records of the Colony of Rhode Island and Providence Plantations in New England*, vol. 1 (Providence, 1856), 290.
57 Williams, *Key*, 83.

FEAR AND SELF-LOATHING: JOHN ELIOT'S *INDIAN DIALOGUES*

1 See John Garrett, Roger Williams, *Witness Beyond Christendom, 1603–1683* (New York: Macmillan, 1970).
2 For a description of Eliot's first meeting with Waban, see his *The Day-Breaking if not the Sun-Rising of the Gospell with the Indians in New-England* (London, 1647); *Collections of the Massachusetts Historical Society*, 3rd ser, 4 (1834), 3. Nishohkou eventually converted; for the texts

of Waban's and Nishohkou's confessions see *Tears of Repentance: Or, a Further Narrative of the Progress of the Gospel amongst the Indians in New England* (London, 1653); *Collections of the Massachusetts Historical Society*, 3rd ser, 4 (1834), 231 and 251.

3 The quote is from the charter of the Massachusetts Bay colony. Quoted in Alden Vaughan, *New England Frontier: Puritans and Indians, 1620–1675* (Boston: Little Brown, 1965), 236.

4 C. H. Firth and R. S. Rait, eds., *Acts and Ordinances of the Interregnum, 1642–1660* (London: His Majesty's Stationery Office, 1911), vol. 2, 197–200. In this act, Parliament ordered all of Britain's ministers to read the act in their parishes "upon the next Lords-day after the same shall be delivered unto them, and to exhort the people to a chearful and liberal contribution."

5 See William Kellaway, *The New England Company 1649–1776. Missionary Society to the American Indians* (London: Longmans, 1961), 26. While for understandable reasons the parliamentary act which created the Society for the Propagation of the Gospel avoided reference to the political turmoil, it made pointed reference to the pure holiness of the missionary work: "a work so much tending to the honor of Almighty God." See Firth and Rait, *Acts and Ordinances*, vol. 2, 198.

6 George P. Winship, *The Cambridge Press* (Philadelphia: The University of Pennsylvania Press, 1945) 67.

7 *Ibid.*, 151.

8 See Michael Walzer, *The Revolution of the Saints: A Study in the Origins of Radical Politics* (Cambridge, MA: Harvard University Press, 1965), 150 and 168.

9 In addition to the men I discuss in this paragraph, also signing the Preface were William Carter, Joseph Caryl, George Griffith, Sidrach Simpson, William Strong, Ralph Venning, and Jer. Whittaker. Readers familiar with the history of Nonconformity during the middle of the seventeenth century will no doubt recognize some, if not all, of these names.

10 On the controversy surrounding this publication of Hooker's sermons, see Andrew Delbanco, *The Puritan Ordeal* (Cambridge, MA: Harvard University Press, 1989), 175. For a discussion of the beliefs of Goodwin and Owen, see Geoffrey F. Nuttall, *The Holy Spirit in Puritan Faith and Experience* (University of Chicago Press, 1992), 34–47.

11 See Walzer, *The Revolution of Saints*, 150.

12 On Gouge, see *ibid.*, 280. And on Greenhill, see Stephen Foster, *The Long Argument: English Puritanism and the Shaping of New England Culture, 1570–1700* (Chapel Hill: University of North Carolina Press, 1991), 88.

13 See N. H Keeble, *The Literary Culture of Nonconformity in Later Seventeenth-Century England* (Athens: University of Georgia Press, 1987),

26. Also meeting with the King were, among others, Richard Baxter, Edmund Calamy and Simeon Ashe.

14 See Perry Miller, *Errand into the Wilderness* (Cambridge: Harvard University Press, 1956), 13–14.

15 See John Eliot, "The Cleare Sun-shine of the Gospel Breaking forth upon the Indians in New England" in *Collections of the Massachusetts Historical Society*, 3rd Series (1648; London, 1834), 27 and 29.

16 There are of course many references to the friction between the English and the Spanish during the 1650s. One might look, for instance, at Andrew Marvell's poem, "The First Anniversary of the Government under His Highness the Lord Protector, 1655" to find him accusing the Spanish of mistreating the Indians: "But Indians, whom they should convert, [they] subdue." We should also remember that the 1650s saw a reprinting of Las Casas's infamous account of Spanish atrocities, which I discussed in ch. 1. For a more complete discussion of the colonial dimensions of the Anglo-Spanish rivalry, see J. Leitch Wright, Jr, *Anglo-Spanish Rivalry in North America* (Athens: University of Georgia Press, 1971), *passim*.

17 See David Cressy, *Coming Over: Migration and Communication between England and New England in the Seventeenth Century* (Cambridge University Press, 1987), 210–11.

18 See Matthew Sylvester, *Reliquiae Baxterianae or, Mr Richard Baxter's Narrative of the Memorable Passages of his Life and Times* (London, 1696), part 2, 290.

19 See Kellaway, *The New England Company*, 36–45 and 54 ff., for a detailed account of the rechartering process and the legal battle to retain the sequestered estates.

20 See Winship, *The Cambridge Press*, 242 ff. Also see *Reliquiae Baxterianae*, part 2, 290. It is interesting to note an example of the converse of Baxter's "sanitizing" operation, which was the involvement of Shaftesbury and Locke in drafting the constitution of North Carolina.

21 See Eliot, "Tears of Repentance," 266–7.

22 Henry W. Bowden and James P. Ronda, eds., *John Eliot's Indian Dialogues, A Study in Cultural Interaction* (Westport, CN: Greenwood Press, 1980), 122–23.

23 See Sir Roger L'Estrange, *The Fables of Aesop and Other Eminent Mythologists; With Morals and Reflexions* (London, 1692); John Ogilby, *The Fables of Aesop Paraphras'd in Verse* (London, 1651); and William Caxton, *Fables of Esope* (1494). All of these collections are available in modern editions. See L'Estrange, *The Fables of Aesop* (New York: Dover, 1967); and R. T. Lenaghan, ed., *Caxton's Aesop* (Cambridge, MA: Harvard University Press, 1967). A facsimile of Ogilby's 1668 edition of Aesop was published by the William Andrews Clark Memorial Library at the University of California at Los Angeles in 1965.

24 See Annabel Patterson, *Fables of Power: Aesopian Writing and Political History* (Durham: Duke University Press, 1991), 61.

25 Edmund Spenser, "The Shepheardes Calender" *Poetical Works*, ed., J.C. Smith and E. De Selincourt (New York: Oxford University Press, 1912), 435.

26 For a more complete discussion of the political context of the May eclogue as well as *The Shepheardes Calender* as a whole, see Patterson, *Tables of Power*, 59.

27 Eliot, *Indian Dialogues*, 121.

28 *Ibid.*, 149.

29 *Ibid.*, 121.

30 *Ibid.*, 127.

31 For another version of this argument, see James Holstun, *A Rational Millennium, Puritan Utopias of Seventeenth Century England and America* (New York: Oxford University Press, 1987), 122ff.

32 Eliot, *Indian Dialogues*, 134.

33 *Ibid.*, 135. Although I will be making a much stronger argument in a moment for the connection of this dialogue to the question of toleration, I will point out that this sachem's reasoning mirrors that of those who opposed toleration in England during the 1660s. Those who argued against toleration did so not simply on the basis of theology. Many worried that the legalization of dissent would lead to massive confusion on issues such as land rights and tithing. For a discussion of this problem, see Richard L. Greaves, *Enemies under His Feet: Radicals and Nonconformists in Britain, 1664–1677* (Stanford University Press, 1990), 224ff.

34 See Martin Luther, "An Appeal to the Ruling Class of German Nationality as to the Amelioration of the State of Christendom," in *Martin Luther, Selections from His Writings*, ed. John Dillenberger (New York: Anchor Books, 1961), 412–13.

35 See John Eliot, *The Christian Commonwealth*. For an interesting discussion of this work, see Holstun, *Rational Millenium*, 108–162. He argues that *The Christian Commonwealth*, while not published until 1659, was probably written in 1651 or 1652 as an intervention in the "Engagement Controversy." Eliot's tract, Holstun argues, was thus a response to the resolution passed in Parliament on 11 October, 1659, which required all men to swear their fidelity to the Commonwealth of England (146–7). Although Holstun does not cite a source for this story about the burning of copies of *The Christian Commonwealth*, see Kellaway, *The New England Company*, 88; also see Holstun, *Rational Millennium*, 159. For another account of Eliot's intentions and goals in *The Christian Commonwealth*, see Theodore Dwight Bozeman, *To Live Ancient Lives: The Primitivist Dimension in Puritanism* (Chapel Hill: University of North Carolina Press, 1988), 264–80.

36 Eliot, *Indian Dialogues*, 137.

37 See John Milton, *The Complete Prose and Major Poems*, ed. Merritt Y.

Hughes (New York: Macmillan, 1957), 885. I should point out that in the passage I cite here Milton is primarily concerned with the financial burden of monarchy. But as Milton makes clear, financial issues are not easily separated from religious ones when it comes to the question of a king and his court.

38 Henrietta Maria even went so far as to attempt a "death-bed conversion" of her elder daughter, Mary. See J. R. Jones, *Charles II, Royal Politician* (London: Allen and Unwin, 1987), 52–3. For a description of the negotiations leading up to Charles's marriage, see Ronald Hutton, *Charles II, King of England, Scotland, and Ireland* (New York: Oxford University Press, 1989), 158–61.

39 See Jones, *Charles II, Royal Politician*, 62. Clarendon used Father Goffe as an example of a Catholic priest who might benefit from Charles's declaration. Goffe, who had been an Anglican before the Commonwealth, was chosen as the one to deliver the news to Charles that his father had been executed. Subsequently, in 1651, Goffe converted to Roman Catholicism. The persistence of characters such as Goffe in Charles's inner circle help to keep alive the fears of his own impending conversion.

40 On the Treaty of Dover, see *ibid.*, 89–90. Hutton discusses in some detail both the treaty and Charles's promise of conversion (*Charles II, King of England*, 263–6). On the second Declaration of Indulgence, see Jones, *Charles II, Royal Politician*, 97–8 and Hutton, *Charles II, King of England*, 284 ff. For an interesting discussion of the literary reaction to the second Declaration of Indulgence, see Keeble, 57–9.

41 See Holstun, *A Rational Millennium*, 122.

42 Eliot, *Indian Dialogues*, 59.

43 *Ibid.*, 61.

44 See Kellaway, *The New England Company*, 93. See also Francis Jennings, *The Invasion of America: Indians, Colonialism, and the Cant of Conquest* (Chapel Hill: University of North Carolina Press, 1975), who quotes Hugh Peter (who had migrated to Massachusetts and then moved back to England where he was executed at the Restoration) as saying that the mission work in Massachusetts "was but a plain cheat, and that there was no such thing as a gospel conversion among the Indians" (250). Elsewhere, Jennings argues that Eliot blatantly misrepresented himself and his work. Passing himself off as an expert in the Algonquin language, and portraying his hitherto failed attempts to preach to the Indians as successes, he shamelessly solicited funds from his brethren in England. See "Goals and Functions of Puritan Missions to the Indians," *Ethnohistory*, 18 (1971), 204ff. Also see Ola Elizabeth Winslow, *John Eliot "Apostle to the Indians"* (Boston: Houghton Mifflin, 1968), 144. Winslow mentions Hugh Peter's accusations in the context of a discussion of the less than enthusiastic reception Eliot's work received from his fellow settlers.

45 Eliot, *Indian Dialogues*, 60.

46 It is also important to remember that the issue of land was crucial in the English attempt to distinguish their colonial behavior from other countries (especially Catholic Spain). "That when other Nations who have planted in those furthest parts of the Earth, have only sought their owne advantage to possesse their Land, Transport their gold, and that with so much covetousness and cruelty, that they have made the name of Christianitie and of Christ an abomination, that the Lord should be pleased to make use of our Brethren that went forth." See *Strength out of Weaknesse; Or a Glorious Manifestation of the Further Progress of the Gospel among the Indians in New England* (London, 1652); *Collections of the Massachusetts Historical Society*, 3rd series 4 (1834): 158.

47 Eliot, *Indian Dialogues*, 71.

48 *Ibid.*, 71–2.

49 *Ibid.*, 59.

50 I realize that the question of the declension of the younger generations is by no means agreed upon by a consensus of contemporary scholars. Several scholars have revised or rejected Perry Miller's analysis in *The New England Mind: From Colony to Province* (Cambridge: Harvard University Press, 1953), where he argued that the Half-Way crisis was indeed a sign of a declension of sorts. For instance, Edmund S. Morgan in *Visible Saints: The History of a Puritan Idea* (New York University Press, 1963) and Robert G. Pope in *The Half-Way Covenant* (Princeton University Press, 1969) argue that the second generation of Massachusetts Puritans was more scrupulous about religious experiences than the first, and so there was the appearance of declension. More recently, Sacvan Bercovitch argues that the apparent signs of declension, such as the Jeremiad, were in fact signs of the health of Puritan culture, not its decline. In any event, I want to argue that whether or not Eliot believes in declension, he is certainly using its language. I would not go so far, however, as to suggest that we read the *Dialogues* as a jeremiad because as I will make clear in a moment there is finally a much more positive and hopeful tone to them.

51 Again, see Winslow, *John Eliot*, 144 ff.

52 Kellaway, *The New England Company*, 89.

53 See Holstun, *A Rational Millennium*, 111. While I will modify Holstun's argument in a moment, I would direct readers to the preface of Eliot's *Christian Commonwealth* (London, 1659), where he does exactly what Holstun here says he does: Eliot argues that the very arrival of the English is a piece of grace for the Indians, and the fact that some Indians treat it as such is a sign that this is indeed the case.

54 Interestingly, the Parliamentary Act creating the Society for the

Propagation of the Gospel in October of 1649 explicitly describes how the Indians themselves showed at least some agency in their own conversions: "Whereas the Commons of England assembled in Parliament have received certain intelligence, by the testimonial of divers faithful and godly Ministers, and others in New-England, that divers [of] the Heathen Natives of that Countrey, through the blessing of God upon the pious care and pains of some godly English of this Nation, who preach the Gospel among them in their own Indian Language, who not onely of Barbarous are become Civil, but many of them forsaking their accustomed Charms and Sorceries, and other Satanical Delusions, do now call upon the name of the Lord, and give great testimony of the power of God. . ." See Firth and Rait, *Acts and Ordinances*, 197. I would suggest that such phrasing of the act is quite deliberate. In 1649, the Parliament could never have supported an act that called for an Arminian ministry to the Indians.

55 See Morgan, *Visible Counts*, 124.

56 See "Some Unpublished Correspondence of the Rev. Richard Baxter and the Rev. John Eliot, 'The Apostle to the American Indians,' " *Bulletin of the John Rylands Library*, 15 (1931): 168.

57 Roger Williams was indeed an exception. See my argument in ch. 5.

58 See Increase Mather, *A Discourse Concerning the Subject of Baptisme* (Cambridge, 1675), 30–1.

59 There were two classes of church participants that fell short of full church membership: covenant assenters and covenant owners. The former merely assented to be governed by the church, while the latter showed a greater commitment, although they were still not allowed to vote on church matters. For a fuller description of these categories see Ross W. Beales, "The Half-Way Covenant and Religious Scrupulosity: The First Church of Dorchester, Massachusetts, as a Test Case," *William and Mary Quarterly*, 3rd ser., 31 (1974): 472ff. In his article, Beales disputes the claims of Morgan and Pope that the Half-Way Covenant was the product of an overly scrupulous attitude toward the individual's evidence of grace and conversion.

60 See Mather, *A Discourse Concerning the Subject of Baptisme*, 50.

61 For an interesting commentary on the above passage from Mather, see E. Brooks Holifield, *The Covenant Sealed: The Development of Puritan Sacramental Theology in Old and New England, 1570–1720* (New Haven: Yale University Press, 1974), 183ff. Holifield points out that in this passage Mather directly contradicts his father who had held that Indians were to be first formed into a church and then baptized – the accepted notion of how to handle Indian conversions.

62 See for instance Eliot's account and his justification of his method in *Tears of Repentance*, 227ff.

63 See Morgan, *Visible Saints*, 137.

64 Neal Salisbury, "Red Puritans: The 'Praying Indians' of Massachu-

setts Bay and John Eliot," *William and Mary Quarterly*, 3rd series 31 (1974): 45.

65 James P. Ronda, "'We Are Well as We Are': An Indian Critique of Seventeenth-Century Christian Missions," *William and Mary Quarterly*, 3rd series 34 (1977): 67.

66 See Eliot, *Indian Dialogues*, 79.

67 See *ibid.*, 89.

68 See *ibid.*, 107.

69 See *ibid.*, 108.

70 See *ibid.*, 143.

71 See *ibid.*, 147.

72 See *ibid.*, 151.

73 See *ibid.*, 157.

74 See *ibid.*, 160–1.

Index